THE ROUTLEDGE CREATIVE WRITING COURSEBOOK

Paul Mills

LONDON AND NEW YORK

First published 2006
by Routledge
2 Park Square, Milton Park, Abingdon, Oxon OX14 4RN

Simultaneously published in the USA and Canada
by Routledge
29 West 35th Street, New York, NY 10001

Reprinted 2007

Routledge is an imprint of the Taylor & Francis Group

Typeset in Garamond and Gill Sans by Taylor & Francis Books Ltd

Printed and bound in Great Britain by
MPG Books Ltd, Bodmin

British Library Cataloguing in Publication Data
A catalogue record for this book is available from the British Library

Library of Congress Cataloging in Publication Data
Mills, Paul, 1948-
The Routledge creative writing coursebook / Paul Mills.
p. cm.
Includes bibliographical references and index.
ISBN 0–415–31784–3 – ISBN 0–415–31785–1 (pbk.) 1. English language—Rhetoric—Study and teaching. 2. Creative writing—Study and teaching. I. Title.
PE1404.M56 2005
808' .02—dc22
2005012238

ISBN10: 0–415–31785–1 ISBN13: 978-0-415-31785-6 (pbk)
ISBN10: 0–415–31784–3 ISBN13: 978-0-415-31784-9 (hbk)

For Elizabeth

CONTENTS

PREFACE

Somewhere between a second edition and a sequel, the present book follows *Writing In Action,* with a focus exclusively on *creative* writing. It aims to offer fresh approaches and some new terms to match. Whilst writing this book I became aware of new ground to be discovered, and the constant need to rethink what happens when we read and write creatively.

Creative writing as a taught discipline is on the move; it is going places, and I hope I've provided some opportunity to think about interesting new directions. As well as that, my method, as in *Writing In Action,* has been to encourage genuine pleasure in the things good writing can do, and to move from given examples to suggestions for writing. Excitement and pleasure in written words generates momentum without which technical advice would be sterile. The plan of each chapter is therefore quite straightforward, and offers, I hope, enough but not too much guidance.

I acknowledge that what I have written in every chapter stems from my personal experience as a writer and reader. The whole idea is to stimulate not just good writing but open discussion, assuming that one leads to the other, and so leave room for tutors and students to make their own discoveries. With this point very much in mind, I am pleased to acknowledge how much I myself have benefited from the influence of students, colleagues and friends, many of whom are writers themselves, whose insights are mirrored here in so many ways.

Paul Mills, July 2005

ACKNOWLEDGEMENTS

Paul Mills, 'Mile End Opera', from *Dinosaur Point*, 2000, Smith/Doorstop Books. Reproduced by kind permission of the publisher (www.poetrybusiness.co.uk).

'Strayed Crab', from *The Complete Poems: 1927–1979*, by Elizabeth Bishop. Copyright © 1979, 1983 by Alice Helen Methfessel. Reprinted by permission of Farrar, Straus and Giroux, LLC.

'Sandra Lee Scheuer', Copyright © Gary Geddes. 'Active Trading', 1996. Reproduced by permission of Peterloo Poets.

Fred D'Aguiar, 'Home', from *British Subjects*, Bloodaxe Books, 1993. Reproduced by permission of the publisher.

Peter Dixon, excerpts from 'W-H-A-M', from Munden and Wade (eds), *Reading the Applause*, National Association of Writers in Education (www.nawe.co.uk). Reproduced by kind permission of the author and publisher.

Nicholas Tredre, excerpts from 'Flatmates from hell', The *Observer*, 22 January 1995. Reproduced by permission of Guardian Newspapers Ltd.

Julia Copus, 'Breaking the Rule', from *In Defence of Adultery*, Bloodaxe Books, 2003. Reproduced by permission of the publisher and author.

Excerpts from draft version of 'Farewell on the Town Hall Steps', by Susan Burns. Reproduced by kind permission of the author.

From *Keeping a Rendezvous*, by John Berger, copyright © 1988, 1991 by John Berger. Used by permission of Pantheon Books, a division of Random House, Inc, and the author.

Excerpts totalling 525 words from 'Ocean 1212W', from *Jonny Panic and the Bible of Dreams*, by Sylvia Plath. Copyright © 1952, 1953, 1955, 1956, 1957, 1960, 1961, 1962, 1963 by Ted Hughes. Reprinted by permission of HarperCollins Publishers Inc. and Faber and Faber, Ltd.

'Proletarian Portrait', by William Carlos Williams, from *Collected Poems: 1909–1939*, Vol. 1, Copyright © 1938 by New Directions Publishing Corp. Reprinted by permission of New Directions Publishing Corp. and Carcanet Press Limited.

Daniel Weissbort, 'Peonies Again', from *Leaseholder*, 1986. Reproduced by permission of Carcanet Press Limited.

'The Hand' from *The Wellspring*, by Sharon Olds, copyright © 1996 by Sharon Olds. Used by permission of Alfred A. Knopf, a division of Random House, Inc.

'The Hand' from *The Wellspring*, by Sharon Olds published by Jonathan Cape. Used by permission of The Random House Group Limited.

'Sunday Night' from *All of Us*, by Raymond Carver published by The Harvill Press. Used by permission of The Random House Group Limited and © Tess Gallagher.

'Sunday Night' from *New Path to the Waterfall*, by Raymond Carver. Reprinted by permission of International Creative Management, Inc. Copyright © 1989 Tess Gallagher.

Miroslav Holub, 'The Fly', from *Poems Before & After*, translated by Ian and Jarmila Milner, Edward Osers, George Theiner, Bloodaxe Books, 1990. Reproduced by permission of the publisher.

'Funeral Blues', copyright 1940 and renewed 1968 by W.H. Auden, from *Collected Poems*, by W. H. Auden. Used by permission of Random House, Inc. and Faber and Faber Ltd.

Excerpts from 'February-Not Everywhere' by Norman MacCaig, from *Voice Over*, 1988, Birlinn. Reproduced by permission of Birlinn, Polygon and John Donald.

Excerpts from 'Swami Anand' by Sujata Bhatt from *Point No Point*, Carcanet Press, 1997. Reproduced by permission of Carcanet Press Limited.

Paul Mills, 'Alex Kidd in Miracle World' from *Half Moon Bay*, Carcanet Press, 1993. Reproduced by permission of Carcanet Press Limited.

Excerpts from 'No Legal Existence' by Anne Spillard from *Stand* 21 (3), 1980: 63, reproduced by permission of *Stand*.

Extracts from *The Complete Short Stories*, by V. S. Pritchett published by Chatto & Windus. Used by permission of The Random House Group Limited.

Mark Haddon, excerpts from 'For adults: for children', The *Observer*, 11 April 2004. Reproduced by permission of Guardian Newspapers Ltd.

Excerpts from *The Weir*, Copyright © 1997,1998 by Conor McPherson. Reprinted with permission of the publishers: www.nickhernbooks.co.uk

Excerpts from the programme notes for *Skellig*, May-June 2004 at the Young Vic Theatre, London (www.youngvic.org). Reproduced by kind permission of Trevor Nunn.

CHAPTER 1

WRITING AS ART

Writers build up worlds, make them real, emphasise and illuminate them through images. Through voices they hold our attention, remind us of the varying tones of speech. Through stories told and heard they show the way our thoughts are shaped by narrative, how we shape the thoughts and lives of others and ourselves. From among the features by which we identify writing as an art form, in this first chapter I have selected four that produce a consistently powerful impact for writers and readers. These are **voice**, **world**, **image** and **story**. Without these elements our practice as writers would become disadvantaged. Creative language would not be as it is, neither would we read with the special attention and pleasure it generates.

Story implies structure, and structure meaning. Stories are told by voices creating images; voices also build and inhabit worlds. A writer staying close to the voices of characters has more chance of crossing over into their rhythm of living, of involving readers in that rhythm, so that as readers we feel we know it for ourselves. The use of speaking and thinking voices in writing seems to be a key quality, perhaps the most important skill of all for a writer to learn. But then, if we think about it, the voices that most hold our attention are those that tell stories, generate images, make their world as real to us as our own.

In this chapter I shall begin my exploration of how these qualities interact. Not one of them stands alone as the central foundation. But it may be that each of the five genres I cover in this book – memoir or personal narrative, poetry, fiction, children's writing and drama – typically favours one quality above others. We might see *image* as the domain of poets. We might expect *voice* to be the foremost interest of any dramatist, while *story* dominates every instance of prose fiction or memoir. It will help, however, if we *don't* make these assumptions. A successful poem can be written as dramatic story. A piece of short fiction might have very little in the way of narrative. Voices might not always be appropriate. Obviously there will be differences within genres, between writers. While Alan Ayckbourn writes by devising a carefully plotted story, Harold Pinter describes a play as 'an evolving and compulsive dramatic image' (Pinter, 1976: 12). The emphasis may change from writer to writer, but to value their impact we need to experience voice, world, image and story as strengths, qualities, amazing creative inventions. What is it that they do? How do they work? This chapter will be the first step in discovering some answers to these questions.

VOICE

Writing as art helps us to recognise the voices, images, worlds and stories we inhabit – and which inhabit us – in other words, our acquired culture. But it usually does this not through explanation or analysis, but by encouraging us to listen and see. In the following passage from her novel *The Bluest Eye*, the black American writer Toni Morrison paints a picture of weekends in a family household in Ohio. The child narrator remembers the impact of her mother's voice. She recreates her singing, her idioms of speech, the actual words spoken in the house. The picture has been painted for us in sound:

> Saturdays were lonesome, fussy, soapy days. Second in misery only to those tight, starchy, cough-drop Sundays, so full of 'don'ts' and 'set'cha self downs'.
>
> If my mother was in a singing mood, it wasn't so bad. She would sing about hard times, bad times, and somebody-done-gone-and-left-me-times. But her voice was so sweet and her singing-eyes so melty I found myself longing for those hard times, yearning to be grown without 'a thin di-i-me to my name'. I looked forward to the delicious time when 'my man' would leave me, when I would 'hate to see that evening sun go down...' ... Misery coloured by the greens and blues in my mother's voice took all the grief out of the words and left me with a conviction that pain was not only endurable, it was sweet.
>
> But without song, those Saturdays sat on my head like a coal scuttle, and if Mama was fussing, as she was now, it was like somebody throwing stones at it.
>
> (Morrison, 1994: 25–6)

This last image (of the mother fussing at her children), even without mentioning voice directly, represents it to us as something terribly uncomfortable: we see hands going up over ears to block it out. In the passage we also hear the narrator and catch a sense of her own speech-rhythms. Morrison has got right inside this child's voice. The story at this point is being told to us through a distinctly spoken language: 'lonesome ... fussy, soapy ... starchy, cough-drop Sundays.' This narrator is inclined to speak very much in her own fashion – independent, awkward to handle, yet also sensitive, sympathetic. Other voices come through to us: the first line of a lyric from the black jazz singer Bessie Smith, 'I hate to see that evening sun go down'.

Exploring the voice has uncovered a rich field in contemporary writing. In *The Bluest Eye* Morrison describes a conversation 'like a gently wicked dance: sound meets sound, curtsies, shimmies, and retires. Another sound enters but is upstaged by still another: the two circle each other and stop' (Ibid: 15). Yet a fascination with voices and speech has been present in fiction for over two centuries. The personal letter, a form where writing comes closest to natural speech, made its appearance in one of the earliest examples of fiction. *Pamela* by Samuel Richardson (1740) contains a series of letters written between women on the subject of love. Authentic, spontaneous, as if close to real, unedited experience, it was partly through its use of the letter (we call this an 'epistolary style') that fiction placed its emphasis on speech. In a recent, unusual example of such emphasis, Iris Murdoch begins her novel *A Fairly Honourable Defeat,* written and set in the 1960s, by inventing a conversation which continues for almost twenty pages, with only one short interjection by the author setting the scene. If one rule of fiction is to discover *what most interests the characters*, then one such interest could be love, but another might be conversation itself. As she demonstrates, talk, conversation, interests this husband and wife because it is their way of shaping experience. We hear their voices because, for them, voices are important. Talking matters.

Dialect and Diversity

In the middle of the last century, the Russian literary critic Mikhail Bakhtin called attention to voices used creatively by writers. 'Diversity of speech', he wrote, 'is the ground of style', and commenting particularly of the novel: 'For the prose artist the world is full of other people's words, among which he must orient himself and whose speech characteristics he must be able to perceive with a very keen ear' (Bakhtin, 1984: 200–1). In his book *After Bakhtin*, David Lodge, himself a prolific novelist, draws attention to this feature in the novels of Dickens, George Eliot and D. H. Lawrence.

But the uses of voice don't confine themselves only to fiction. In our time poetry has also widened its appeal by developing its range of speaking voices, tones, registers, accents, slang expressions. Writing in all its creative forms no longer limits itself to the voice of one dominant authority, or to a form of address by a single speaker; that is, white, middle-class, educated British-American. Writing as art is now practised by people from a wide range of racial and ethnic backgrounds, representing differences of age, gender and sexuality. All these voices are actively sought by audiences and readers whose numbers reflect a similar range of culture and experience.

When it comes to the question of how much or how little we know about other people, it is hardly surprising that voices provide one of the first signals of difference or similarity. We might indeed remember a voice more than a name or face. City neighbourhoods often consist of people from a variety of ethnic backgrounds. Living on the same staircase as an Asian family, the Scottish poet Liz Lochhead wonders about the mother's position in terms of her speech and location. Spoken language can differ between generations in the same household: 'How does she feel? / her children grow up with foreign accents, / swearing in fluent Glaswegian' ('Something I'm Not', in Crawford and Imlah, eds, 2000: 505). In a radio play by Benjamin Zephaniah, a young boy with a natural-born English Midlands accent wonders about his father's black Caribbean preacher-voice holding forth in a manner astonishing to him – one is obsessed with football, the other with the Bible.

In his poem 'The Shout', Simon Armitage describes how he and another boy at school were testing 'the range of the human voice'. How far does a voice carry? was the question they asked themselves:

> He called from over the park – I lifted an arm.
> Out of bounds,
> he yelled from the end of the road...

Neither, however, could have foreseen the end of the test:

> He left town, went on to be twenty years dead
> with a gunshot hole
> in the roof of his mouth, in Western Australia.
> (Armitage 2003: 2)

'You can stop shouting now, I can still hear you', Armitage writes in the final line of the poem. The real question was not about distance but difference: of age and of experience. Can voices ever overcome the sense of growing apart? The news of suicide carries further than any shout could reach. The voice has stopped, yet in a truer sense it persists.

Deception and Evasion

For some strange reason we often associate creative literature with truth, yet novels and plays are full of characters who fail to tell it, deliberately avoid it, prefer to tell what they wish was the case rather than what actually is. Plays by Tennessee Williams, Arthur Miller, like those by Chekhov and Ibsen, typify what we might call the literature of evasion. The truth, of course, finally gets spoken, but not until a voice for it can be found. In terms of structure their plays are about discovering that voice, but sometimes the reverse happens, and we hear an especially courageous voice begin to founder and almost silence itself. The voices in Beckett's plays seem to prefer silence. Another voice known for its bleakness and humour is that of Holden Caulfield in Salinger's novel *The Catcher In The Rye:*

> I thought what I'd do was, I'd pretend I was one of those deaf mutes. That way I wouldn't have to have any goddam stupid useless conversation with anybody. If anybody wanted to tell me something, they'd have to write it on a piece of paper and shove it over to me. They'd get bored as hell doing that after a while, and then I'd be through with having conversations for the rest of my life. Everybody'd think I was just a poor deaf-mute bastard and they'd leave me alone.
>
> (Salinger, 1995: 178–9)

Holden's ideal world is *without* voices – even without his own. Even so, we can hear his voice speaking. His bond with the reader overrides his desire to stop communicating. It goes on despite his urge to escape to a permanent deaf-mute state. The voice we recognise – slangy, immediate, often perverse – speaks to us even when he explains he'd rather not. To neutralise one's voice, as here, could be a form of cancelling out one's story. Holden hasn't committed vocal suicide, even though the story he tells contains moments when he's seriously tempted.

In the following extract from a novel by Tim O'Brien, *In The Lake of the Woods,* again the setting is the United States, and the voices project an imagined alternative space, an ideal:

> As a kind of game they would sometimes make up lists of romantic places to travel.
>
> 'Verona,' Kathy would say, 'I'd love to spend a few days in

> Verona.' And then for a long while they would talk about Verona, the things they would see and do, trying to make it real in their minds. All around them the fog moved in low and fat off the lake, and their voices would seem to flow away for a time and then return to them from somewhere in the woods beyond the porch...
>
> They would go on talking about the fine old churches of Verona, the museums and outdoor cafes where they would drink strong coffee and eat pastries. They invented happy stories for each other. A late-night train-ride to Florence, or maybe north into the mountains, or maybe Venice, and then back to Verona, where there was no defeat and nothing in real life ever ended badly. For both of them it was a wishing game. They envisioned happiness as a physical place on the earth, a secret country, perhaps, or an exotic foreign capital with bizarre customs and a different new language. To live there would require practice and many changes, but they were willing to learn.
>
> (O'Brien, 1995: 2–3)

These two characters create a world – they call it 'Verona' – simply by talking about it. It becomes their own 'secret country' an 'envisioned happiness'. It's important, of course, that they don't actually go to the real place, don't make actual, practical plans. Would they agree with the author's explanation – that their talk hardly amounts to more than 'a wishing game'? They probably would. His voice overlaps with theirs. They half-know, half-suspect this Verona is an evasion, an easy escape-route. From what? They probably wouldn't be willing or ready to say. Voices can be used to show concealment; sometimes this is precisely what speech is about.

This merging of the writer's voice with the voices of characters in fiction is known as free indirect speech, a valuable device in third person narrative, as shown above. As readers it keeps our attention where it should be, not on the writer's views and opinions, but on the characters in the story. We listen to *them*, engage with what is happening in their minds *below* the level of conscious, articulate speech. The writer enables us to see, hear and feel their hidden sensations, first intimations (for example) of doubt or of desire, before these become conscious or can be spoken about directly.

Finding a Voice

If creative language frequently makes use of *voiced* forms, does this mean each writer is burdened with the quest to discover his or her unique voice, something expressly *original* among this huge polyphony of voices? The notion of 'your own voice', 'finding a voice', refers to a writer's stance towards all the creative features of writing as art, including, of course, voice itself. Your voice will be generated by what you write about, the recurrent places, aspects and qualities of the world you represent, by the images you choose to highlight, the types of story or story-like events that hold for you a special fascination.

Some readers might think certain idioms, slang expressions and regional speech qualities to be a handicap. To others the possession of an accent suggests vitality. Conor MacPherson's play *The Weir* (see Chapter 6, p. 214) is a play written to celebrate voices (and stories) from the northwest of Ireland. But how do we choose our words, the right words? I don't like the word 'handicap', for instance, even though I found myself using it in a sentence above. Somehow it doesn't have quite the right sound to it, possibly because it's actually disappearing from spoken use. I really want something less old-fashioned sounding: 'dysfunction'? This is a euphemistic term, now therapist-journalese. Another possibility might be 'encumbrance', another 'liability'.

Choice of words depends more than we think on the currents and undercurrents of speech. Creative language incorporates what people say and how they speak – to themselves, to each other – and builds up a rich supply of spoken rhythms. Inside each single voice are many voices, some angry or calm, moral or perverse, some native, others overheard. One of the skills of the writer is learning how to listen to voices – those all around us and within us, those of characters in a story or play. It is as if the writer's job is to write down what his or her characters are saying, remaining wholly faithful to the way *they* speak. Maybe that is one way, paradoxically, of finding one's own voice – by hearing and recording those of others.

Voices under Pressure

MacPherson's play is set in a pub in a remote part of Ireland. Voices of people in a bar in any region will be influenced by their surroundings. Is there a pool table, wide-screen TV? Background noise, even background silence? Degrees of relaxation and tension influence speech, just as they do other types of behaviour. Talking never happens in the abstract. He said it on that day, in that place, and had these been different ... who knows? This question applies to writers, too.

All writing is influenced by the conditions of its production. These conditions might be political or personal, close at hand, far in the background, almost invisible, unknowable, or very much in the foreground and invasive. Coleridge famously records how the arrival of an unwelcome guest – the 'person from Porlock' – interrupted the flow of his inspiration. Can we tell from a piece of writing anything about the immediate, practical conditions and pressures that helped or hindered, or at least influenced, the tone, form and content of it as a text? Might it encourage a certain reading by hinting (through its degree of formality/informality, its voice under pressure) at what might be called its *implied* circumstances? Can we tell if a poem was made spontaneously, *in the moment*, or heavily revised?

For writers and teachers of writing, such issues are quite specific and practical. A good many poets have developed the skill of writing as if in the presence of the scene, place, person they are describing, a style we might call responsive or expressionist. Ted Hughes' poem 'The Thought Fox' describes not just a subject but a method, and one he recommends in his book on writing, *Poetry In The Making.* Against this is the measured, careful phrasing found in the work of other poets – the 'midnight oil' of the study Yeats refers to in his poem 'Among School Children'. Poems such as 'The Thought Fox' operate by describing a physical location – snow, shadow, movement – in a way that makes the physical location so real it seems to replace the actual conditions under which the poem was written, conditions we don't actually know about unless we were there with the poet when he was writing. But in another sense we are there with the poet, looking at that landscape, that fox, through the transforming force of imagination. Certain poems appear to have been written all at once, in one sitting, with few corrections, whether they have or not, while others show a formal care that seems to rule against a sense of such immediacy. When Sylvia Plath in the title poem of her book *Ariel* writes the line 'The child's cry / Melts in the wall', was this a response to the real thing happening in an adjacent room as she was writing the poem? Do her poems carry a trace of being written 'Between five in the morning and the milkman rattling his bottles' as she explained in an interview? Was an alertness to sound in the pre-dawn winter of 1963 a conditioning influence on her poems in *Ariel*? Or was she aiming, for the best of reasons, to give us that impression?

The English poet Sir Thomas Wyatt in the sixteenth century wrote under constant threat of imprisonment, possibly even execution, in the court of Henry VIII. Does his verse betray such conditions, or attempt to conceal them? Would a judicious degree of formality guarantee his survival, or should he adopt the disguise of careless spontaneity? In plays and films we expect physical and social conditions to influence the way characters speak. In David Mamet's play *Glengarry Glen Ross*, a real-estate salesman's loss of confidence leads to abusive, sexist slang, deformed, unfinished sentences. This is a voice *under pressure*:

> LEVENE: I tell you why I'm out. I'm *out*, you're giving me toilet paper, John. I've *seen* those leads. I saw them when I was at Homestead, we pitched those cocksuckers Rio Rancho nineteen sixty nine they wouldn't buy. They couldn't buy a fucking *toaster*. They're *broke* John. They're deadbeats, you can't judge on that. Even so. Even so. Alright. Fine. Fine. Even so. I go in, FOUR FUCKING LEADS they got their money in a sock. They're fucking Polacks, John. Four leads. I close two. *Two*. Fifty per...
>
> WILLIAMSON: ... they kicked out.
>
> LEVENE: They *all* kick out. You run in streaks, pal. *Streaks*. I'm... I'm... don't look at the *board*, look at *me*. Shelly Levene. *Anyone* Ask them on Western. Ask Getz at Homestead. Go ask Jerry Graff. You know who I am... I NEED A SHOT. I got to get on the fucking board. *Ask* them. Ask them who ever picked up a check I was flush. Moss, Jerry Graff. Mitch himself ... Those guys *lived* on the business I brought in.
>
> (Mamet, 1984: 7)

In his book on writing plays, *The Crafty Art of Playmaking*, Alan Ayckbourn notes the importance of punctuation in speech: 'Sometimes the speeches are broken up (quite grammatically incorrectly) in order to give an indication to the actor of the preferred delivery' (Ayckbourn, 2002: 62). He then quotes a speech from his play *Woman in Mind* as an example, and adds – the speaker is Susan – 'her pattern is breaking up like her personality'.

A huge advantage of bringing the voice and voices to the fore in any piece of writing will be that readers engage with a text more sympathetically; also, they are going to connect with its verbal energy. If a character in a poem or play says something – to themselves or to somebody else, tells a story, reports or records an experience in their own words – there is a sense of human fragility, of excitement, danger, possible misunderstanding and risk. And it could well be that in creative writing this sense of risk, far from being a fault or a weakness, is the very stuff that makes us sit up and take notice.

Orality and Literacy

One final thought about voices. This section's title above repeats that of Walter Ong's book about the differences between words as sounds (orality), and written words. As Ong explains, 'Writing ... was a very late development in human history. Homo Sapiens had been on earth perhaps some 50,000 years' (Ong, 1995: 83). The visual field of the written word (writing has to be seen, spatially mapped) differs fundamentally from sound sensations. We can only read print as individuals, while we hear collectively as an audience. Voice is produced by, and resonates with, the body, it 'vanishes as soon as it is uttered', while writing 'separates the word from the living present, where alone spoken words can exist' (Ibid: 31–3). I hope it's clear, even from the few examples I've chosen, that writing *as* speech, writing *about* speech, adds vital qualities to a text, and we might even claim that *creative* writing, developing as it has done from an oral tradition, not only reduces the separation between writing and voice, but thrives on their proximity. If speech 'vanishes', creative writing keeps alive the traces of its vanishing.

WORLD

Whenever writers create credible worlds, each of these imagined spaces holds the attention of readers and audiences by making us share, care about and appreciate the actions and events that happen within its borders. Such borders might be close to the real world, adjacent to it, or far away from it. The distance is less relevant than the convincing representation of this space as authentic, consistent, believable, so that we feel our interest will be rewarded. Cinema audiences watching films whose setting is contemporary, respond to shots of cities, highways, deserts, rivers, streets and home interiors. These spaces connect with spaces they feel they could travel to and from. Fiction writers have to do this through words. The novelist Margaret Atwood remembers being told early on in her career, 'Respect the page – it's all you've got'! All forms of creative writing, including poems, need to persuade readers to keep attending, because the world of their invention has a distinct reality. A basic element of this hold on the reader is the skill of verbal realisation.

Stories can't happen without places made real to us as we read. As the writer John Berger explains, 'When we read a story we inhabit it. The covers of a book are like a roof and four walls' (Berger, 1992: 15) But this feature applies just as much to other creative forms, as in this poem by the Canadian poet Gary Geddes:

'Sandra Lee Scheuer' (Killed at Kent State University on May 4th, 1970, by the Ohio National Guard)

You might have met her on a Saturday night
cutting precise circles, clockwise, at the Moon-Glo
Roller Rink, or walking with quick step

between the campus and a green two-storey house,
where the room was always tidy, the bed made,
the books in confraternity on the shelves.

She did not throw stones, major in philosophy
or set fire to buildings, though acquaintances say
she hated war, had heard of Cambodia.

In truth she wore a modicum of make-up, a brassiere,
And could, no doubt, more easily have married a guardsman
Than cursed or put a flower in his rifle barrel.

While the armouries burned she studied,
Bent low over notes, speech therapy books, pages
Open at sections on impairment, physiology.

And while they milled and shouted on the commons
she helped a boy named Billy with his lisp, saying
Hiss, Billy, like a snake. That's it, SSSSSSSS,

Tongue well up and back behind your teeth.
Now buzz, Billy, like a bee. Feel the air
vibrating in my windpipe as I breathe?

As she walked in sunlight through the parking lot
at noon, feeling the world a passing lovely place,
a young guardsman, who had his sights on her,

Was going down on one knee as if he might propose.
His declaration, unmistakable, articulate,
flowered within her, passed through her neck,

Severed her trachea, taking her breath away.
Now who will burn the midnight oil for Billy,
ensure the perilous freedom of his speech?

And who will see her skating at the Moon Glo
Roller Rink, the eight small wooden wheels
making their countless revolutions on the floor?
(Geddes 1996: 27)

Although this poem's setting is Ohio, USA; Baghdad, Bejing, London – nowhere is protected in the present state of the world. But the poem's ability to deliver this message is effective because it shows us 'a green two-storey house ... speech therapy books' because it records a voice saying, 'SSSSSSSS ... Feel the air / vibrating in my windpipe as I breathe'. The details are there in close-up realisation. The poem builds a world, her world, and allows us to inhabit it with her. As we read, we are there, able to listen and hear, to see. The subject of this poem could and probably did originate as a report in a newspaper or on television, yet events recorded in the media generally reveal very little that could help us experience them with such intimacy and exactness.

The subject of the next extract has no obvious link with news or the media, although some images may be familiar through films. From the start of the poem I am aiming simply to build up a scene, recreate its impact. Here, a family is making their first visit to San Francisco:

from 'The Bridge'

The day we chose to let America show us its first city,
north of Santa Cruz, Half Moon Bay, Pacifica,
driving the coast route to the Golden Gate,
out of the fog, our glimpse of it
was of two swaying masts, a pilot craft
moored to San Francisco,
moving the whole city out of harbour,
ready to break free, cut loose, vanish
into a river of light.
Other ships were moving fast upstream,
a floating Toyota factory out of Japan.
Out on the flat shining plane of the bay
Alcatraz like a cubist mirage.

Downtown crowded us with streets, steepness,
the entire city a huge lift to the top
of the Trans-America Pyramid and its window, like thick
aquarium-glass, as if the gold of the sun swam in America.
Houses flung on the hills like litter Every space used up.
(Mills, 2000: 36)

Although the people involved are not referred to in this opening, we still might be able to sense their reactions, as if they can hardly believe that they are there. Re-reading the lines I can recapture the excitement I felt when writing them. They aim to produce the sense of being in a place and a moment unlike any other.

De-familiarisation

Writers sharpen our sense of the world by making us hear and see with intensified clarity at times when otherwise we might just take things for granted. The Golden Gate Bridge probably doesn't need de-familiarising, while other, more common, experiences, will. The poet Peter Sansom, for example, instead of saying 'drove off at speed', writes of a 'floored accelerator waking the whole street'. Rather than 'looking a mess' D. B. C. Pierre writes: 'Ella's just skinny, with some freckles, and this big ole head of tangly blond hair that's always blown to hell, like a Barbie doll your dog's been chewing on for a month' (Pierre, 2003: 126).

Why do writers build worlds, struggle to make them real to readers? One reason might be to intensify the sensation of being alive, as the Russian formalist critic Victor Shklovsky explains in his essay 'Art as Technique': 'to increase the difficulty of length and perception, because the process of perception ... must be prolonged' (Shklovsky, 1917). To find new ways of being in spaces that are otherwise familiar, putting readers in touch with a reality we might easily ignore, as in Gary Geddes's poem. Another might be sheer pleasure as in 'The Bridge'. Building a world is a means of welcoming readers, enabling them to inhabit the scene of a poem, novel or play, and writers do this by opening doors, letting readers in, rather than just by telling them what this or that place signifies. The word 'excitement' doesn't appear in 'The Bridge'. In Gary Geddes's poem no one is being instructed what to think. The setting, the unique presence of Sandra Lee Scheuer, is realised without any attached authorial commentary. Words that sum up a feeling-response – anger, injustice, waste of life – don't get a look in. The business is to make things real, to surprise us. The doors that are opened don't have signs on them: excitement, pleasure, outrage or evasion, or the name of the writer. No matter how public or private these worlds seem, they are made open to everyone through the art of looking and listening more closely, and turning the sensation into words.

Public and Private

As well as the worlds writers create, there is the world out there in its present existence, and sometimes writers feel the need to comment on it, give their opinion, intervene directly and unambiguously. Here is a list of slogans mounted on placards during a recent demonstration in America:

Go Solar, Not Ballistic
God Does Not Bless Only America

How Did Our Oil Get Under Their Soil?
How Many Lives Per Gallon?
Justice Or Just Us?
Let's Try Pre-emptive Peace
Make Alternative Energy Not War
Rich Man's War Poor Man's Blood
Stop Mad Cowboy Disease
Our Grief Is Not A Cry For War

Parallelisms, reversals, verbal play – do these lines, singly or together, make up writing we might call 'creative'? In a world that faces increasing numbers of unsolved public questions, should writers aim to preserve a distance, not get involved, or, on occasions when involvement beckons, stick to the well-tried writing-workshop approach of 'show' don't 'tell'? The slogans exhibit features we might well describe as creative, not least because to awaken response they make strange what was familiar: 'Let's try *Pre-emptive Peace*.'

In the words of the American poet and essayist Eliot Weinberger, 'In all the anthologies and magazines devoted to 9/11 and its aftermath, nearly every single writer resorted to first-person anecdote: 'It reminded me of the day my father died…'; 'I took an herbal bath and decided to call my old boyfriend…'. Barely a one could imagine the event outside the prison cell of their own expressive self.'

Weinberger's comments ask serious questions. Should students of creative writing continue to be encouraged to focus on personal experience as their foremost subject, and so risk neglecting themes such as war, poverty, terrorism, global warming, human rights, racism, marginality? Can the right 'anecdote' bridge the gap? Is the 'expressive self' indeed a prison? Must sloganised writing be the alternative, and, if so, is it desirable? Or is there still room for the personal voice whether or not this is attached to an issue or a position? My own reaction to these dilemmas is that they should be debated. Two points of guidance spring to mind.

Imagination

The first is that no one can write anything of significance – to themselves (and therefore, it follows, to anybody else) – unless *imagination* is allowed to play a major part in the process. Worlds and spaces in writing as art can't be made real without the imaginative play of the mind remembering, selecting, attending. Memory is often the primary source of imaginative experience. Not all memories stored away in the inaccessible filing-system of our ordinary minds attract the same level of attention. Some things stand out, stay with us consciously or half-consciously. Here, in the introduction to an essay on Ted Hughes's *Birthday Letters*, I explain the process of retrieval:

> As a poet and teacher of creative writing, at some point I ask my students to retrieve from memory places, things, experiences or events which have become lodged in their imagination. Some things will have been stored at the back of their minds – something in childhood, something which might have happened only a week, a day, or even just hours before. There will be things that aren't just memory but which will have acquired a particular colour, an unusual resonance. Ordinary memory will have transferred certain impressions into imagination, and these will be part of ourselves as individuals, also of who we are as a culture. We might not know why these things are transferred, or why certain events feel so different. Knowing why isn't really the business. Writing about them, and making them real, is, however, and if attention is given to the imagination in this way, the idea is that it will collect more and more experiences, more and more significance will be available. The idea behind this method is a belief – that imagination acts as a shaping force, is more intelligent than our ordinary minds. Imagination is present in each one of us. It is what defines us as a species. To write, paint, or do whatever imagination offers, requires a kind of listening to its suggestions.
>
> (Mills 2002: 170)

Imagination, then, is the main directive. It selects; we follow. We may be led to illuminate worlds that are public in the media sense of the word – war, poverty, racism – or we may not. But unless we are actually driven to explore them, it's difficult to see how these can become imaginative spaces realised through an adequate state of attention. Imagination, starting with memory, does lead to a widening out beyond the confines of an inert privacy. Or we might say that personal meaning itself has been extended.

The second point asks the question: 'How do we know our world?' While technologies seem to expand our knowledge, we feel a growing mistrust about what we are told, what we are shown, what in fact is the case. Much of our seeing and knowing is second-hand, received by secondary means. In these conditions, validation through direct experience happens in isolation or by chance. This phenomenon has implications that go far beyond the issues of writing. To take the example of climate change: the problem is that when we come to know it directly, locally and personally, protest could be too late. Obvious, too, is the likelihood that so-called 'experience' can no longer be separated from secondary information. Such information – whether we call it news, science, rumour or myth – will always be there as background noise, distorting what we like to protect as our own subjective response.

The poet's view of Sandra Lee Scheuer will be, like all others, incomplete. Nothing can ever be a last word. People are complex. What is hidden? How do we know each other or ourselves? These are questions keenly felt in the work of contemporary writers. While the work of many writers explores this secondary position – control through media, the fictive as real – a parallel movement continues. Creative writing resists the cliché, rejects the sentimental, builds new links between self and world. So much writing continues to bring the localised and specific into focus.

The act of making alike, *assimilation*, might seem to be one aim of the writing process. Simile and metaphor, we might argue, are its basic devices – the art of seeing one thing in terms of another, fusing their identities, explicitly in a simile, implicitly in the case of metaphor. But to describe Alcatraz as a cubist painting, or say of the young guardsman that his 'declaration ... flowered within her' is to enhance the actual *difference* between things compared, to reinforce our sense of their strange otherness and importance. Whenever we experience something in its full vividness, assimilation is forced into retreat. Art cultivates edge, contrast, and the respect for difference.

Experience beyond the personal range of the writer can still be felt – through imagination. Another of its attributes is the desire to reach and acknowledge as real other people's worlds. In poetry, for example, the use of a personae (see Chapter 3, p. 87) has helped to refashion our understanding of world events, bringing distant experiences up close. 'All night pitiless pilotless things go shrieking / above us somewhere', writes the American poet Adrienne Rich, '... when fear vacuums out the streets / when the whole town flinches' (Rich, 2004: 23).

IMAGE

Words as Images

All writers fall in love with words. They realise words can do something amazing. Sometimes this love-affair goes on in front of our eyes. In Pinter's plays we sense the writer collecting certain words and phrases out of the mouths of his characters, holding them up to the light, making a display of galleried language even while he's equally interested in two old women, for example, talking in a café late at night, or a husband and wife discussing the strength of the sun on a hot afternoon in London. The writer can be sensed mounting his display of phenomenal words, while the characters talk with no apparent awareness of this exhibiting, no awareness whatsoever of audience.

A fascination with Pinter's language comes about whenever his characters generate images through words. They do this as though they might not be fully aware of what they are doing, which is one reason why his plays have achieved a lasting appeal to audiences as well as to directors and actors. Everyone wonders what these characters sense, whether or not they, like the writer, are involved in a kind of expert exhibitor's display – or whether they are simply talking. A half-mocking, verbal imaging shifts in and out of his characters' voices, in and out of the playwright's creative attention. Who is who? Nobody can be certain.

Writers too may talk and talk, but unless they are able to focus our minds through images, much of what they say to us will be lost. Metaphor, icon, symbol; together these words convey the range of meaning attached to *image,* but we don't need to consider exact definitions at this point. What we do need to think about is impact, resonance, how images work, and, as in the following extract from Pinter's play *The Lover*, what dramatic function they perform.

In the following scene Richard and Sarah, a married couple in their thirties, are talking about Venetian blinds. Richard has just returned from a day at the office. What has Sarah been doing with her day? (*The Lover* was written in 1966.)

> Richard: What about this afternoon? Pleasant afternoon?
> Sarah: Oh yes, quite marvellous.
> Richard: Your lover came did he?
> Sarah: Mmnn. Oh yes.
> Richard: Did you go out or stay in?
> Sarah: We stayed in.
> Richard. Ah! (*He looks up at the Venetian blinds*) That blind hasn't been put up properly.
> Sarah: Yes, it is a bit crooked isn't it?
>
> *Pause*
>
> Richard: Very sunny on the road. Of course, by the time I got on to it the sun was beginning to sink. But I imagine it was quite warm here this afternoon. It was warm in the City.
> Sarah: Was it?

> *...He pours drinks*
>
> Richard: I see you had the Venetian blinds down.
> Sarah: We did, yes.
> Richard: The light was terribly strong.
> Sarah: It was, awfully strong.
> Richard: The trouble with this room is that it catches the sun so directly, when it's shining. You didn't move to another room?
> Sarah: No. We stayed here.
> Richard: Must have been blinding.
> Sarah: It was. That's why we put the blinds down.
>
> *Pause*
>
> Richard: The thing is it gets so awfully hot in here with the blinds down.
> Sarah: Would you say so?
> Richard: Perhaps not. Perhaps it's just that you feel hotter.
> Sarah: Yes. That's probably it.
>
> (Pinter, 1963: 51–2)

During her lover's visit, the blinds were down. Now they are up, but a bit crooked. The sun was strong. Now it has sunk. Sarah and her lover didn't decide to move to another room, possibly a bedroom. ('No, we stayed here.') How 'hot' was the encounter in this living-room? The word 'hot' has become detached from the sun or the light, and might be referring to something else – the activities in the room hidden by blinds. The sun, rooms, heat, the City become an extended topic of conversation, but the reason for such extension is to establish a set of images surrounding an otherwise simple and innocuous object – a blind. As well as an object shutting out light, 'blind', of course, is a word in its own right. Who is blind? Who is blinding who? Does Richard know what he's saying, asking, suggesting? The audience can't be sure.

Reading Images

An image can be something we feel invited to walk around, view from different angles like a sculpture. Something has been carved out so that each view of it is equal to any other. No single perspective has the last word. No matter how powerful images are, their reception may still be unclear, and that uncertainty can prove creative. In creative writing, the audience or reader needs to feel actively involved in the construction of meaning. In Margaret Atwood's story 'Death by Landscape' the central character, Lois, has accumulated a collection of paintings over many years:

> They are pictures of convoluted tree trunks on an island of pink wave-smoothed stone, with more islands behind; of a lake with rough, bright, sparsely wooded cliffs; of a vivid river-shore with a tangle of bush and two beached canoes, one red, one grey; of a yellow autumn woods with the ice-blue gleam of a pond half-seen through the interlaced branches.

The paintings have increased in market value, but

> She bought them because she wanted them. She wanted something that was in them, although she could not have said at the time [of buying them] what it was. It was not peace: she does not find them peaceful in the least. Looking at them fills her with a wordless unease. Despite the fact that there are no people in them or even animals, it's as if there is something, or someone, looking back out.
>
> (Atwood, 1992: 110).

In the narrative that follows, Atwood shows us a scene where Lois and her friend Lucy, girls in their teens, make an excursion to an island during a summer camp expedition in the Canadian wilderness. During this episode Lucy unaccountably vanishes without trace. Her disappearance leaves no evidence behind and no explanation. Only through her collection of paintings can Lois find any way of accommodating her loss or making it real. Atwood makes the point that these are not 'landscape paintings in the old, tidy, European sense ... mountain in the background, a golden evening sky'. Instead they are images of wilderness, neither of possession nor of control but rather dispossession.

> There are no backgrounds to these paintings, no vistas, only a great deal of foreground that goes back and back, endlessly, involving you in its twists and turns of tree and branch and rock. No matter how far back in you go, there will be more. And the trees themselves are hardly trees; they are currents of energy, charged with violent colour...
>
> Everyone has to be somewhere, and this is where Lucy is. She is in Lois's apartment, in the holes that open inwards on the wall, not like windows but like doors. She is here. She is entirely alive.
>
> (Ibid, 1992:129)

The observer (of the wilderness, of the paintings) herself becomes 'lost in all those foregrounds ... holes that open inwards ... like doors'. The passage above ends with the final sentence of the story, completing the mystery while keeping it open.

'Death by Landscape' serves several purposes. One might be to render an impression of the Canadian bush country of Atwood's childhood: this is a place that draws you in and yet resists your every attempt at perspective or understanding. But the story, far from being an essay on wilderness, childhood, landscape art, perspective or its opposite, actually demonstrates its point – which is that images control us; they have power. Artists and writers invent or discover images that will 'involve' us, which might start off as mere objects in a scene (a tree, a lake), yet are delivered in such a way that they become 'doors'. An image is an object with a hinge, and works by opening. Through them, like Lois with her paintings, we might recover an access to lost worlds, find what is still alive there – ourselves, others. 'She [Lucy] is entirely alive.' As a short story the fictional framework itself leaves this generous conclusion ajar, but do we accept it? We walk through, look around, think again about Lois's 'wordless unease'. What fits with what? What is the truth?

The whole point of images is their drama: the way they provoke our active, imaginative involvement. Both writers and readers become participants. Atwood and Pinter invite us to be Lois, Richard or Sarah in a process dominated by images. Things in the world surrounding these characters are highlighted for us as problematic, potentially illuminating, ultimately confounding but compulsive – the subject both of our attention and theirs.

Image-making

How do writers construct worlds where objects become hinged openings, doors, invitations to enter and speculate? In a way I might already have answered this question. Images occur when a mind is closely attending to some object or event in its surroundings. To elaborate, the mind is in an unusual state of attention, so that a once familiar state or condition of things appears to be unfamiliar, surprising, joyful or hazardous. This view will not appeal to everybody. It assumes, it is argued, a 'moment of vision' theory of creativity. It depends upon an abnormal state of emotion, as if real writing happens involuntarily, under pressure, or is induced only in the presence of certain quite specific groups of objects – mountains or glaciers or the moon. In other words, it shows a dangerous tendency to Romanticism, an approach to writing developed by Wordsworth and Coleridge in the final years of the eighteenth century in England – dangerous because it limits our scope of response, directs it, favours a notion of mood as opposed to intelligence. But if we are going to allow imagination a free hand, we don't have to follow Wordsworth's theories. Nor do we need to embrace an opposing alternative. A number of early seventeenth-century poets in England believed that the ultimate image-maker was God, and that symbol, image and metaphor act as echoes of His divinity, or at least derive their power from a connection with it. We don't have to believe that either.

Another approach, based on experiment, takes nothing for granted. Next to me in the room where I am writing is a square, red table, about the same height from the floor as my chair. You can get such tables cheap from IKEA. On this table is an orange tree plant (with fruit on it) and a white circular plate eight inches in diameter. On the plate are flakes of a sausage roll I've just eaten. I am in a moment of *now*, whatever now is, along with chair, table, plate, oranges on a tree. What holds my attention is this plate; why, I don't know. Is it the absence of glaciers or mountains? I don't think so. The question seems irrelevant. As well as flakes of pastry the plate has two areas of shadow – one made by two leaves from the plant which seem to merge on its white surface, the other by the frame of a window interrupting the sun and so holding a third of the plate in shade. So far I have tried not to use metaphors. Even so, the longer I look, the more these start to emerge or become possible. I'm not in any unusual state of emotion, just looking at what is in front of me in this *now* I occupy, noticing white on red, circle on square, flakes, shadows. The flakes are scattered randomly, like ... I want to use a metaphor. The shadow of window frame darkens a gradually smaller section of plate. This is because the planet moves in an orbit, signalled by light. The plate has a flat surface centre and a raised area all the way round. Between the two is another shadow, curved dark like a new moon curved bright. I start to think what else this plate might have held: a melon slice, or an orange – not just the shadow of an orange; I also consider how quickly, unquietly, the plate would shatter. When I look at the flakes I see randomly scattered clumps inside a circle, as if somehow moved around by it. They seem random, yet suppose I were now looking at a map of the universe scattered with clumps of matter, accidental, not accidental, some sticking together – as if I could read its meaning, as if I were looking directly into its future. Everything is evidence, nothing random. The key to physics is in the tiny details of an eaten sausage roll.

What I aim to demonstrate here is the mind's tendency to make images even in the most ordinary of circumstances, under no emotional pressure, only by means of the act of attention itself. Under attention things start to transform, become significant, link up with sets of preoccupations you might not know you possessed. Metaphors happen uninhibited. I make no apologies for the moon.

Under different emotional circumstances I might have produced other metaphors – or my attention might have been interrupted.

The aim is to explore what happens in practice – by researching the issue, and to write in such a way that readers share the experience. By careful looking, alert response, objects emerge from their ordinary background, start to induce a gradual widening out of associations. What these will be is hard to predict. At the very least you will have encountered a bit of the world as real, made it more real than it would be seen through usual functional perception – sausage roll eaten, paragraph finished, time for a cup of tea, etc. The presence of images implies readers will not feel left out. The point at which an object becomes an image: this is the moment of fascination, discovery, more so if the process is shown to us. We need to feel how significance accretes and why, and one way to experiment is with images in the making.

Icons, signs, logos: Eagle signifies USA; 007 a gun-barrel filling with blood; North Sea Gas a trident sprouting flames; the Cross, Golgotha; images of redemption, power, licence to kill, money; yin and yang; pictorial plaque of the Pioneer spacecraft; hammers, sickles; scythes; locks and doors; mother and child in paintings; sculptures; sexual images; the exotic; a Playtex bra ad in Times Square New York – all of these we might call received images. We do not meet with them in their process of making, yet they confirm our sense of shared worlds. Writing frequently draws on images received, while it also renders them as subjective. Sometimes the process of making is close at hand, almost seems to happen before our eyes. The black British poet Fred D'Aguiar describes a return to London, his home city:

from 'Home'

The cockney cab driver begins chirpily
but can't or won't steer clear of race,
so rounds on Asians. I lock eyes with him
in the rear-view when I say I live with one.

He settles at the wheel grudgingly,
in a huffed silence. Cha! Drive man!
I have legal tender burning in my pocket
to move on, like a cross in Transylvania.

At my front door, why doesn't the lock
recognise me and budge? I give an extra
twist and fall forward over the threshold
piled with felicitations of junk mail,

into a cool reception in the hall.

Grey light and close skies, I love you,
chokey streets, roundabouts and streetlamps
with tyres chucked around them, I love you.

Police Officer, your boots need re-heeling.
Robin Redbreast, special request – a burst
of song so the worm can wind to the surface.
We must all sing for our supper or else.

(D'Aguiar, 1993:14)

Get Fred D'Aguiar to an interview, ask him what he thinks about England. Something like this will be his answer. There are no words for any exact, named, specific emotion, only images: 'I love you, / chokey streets...' The poem records a series of awkward obstacles – the taxi driver, the lock, junk mail stuffed with the type of received images we can imagine, a 'cool reception' – meaning the weather? Something else? The image of that 'burst of song / so the worm can wind to the surface'. Is this how the poet/singer feels, is made to feel – victim of a predatory capitalism rendered somehow lyrical: 'We must all sing for our supper or else'? Notice, too, the received images: 'a cross in Transylviania' – held up to ward off harm (held in the form of money), and the lock that has a mind of its own. The poem is so rich in images they become increasingly difficult to count. Some are just recorded observations: 'Grey light and close skies'. Others derive from English folk song tradition, singing 'for our supper', implying in passing a familiarity, revived by love but also alienation. And all these images occur just by putting himself in the mood of return, giving that his attention. We feel them being generated as he speaks, also as we read, and this is the huge advantage of writing – that readers share in the process as it happens.

STORY

Story occurs whenever importance is attached to events in time. This phenomenon happens so frequently that it seems fundamental to how we communicate. The events may have happened to somebody else, not to the speaker or writer. Whatever the listening, speaking, reading situation, we can assume that when any form of storytelling occurs, it has a purpose: to entertain, instruct, inform, enlighten. In the last four stanzas of 'Sandra Lee Scheuer', Geddes imagines two linked interwoven sets of events: a marriage proposal, a shooting – both in their opposite ways momentous. His purpose here isn't hard to detect: one story reveals to us what the natural course of her life might have been, another the unnatural cause of her death. By placing them together in slow motion the poem engages us, so that we feel the moment of impact intensely, almost as if it were happening before our eyes. Story therefore recreates, enacts, doesn't simply state or tell. Even so, it has a purpose. Aesop's fables end with pronouncements: 'Persuasion is better than force.' The underlying point of fables, however, is that story is better than pronouncement, enactment more vivid to us than statement. Story has the better chance of making things matter to us. When we want to clarify the great importance of something, our best way of doing so is through narrative.

Participation, Enactment

Storytelling achieves the clarification of the great importance of something by creating a sense of moments as *momentous,* for those involved, for its audiences and readers. In live performance the storyteller's art succeeds by action and gesture, moulding the voice, body and features into a state of empathy with the people and events, so that the moment of telling allows the story to come fully into existence, thus allowing the listener to participate. This quality I call *enactment*. The characters become habitable spaces, there all the time but coming alive whenever the space is filled by a real actor. Characters in fairy tales, any characters known through previous tellings, pre-exist the performance or reading. 'Hamlet' has become a space inhabited by generations of actors and audiences, and this is so because 'Hamlet' is a voice within a compelling story. Hamlet's condition is one of profound scepticism mixed with adult sexual revulsion. It needs a particular story to bring that out. Once out and enacted, we can see it, feel, empathise with and come to understand the nature of this scepticism – sometimes perverse, sometimes full of insight. We understand it *in time*, not just as abstraction.

Story and Performance: The Oral Tradition

Performance poetry also shares something with the art of narrative enactment. Asked about the influences on his writing, Adrian Mitchell comments, 'I think it goes back to the ballads. I can recall the impact of Sir Patrick Spens. It was that simplicity you find in the old ballads ... then later came the attraction of the voice, the delivery' (Munden, 1999: 32). In oral traditions, songs and ballads declare that something worth our attention has happened. We know the story already, yet whenever the piece is delivered its world pushes aside the stream of unshaped time, replacing it with an inkling of the extraordinary. Writing about Irish Lament poetry and the oral tradition, Aileen La Tourette sees these forms in terms of a physical act:

> I can imagine the poet, the keener, recalling the dead person with all the passion they could summon, and then, in a quieter voice, gently laying them to rest. I imagine the act of corporate keening, the repetition of a cry, as a healing, energetic, physical act. … It lies, like all performance poetry perhaps, on some kind of cusp of drama, ritual, dance – I imagine a swaying and bending of the body – where words meet actions and form gestures and postures almost inextricable from the syllables themselves.
>
> (Ibid., 1999: 29)

Reacting to the momentous, enacting it, the emphasis falls on 'recalling … summoning … where words meet actions …' – the dead are brought to life, then laid to rest, in forms of 'ritual, dance'. Statement is there, yet a statement enacted, as in this poem about Art:

from 'W-H-A-M'

Paintings should not be locked up in galleries
Or pinned to walls with nails of steel.
Paintings should not be dormant and dusted –
Sad as last year's Christmas cracker.
They should be released, set free
Live in trees in sunlit France
Be invited to balls
football matches
symphony concerts
orgies and outings
They should wave to people in the street.

(Ibid., 1999: 88)

The poet John Mole has explained that 'the very act of writing itself, with its continually renewed challenge, becomes my performance' (Munden, 1999: 48) – as though a poem itself were an event, a moment of challenge. In the passage above by Peter Dixon, paintings become events, or like people set free in a world their presence passionately transforms. The poet is using a sense of story. A new world of story is required. The ordinary world of paintings locked in galleries needs story, action, some new event or change of state.

Story and Change

Whereas the other features of creative language operate by bringing us in close, showing more of the world, exposing the inherent attributes of a person or scene, story drives us forward – through and beyond. Richard in Pinter's *The Lover* tries to fix the meaning of 'blind'. Lois's paintings in Atwood's story will always reveal the irreclaimable presence of her friend. The point about making images is to make them stay in place: the statue that will never be dislodged from the public square; the works of art stowed in their museums; D'Aguair's worm that always winds to the surface; his London of chokey streets, grey light, close skies. Story rebels against such continuities. If popular journalism loves images, its addiction to story draws even more followers. The celebrity ideal attracts because story puts it at risk, and so this sense that things can always get better, or worse, feeds an appetite for *discontinuity*. Here is an example from a piece of journalism:

> It starts with the little things: the unscrubbed bath, the unwashed dishes, the socks on the living room floor. Then the little things become bigger; the unpaid share of the gas bill, the 'borrowed' clothes, the continuous late night thump of the stereo system. Gradually you come to realise that you are living with the flat-mate from hell.
>
> (Tredre, 1995)

From an *Observer* article by Nicholas Tredre, this passage implies a point where the person causing these kinds of disruption won't be tolerated much longer. Even though this is the opening paragraph, already the language has started to move us on, tracking a situation as it develops. The writing enacts, builds tension, records time as events not just in a list but as a shape. We are allowed to feel the developments from the viewpoint of someone there in the picture – a picture already changing, moving on.

The 'little things' are getting bigger, yet the tone remains comparatively light. Not so in this next extract from Michael Herr's introduction to the photographer Don McCullin's autobiography, where the setting is a road intersection in North Vietnam:

> This was an elemental crossroads, where body and spirit could meet and then be sheared away from one another in a second. It had been cold and dark for days, and all the light seemed to be weighed with gray, greasy particles. And without breaking it down into its components of smoke, cordite, fear, dust, death, prayers, and the palpable pyramiding misery, the air was just too thick. It was thick along the ground where we were lying, and

> above us it was thick with rounds. We then saw McCullin step into this crossroads with what was, at the very least, a great impersonation of total deliberateness. He referred to his light meter, made some adjustments on his camera, and began taking pictures.
>
> (Herr, 1990: 10)

The rule is: set the scene, move it forward. 'For days...' becomes 'the ground where we were lying...', becomes the first moment of action: 'We then saw...' followed rapidly by more moments of action. The whole style of the passage is an acting out. Whenever events develop in real time, as in reports or records, someone could always be ready to say, '*I was there, and it wasn't like that*'. A writer aims to counter such objections, and does so using reality effects, details that carry an '*I was there*' type element of 'convincingness'. Here we have 'light ... weighed with gray, greasy particles ... the air was just too thick'. Most of us have enough sense of war to accept these details, and it's important we do so because when McCullin does appear he is going to be playing a hero's role, or at least a 'great impersonation' of it. We are being asked to accept this, too, and we do. The passage has slipped from real time into time where heroes arise. Armed with a camera, McCullin appears like Beowulf facing Grendell's ravages in the hall of the Geats. Someone has stepped forward with hero qualities, crossing the borders of real time into a world of story.

Shaping Time: Story Worlds

As well as a moment by moment telling, story also moves us into a world becoming extraordinary. You are a flatmate, then, apparently, you are a *flatmate from hell.* People who are experiencing story find themselves in circumstances no longer safe. The real world is still present, but changed. The shift can be gradual or sudden, wondrous, sometimes deeply horrifying: love, loss, grief, illness, possible recovery, sudden news, travels and expeditions, things from the past erupting into the present. We sense that time is shaped differently from how we thought it was. Buried conflicts surface. Opposite forces face each other, struggle for domination. We ask, 'What's going on?'

In fiction, the extraordinary becomes real, the real extraordinary. But to make the shift from one to the other requires extraordinary skill on the part of the writer. Building up worlds we recognise as authentic helps to enact the shift and make it credible. Harry Potter begins in Privet Drive. The world of story – demons, goblins, witches, wizards, owls – waits to pounce on the normal and rip it apart, which is why the normal has to be there.

'Mr and Mrs Dursley, of number four, Privet Drive, were proud to say they were perfectly normal, thank you very much. They were the last people you'd expect to be involved in anything strange or mysterious, because they just didn't hold with such nonsense' (Rowling, 1997: 1). Rowling's stories usually start with the ordinary, with characters representing its limitations. She makes us want to move forward into the strange, the eventful – to mystery.

'A certain man planted a vineyard, and let it forth to husbandmen, and went away into a far country.' The idea of parables was to speak in images people could understand. Jokes do it too. 'An Alsatian went into a post office ... Can I send a telegram, please, he said.' Extreme disruption, yet against a background of the familiar. Even Harry Potter is unnerved at first by what he discovers, and this is so because his upbringing is still partly Dursley. Faced with Hogwarts, readers will recognise the experience of being inducted into a new school – a big one – where mysterious doors lead you astray, staircases go nowhere, as if the place itself had it in for you.

The American novelist Jean Hegland sees story occurring when characters find themselves in extraordinary circumstances. In her first novel, *Into the Forest*, there is a war somewhere; power stations fail for days and weeks, then months. The moveable point is *circumstances*. The characters – for the most part ordinary just like ourselves – will either cope or die. At first they resist this storyworld, hoping it will end, longing for the familiar to return, and on occasions it seems it almost might. Other writers might be inclined to invent one or more extraordinary *characters*, so that they become the point of movement, circumstances shaped by their actions, thoughts and behaviour. But there must be some impact of strangeness – either the *situation* is strange or the *characters* are. Story will insist this is so. *Into The Forest* begins in one of these modes – it is circumstances – yet ends with the characters. Gradually it is they who become extraordinary, and the special quality of the extraordinary in this case is that instead of remaining dependent children in the face of disaster, together they decide to shape their future. In the following passage, the narrator, a girl of eighteen, writes her diary. Her younger sister Eva is heavily pregnant. Their parents are dead. They live on the edge of a forest in northern California, where only their resourcefulness allows them to survive. Every moment of experience demands this constant effort of survival, yet with occasional rare times for reflection:

> Again the moon grows full. There has been a break in the rain, but the weather is so cold and Eva so enormously big that we stay close to home, close to the stove and pantry and our

> warm mattresses. Eva dozes and drinks the tea I steep for her. She knits odd little gowns from the silks our mother left, while I scan the encyclopedia for the dreams it contains, and write by the light of the round moon and the open stove, my pen scratching its tiny markings onto these last sheets of paper.
>
> This afternoon I read: *The oldest use of the word 'virgin' meant not the physiological condition of chastity, but the psychological state of belonging to no man, of belonging to oneself. To be virginal did not mean to be inviolate, but rather to be true to nature and instinct, just as the virgin forest is not barren or unfertilised, but instead is unexploited by man.*
>
> *Children born out of wedlock were at one time referred to as 'virgin-born'*
>
> (Hegland, 1998: 208)

This new state of being and action is their story and one they approach, as here, with increasing conviction and commitment. We might call it their story-world, one of danger, insecurity, but also determination, drive, anxiety and desire. Nothing is certain. To enter the forest, let go of the past, means to become virginal as defined by that encyclopedia: 'belonging to oneself'.

In sharp contrast with Hegland's gradual induction of her characters, Stephen King's novels move swiftly into their story-world. Yet he also prefers to make circumstances the driving point of a story. As he explains, too much focus on characters entangles him in a need for complicated plots, a feature of fiction King would rather avoid:

> A strong enough situation renders the whole question of plot moot, which is fine with me. The most interesting situations can usually be expressed as a *what if* question:
>
> What if vampires invaded a small New England village (Salem's Lot)
>
> What if a young mother and her son became trapped in their stalled car by a rabid dog (Cujo)
>
> ...In my view, stories and novels consist of three parts: narration, which moves the story from point A to point B and finally to point Z; description, which creates a sensory reality for the reader; and dialogue, which brings characters to life through their speech.
>
> (King, 2001: 196)

Realism

The first character in fiction to experience 'belonging to oneself' was Robinson Crusoe. There are similarities between Hegland's story and Defoe's novel, one of the earliest examples of modern fiction, written near the beginning of the eighteenth century.

As well as a new attention to self and surroundings, modern fiction writers aimed to position their story-worlds close to the common experience of living readers. This stylistic development is usually defined by the term *realism*. King also insists on 'sensory reality'. However strange, the world of the story must be made habitable, believable. If it were not, his peculiar horrors wouldn't be able to threaten or attack. In terms of technique, King, too, is a realist. Indeed it might be that all modern fiction requires a credible state of sensory reality, and that this is its difference from the world of religious allegory and seasonal myth whose authorship is often anonymous and whose main purpose doesn't require a world of credible illusions. This was a quality that myths and fables didn't even need to consider. Fiction in the modern world has to earn its right to credibility, and does so in a style that uses reality effects and constant researched reference to the actual. It has to convince by experience, not by authority or tradition. Story thereafter aims to give *real* experience a shape, to remind us constantly of ourselves as its potential heroes and heroines, victims and criminals, witnesses and participants. Instead of demons, dragons, prophets and saints, it is ourselves who inhabit the new world of story.

We will explore realism and its developments in other chapters on prose narrative. What are its implications for fiction writing, writing for children, writing autobiography? Should we think of a split between realism and fantasy or myth, or does all narrative share a common root? Were the events in Beowulf true? Was there a dragon? Did Jane Austen's Emma really believe Mr Knightly wanted to marry Harriet? Like a jury we use our sense of what evidence counts, even though we know for a fact there wasn't any Emma or Beowulf. These characters become real to us through a manner and style of presentation, through the rhythm of words, through our notions of what forms of story we can accept, through our own relationship with time. We have to believe that somehow their realness will be to our advantage, that we will, as a result, understand ourselves and our own shaping; that we will do this by hearing, moment by moment, how their experience shapes time.

The Moving Edge

By the time you read this book, events dominating the present news in the world will be history. Mostly we are living in ordinary time – then something happens, a break with what we expected or thought predictable. We pass into the extraordinary, into story. Once across the threshold we find suspense, crisis, resolution, closure or lack of closure, the conventions of oral and written stories that correspond to shaped time in experience. Love and loss, illness and recovery, departure, return, triumph and disappointment: if we are undergoing these shifts of position then we might describe ourselves as being *in a story*. Ordinary time, by contrast, leaves us stranded in routines, habits, timetables – the familiar. In story-worlds our sense of the moving edge of time reaches uncomfortable heights, becomes intense, threatens to overwhelm us. All of us live at the moving edge of time. In fiction, drama, poetry, writing enacts that sense of an edge. Writers in the creative genres give a consistent emphasis to the moment, the moving edge, in subjective experience.

What if Time Stopped?

> Fair youth, beneath the trees, thou canst not leave
> Thy song, nor ever can those trees be bare;
> Bold lover, never, never canst thou kiss,
> Though winning near the goal – yet, do not grieve;
> She cannot fade, though thou hast not thy bliss,
> For ever wilt thou love, and she be fair!
> (Keats, 1996: 848)

Keats was obsessed with time and here in 'Ode On A Grecian Urn' he puts his finger on its pulse so that it does stop. He chose a moment when it was beating fast. Bliss is deferred until the next moment, yet he keeps his finger there. Why? Keats was trying to reshape time. Death is the end of time; he knows this, so why not reverse it back to a moment of bliss? Why not reverse it further back to the moment *before* bliss? That was what he aimed to do. Keats was using his feeling of story to show a moment overshadowed not by death, age, disease or change, but instead by what is *about* to happen – the lovers' kiss. Beauty is truth.

This exclusive focus on the moment is found in many contemporary poems written nearly two centuries after Keats wrote his. The use of the present tense in poetry has become almost a compulsory feature of style. It allows the poet to get close to the detail of an experience, show it in close-up, pause it for the eye's searching scrutiny. Whether or not the aim is to hold the moment at flash-point, hold it in life and so avoid what Philip Larkin called the 'long perspectives' – which lead to death – we can't be sure, but this technique still usually involves a sense of story, an overshadowing. Poets using the present tense can focus on events long in the past, thus making these present and immediate, as in these first lines from the winning poem of a recent National

Poetry Competition, where the poet, Julia Copus, revisits the thoughts of a medieval illustrator of a Book of Hours:

from 'The Art of Illumination'

At times it is a good life, with the evening sun
Gilding the abbey tower, the brook's cold waters

Sliding past and every Hour in my book
a blank page, vellum pumice-storied

to chalky lustres which my inks suffuse:
saffron and sandarach and dragon's blood,

azure and verdigris. Monsters and every type of beast
curl round the words. Each man here has a past,

and each man reason for his faith. I wronged
A woman once and nothing I did after could atone

or throw a light upon the blackness of that deed
whose harm lay in the telling, not the doing.

(Copus, *IOS*, 13 April 2003)

This speaker's past curls round his words just as the dragons do round those he inscribes. In subjects approached with a sense of story, moments in a poem's present will have a past and future, a shadow cast by one or other of these. Another example, the following poem by Susan Burns, successfully demonstrates this type of perception. The version printed here is in draft form, yet we can see the poet already working to create habitable worlds using reality effects, voices, images, and most of all a sense of story:

'Farewell on the Town Hall Steps'

It's as good a place as any to end it.
A July gone cold, the middle of an overcast night.
You're walking me home but we won't reach
Brixton Water Lane and we both know
There won't be a fight.

We sit on the concrete steps, roll a cigarette.

I can hear the goods trains at Loughborough junction,
Distant sirens and your reasoning, sketching the air
With a thin white cigarette paper. I don't cry then
As I have made up my mind,
As you are drunk to your bitten fingernails,
As you can't bring the paper to your dry mouth.
I take it, fumble with tobacco. Your voice thick

With tears, your chin on your knees, unfolding
The usual: how useless a father, how reckless a lover;
How just one more drink, how I don't deserve.

I half-listen; it's always that way with you.
I concentrate on the upturned collar of your jacket.
The truth is always in what's not being said.

Unexpectedly, across the street, an alfresco party,
The end of a wedding. A woman in red satin,
Confetti still in her hair, laughs at the wide sky.

Six stops away from the Victoria line, the hostel
In Copenhagen Street, Chris on the night shift,
Miracle worker, rearranges the confiscations,
The cans of Special, the pocket knives.

As well as the basic narrative of what happened, who said what to whom, where and when, this poem is variously overshadowed by other events. What happened echoes what happened once, what was said – or not said – before. The poet has chosen a moment which shapes time – afterwards things will not be as they were. Other events happening in the present and simultaneously – the party across the street, the night shift – cast their shade and light on the situation, but it may be that the final stanza misses it, becomes a new scene, not an overshadowing. Drafts are important, especially in workshop situations. Should this last stanza be omitted? Some might think so, others feel less certain, but everyone knows the writer herself will have the last word.

No Story?

In the extracts below, the Australian poet Les Murray explores an absence of story, giving it a specific setting that might apply more widely. Moments are seen in a type of life without overshadowing or shape:

from 'Driving Through Sawmill Towns'

... You glide on through town,
Your mudguards damp with cloud.
The houses there wear verandahs out of shyness,
All day in calendared kitchens, women listen
For cars on the road,
Lost children in the bush,
A cry from the mill, a footstep –
Nothing happens.

> ... Sometimes a woman, sweeping her front step,
> or a plain young wife at a tankstand fetching water
> in a metal bucket will turn round and gaze
> at the mountains in wonderment,
> looking for a city.
>
> ... As night comes down, the houses watch each other,
> A light going out in a window has a meaning.
> ... Men sit after tea
> by the stove while their wives talk, rolling a dead match
> between their fingers,
> thinking of the future.
>
> (Murray, 2001: 2–4)

Murray shows us lives stalled at the point of hunger for story. Nothing happens, yet the lack of story is overpowering – in the people, in the minimal instances of their lives: 'calendared kitchens ... metal bucket ... rolling a dead match.' Nothing distracts them from the passage of time. Nothing either shapes it or reshapes it. The women 'gaze at the mountains in wonderment / looking for a city'. For the word 'city' here we might read 'story'.

Summary

Can we identify the special qualities that make a piece of writing *creative* writing? In this chapter I have tried to answer this question, but in ways that will open doors to writing as practice. Most of us will be readers and listeners before we become writers, but reading and listening are for writers active and ongoing. We need to become experts in listening to voices, in sensing what it takes to make a story, in discovering images that stay with us and somehow compel our attention, in knowing about the worlds people inhabit – those they wish for, those they visit or live in from day to day.

What makes certain voices, images, worlds and stories important to a writer, and others less so? My term for this power of shaping and selecting is *imagination.* To know what we enjoy in other people's writing means that our imagination is already at work, and that we ourselves are selecting the stories, styles, characters and settings that will go on attracting this power and winning its approval. Sometimes an unusual combination of words can stir the imagination, sometimes a dramatic scene in a story, poem, play or film, or in a real life experience.

Reading is therefore important to all writers, and in this first chapter I have endeavoured to introduce some of the ways we might read *as writers.* The question a writer will always ask is:

'What can I learn from this or that piece of writing as art; how can it influence my own work?' But there will be other questions too, about how a character's experience of time is shaped for him or her, how a writer gets across the sense of a real experience, how he or she builds up a story's world, creates the sense of voices under pressure. How does the writer attract and hold our attention – in this poem, in this scene of a play?

But just as important as reading is the fact that we need to be alert to the real world, to the way people and places make us feel, in other words, to actual experience and its sensations in time – the stuff, basically, which art transforms. The passages I have chosen all demonstrate – in one way or another – not just a fascination with experience but a need to make it worth our attention.

The chapters that follow are organised according to genres, beginning with memoir or life-writing, but as this introductory chapter suggests, we can, if we choose, begin to see in every genre the same features that make writing creative: **voice**, **world**, **image** and **story**.

Getting Started. Ideas for Good Practice

Start a writer's workbook. Start looking and listening more closely to what is around you. Begin to write brief sketches of scenes witnessed, for example, in a street, among people, at a public event. Try to find the best words to capture things glimpsed fleetingly. Include as many sense impressions as you can.

Write in your workbook regularly every day. If you don't have anything you want to write, try free-writing, letting your pen take you where it wants to go. Don't worry about being coherent or writing on a particular subject. Don't worry either if you find you *are* writing about something in particular. Just write.

Become a word-hoarder. Make good use of thesauruses and etymological dictionaries. Think about the shifting usages of words.

Collect 'found' texts: the names of shops, words on placards, graffiti, signs in the streets, epigraphs on tombstones, names of moored boats, snippets of overheard conversations, bits of texts from newspapers, anything that strikes you as an interesting, typical/untypical use of language.

A line from something you're reading, whether it's factual, philosophical, political or literary, can be the starting point to trigger some writing of your own. Words themselves are triggers.

The novelist Paul Auster has commented: 'The one thing I try to do in all my books is to leave room in the prose for the reader to inhabit it. ... There's a way in which a writer can do too much, overwhelming the reader with so many details that he no longer has any air to breathe.' Find some examples from poems, novels, and stories you have read where you think the reader is given room to breathe and can inhabit the writing. How is this done? Start to read as a writer, make a note of effects you like in texts. Start thinking about the way opening lines work, about the structures and shapes writing has. Think about the changing pace and patterning of the language, the significance of images and how they're used. Whatever its mode, think about those moments in a text that surprise you and how they are achieved. Think about the way texts conclude, how much is suggested rather than stated, where the spaces are for you as a reader to enter the text, how you can achieve that as a writer.

Start to examine your own life as a source of insight and information about the world. Think about the sorts of worlds you inhabit now and have inhabited in the past, your own particular family, home, workplace. Go back to other places you have lived in. Focus closely on a particular interior, its detail and mood, the reality-effects that make it memorable. How important are seasons, time of day? Think of jobs you have done: Just what was it like in the kitchen of that pizza place? Serving awkward customers in the shoe shop? Working on the early morning post? What about the world of the leisure centre, or disco, or martial arts group? All these places will have their own routines, their own jargons and rituals. Try to describe a typical scene. How are people dressed, how do they speak, relate to each other? Think about the dynamic between members of the group. Who's in charge? What are the unspoken rules? Where are the tensions? You are an authority on your own world(s) that are wider than you think. Try to find a fresh way of describing the ordinary. What's everyday to you will be unusual to someone else. When you have got your 'reality effects' you have basic material you can work on, not only for writing memoir but to develop into fiction, poetry or drama.

Suggestions for Writing

The conditions under which writing happens, both physical and emotional, is a topic of much fascination and little certainty. We can only guess what causes the seeds to grow. But we do know that writing workshops sometimes allow the imagination a chance to create those conditions. The imagination acts as a form of flight simulator, so that although you are actually sitting at a desk and writing, you are also, in your imagination, somewhere else, writing in the voice of someone else, maybe a character or persona, or reliving an experience of your own. You are also learning at the controls what happens when language is used creatively. The suggestions below, as with others in this book, are intended to advance your confidence, and help you both to explore new possibilities, and to devise your own simulations using these as examples.

Read the following passage by Elizabeth Bishop. Bishop lived and wrote in South America. The animal in this prose poem is a real creature and here she has given it a voice.

> *from 'Strayed Crab'*
>
> This is not my home. How did I get so far from water? It must be over that way somewhere.
>
> I am the color of wine, of *tinta*. The inside of my powerful right claw is saffron-yellow. See, I see it now; I wave it like a flag. I am dapper and elegant; I move with great precision, cleverly managing all my smaller yellow claws. I believe in the oblique, the indirect approach, and I keep my feelings to myself.
>
> But on this strange, smooth surface I am making too much noise. I wasn't meant for this. If I maneuver a bit and keep a sharp lookout, I shall find my pool again. Watch out for my right claw, all passersby!
>
> My eyes are good, though small: my shell is tough and tight. In my own pool are many small gray fish. I see right through them. Only their large eyes are opaque, and twitch at me. They are hard to catch, but I, I catch them quickly in my arms and eat them up.
>
> What is that big soft monster, like a yellow cloud, stifling and warm? What is it doing? It pats my back. Out, claw. There, I have frightened it away. It's sitting down, pretending nothing's happened. I'll skirt it. It's still pretending not to see me. Out of my way, O monster. I own a pool, all the little fish that swim in it, and all the skittering waterbugs that smell like rotten apples.
>
> Cheer up, O grievous snail. I tap your shell, encouragingly, not that you will ever know about it.
>
> And I want nothing to do with you, either, sulking toad. Imagine, at least four times my size and yet so vulnerable... I could open your belly with my claw. You glare and bulge, a watchdog near my pool; you make a loud and hollow noise. I do not care for such stupidity. I admire compression, lightness, and agility, all rare in this loose world.
>
> (Bishop, 1991: 140)

Notice how Bishop gets right inside the nervous system of the crab and develops its voice accordingly. She is maybe saying something about herself, but indirectly.

1 Write a passage of similar length using an animal as speaker. This animal is in a state of discomfort, possibly dislodged from its usual habitat. Another animal appears. An action takes place.

Write another passage where the speaker is human. Again, in a state of physical discomfort, showing an attitude. Another person or people are present, and at some point – as in the passage above – the speaker is threatened.

2 Write a poem in the voice of a famous person; alive or dead, past or present. Try to enter his or her imagination. Include in your poem three things significant to your speaker; these are an object, a question difficult to answer, another voice.

3 Each of us is involved in a whole range of different activities and any of these could be useful for writing. Using ideas from your workbook, write a short story, a poem, the first scene of a play, or a piece of personal narrative, making use of your special understanding of a work place, surroundings you know well, an individual or group activity. Pay attention to voices, details and reality effects, close-up images, building on your sense of what you know.

4 Try looking out of a window or taking a walk down a street – perhaps it leads somewhere a little unusual, or to somewhere not very surprising. Maybe the window looks out over neighbouring gardens or fields. Whatever you see, describe it, find something in the surroundings interesting to you, something you are looking at with new eyes. Using these and other details, put together a poem or short story with these surroundings as its opening setting.

5 Go into the streets of a nearby town. Write down words from notices, street signs: 'WALK THIS SIDE', 'FOLLOW DIVERSION', 'KEEP OUT' ... Also write down words and phrases from street adverts you can find. Mix these together into a long sequence – one phrase per line – repeating some if you need to. Working in small groups, assemble your list in a way that satisfies you. Be aware of the process and discuss your decisions.

6 Write a piece of dialogue between two characters. Centre this dialogue round an object in a room, for example, a cupboard, a vase of flowers, a suitcase, a chair. Or think up a more unusual object – a toolbox, a screwed-up piece of paper with a message on it, a supermarket trolley, a dismantled motorbike. Write it so that the object becomes an image with real force of significance for the two speakers. At one point one says to the other, 'Don't touch it!'

7 Imagine a photograph of the room in which you are sitting – you are in the photograph too, and there might be other people there with you in the moment of the shot. Write a poem as if *you* are describing this photograph. Use close-up focus, significant details. Make the reader see it. Then write about what it does NOT show: a moment, scene, event or feeling that the photograph leaves out. Also try this using an actual photograph. Decide who is the speaker and the voice.

8 Write a very short story or a poem which centres on a character in a film, but not one of the main characters. Find one of the extras – somebody relatively insignificant. Explore his or her position, viewpoint, and voice.

9 Working in twos, each person tells the other a story. Choose something that has happened to you and has become fixed in your memory, or something that happened to someone you know. Exchange stories with your partner. Pay close attention to what you are being told. Then tell the other person's story to the whole group. Tell it as if it had happened to you personally. You might want to exaggerate certain details, and leave out others. If so, go ahead. Aim to attract the attention of your listeners. Bring the story to life in your own words. Make it animated. If you can, perform the story, emphasising speech and dialogue, elements of suspense, particular images that seem to you important or unusual.

Compare the story as you heard it with the way you told it. Be aware of how these versions differ.

The group will now have a collection of stories, a pool of images to draw on for writing. From this resource, each person chooses something that engages his or her imagination, sense of drama and story, and writes a short piece of fiction (1,000 words limit) or a poem (40 lines limit). You might choose your own story, the one you told, or one you have heard. Use images, voices, close-up focus, reality effects. Think about whether the story has a point or purpose – what is it? Can you make your readers sense what this might be without telling them directly?

10 In the following poem I am describing a small crowd of people in a London tube train. They all believe they are watching a story: two people about to become lovers. A story world seems to be happening right in front of their eyes.

'Mile End Opera'

The man with whiskers of ponytail hair
growing out of the back of his shaved skull,
the woman with the Anna Ford face,
catacombed under London with other strangers.
Cornered, like prison visitors.
Swaying with the machinery.
Also a boy and girl – he's black, she's white.

Beautiful black and white.
He's telling her about his college courses.
Things he likes. She telling him about her.
They are directing such smiles at each other
every one is a hit,
so that everyone in this carriage seems happier,
a shade less absent. People are listening.

Even Anna Ford is feeling distinct.
Even the shaved/unshaved head is alert.
This girl's voice is luminous with this boy.
Whatever she's saying to him she can't stop.
Just listening, just looking at her
is becoming something phenomenal to him.
And, if she's seen that smile – which she has –

she must know what the audience also knows –
that it's real, that these two are somehow
going to get off at the same stop,
that they've only just met but ... what the hell ...
This is it! Though they don't know it
we're all shouting for them, leaning towards them,
giving them space, swaying together,

silently wishing them things which in ourselves
we never knew,
or once or twice have known.
'This is it. Do it. Go for it',
punching the air for them in a whole Yes!

The trains stops, he gets up, goes, he's gone.
She sits staring into the walls of London.
(Mills 2000: 74)

Write a poem describing, for example, two people in a room, your neighbours outdoors or glimpsed through a window, a group of people in the street or in a photograph. Watch them carefully. What are they doing? Why? Can you tell what if anything the real story is? Describe them using a sense of story.

Revision and Editing

Although you may have been using a workbook, you also need to work on pieces of writing that will be read by other people. It's vital to get feedback on your work. Whether you revise and edit your writing as a result is your decision. Even the most negative feedback can sometimes be useful but, practically speaking, your opinion ultimately matters the most. You are in charge.

As you prepare your work for a reader you will need to think about presentation – word processing, line spacing, sentence structure, spelling, punctuation. Errors can interrupt the flow of reading, and, if you are submitting a piece for publication, will definitely look unprofessional.

Check your sentences. Are they too long, too complicated, weakly structured? Can they be followed first time if heard aloud or do they lose their point? Check your paragraphs. If any paragraph is longer than 150 words, see if you can reduce it or make a new paragraph break. See how sentences and paragraphs work in a piece of writing you would like to have written. Finally, check your punctuation. Find out how to use forms you're maybe less familiar with – the colon, semi-colon, dash.

If you are formatting your writing on a word processor, use double spacing for prose, single spacing for poems. Check that your work is easily accessible to the eye of your reader, with consistent font variations – italics and underlines. To save your early drafts, use the 'Track Changes' facility from the Tools menu on the rule bar.

All creative writing will have an oral quality, written for the voice. Test this out by reading your work aloud. How does it sound? Can it be understood clearly by a listener as well as by a reader? If so, you will have made something significant to you and equally meaningful to your audience.

CHAPTER 2

PERSONAL NARRATIVE

The Story of the Self

The sensations of a mind and body, in finite time, moving through a physical universe: if this is one definition of the self, it perhaps becomes more recognisable if we add desires, fears, and, in some cases, prayers for its everlasting salvation. These attributes link each of us to a culture, so that we learn to desire, fear and speak to each other only as we belong to groups of people sharing customs, values and beliefs. The self still remains a neurological mystery, however – in so far as how it can inhabit that cluster of cells somewhere inside the lobes of the brain, how it recognises itself through memory, links up experiences into a story. First memories, first evidence of such linking, are what we think of when it comes to that fascinating question: 'Who am I?' Personal narrative comprises, for many writers, a first acquaintance with images, voices, stories and worlds significant to that act of self-recognition. But the other important attribute of this form is that we can write as we speak. Personal narrative can be like conversation. In the passages below, I particularly admire the way John Berger opens up a discussion with his readers. The subject of his first paragraph is a familiar one:

> Every time I went to bed – and in this I am sure I was like millions of other children – the fear that one or both of my parents might die in the night touched the nape of my neck with its finger. Such a fear has, I believe, little to do with a particular psychological climate and a great deal to do with nightfall. Yet since it was impossible to say 'You won't die in the night, will you?' (when Grandmother died, I was told she had gone to have a rest, or – this was from my uncle who was more outspoken – that she had passed over), since I couldn't ask the real question

and I sought a reassurance, I invented – like millions before me – the euphemism See you in the morning! To which either my father or mother who had come to turn out the light in my bedroom would reply, See you in the morning, John.

After their footsteps had died away, I would try for as long as possible not to lift my head from the pillow so that the last words spoken remained, trapped like a fish in a rock pool at low tide, between my pillow and my ear The implicit promise of the words was also a protection against the dark. The words promised that I would not (yet) be alone.

Autobiography begins with a sense of being alone. It is an orphan form. Yet I have no wish to do so. All that interests me about my past life are the common moments. The moments – which if I relate them well enough – will join countless others lived by people I do not personally know.

(Berger, 1992: 46)

Berger writes with honesty, an approach that carries a sense of risk. He seems wary of the autobiographical, embarrassed by it, preferring to establish links with readers rather than occupy a vacuum: 'This is about me but about you too – all of us.' Maybe readers read personal narrative to find out what they can about that person in the spotlight – the person achieving excellence, standing alone. If so, John Berger's approach gently discourages such an expectation.

Each of the excerpts I have chosen to illustrate the subject of this chapter succeed in ways that have nothing to do with fame or reputation. The writers claim our attention simply because of the way they evoke worlds, capture moments, dig deep into the meanings that made their experiences real to them. The autobiographical no longer needs to associate itself with celebrity and the building of self-image for a public. More broadly it includes memoir or life writing, each of which, as forms of personal narrative, can draw us into particular episodes in the writer's experience, explore their meanings, develop shared insight. Memoir, as the word suggests, means memory, a form of the autobiographical. Autobiography as such may contain information not remembered yet equally vital. An event may indeed have influenced your life, even though you have no memory of it.

Berger's insight into his own purpose – which is to be inclusive, to communicate – allows him to speak directly to his audience and from memory, as if he were in a conversation with his readers. It is this quality which makes memoir so valuable as a form. The writer can narrate, explain, reflect, as well as evoke and illustrate. The writer is thinking through an experience – close to it – not from some far off remote point where what was real now seems easy to map. When a sense of perspective does emerge, it happens because the attention to detail has been accurate, the feeling of engagement – with the experience, with the reader – open and equal. The writer sets out with the aim of making some large or small discoveries, not because they are in place beforehand. The writer needs to bring us these discoveries as they happen, as if the writing were in the act of producing them before us – which indeed it is. While autobiography covers a whole lifetime up to the place and moment of writing, memoir offers a sense of close-upness, of the specific, the episodic. It may concentrate on one or more linked episodes. The most important quality, however, is *tone.* You need to bring the experience to your reader as you would in a real conversation.

Berger's memoir, entitled, 'Mother', was written quite soon after her death. Here is how it continues:

> Six weeks ago my mother asked me to come and see her; it would be the last time, she said. A few days later, on the morning of my birthday, she believed she was dying. Open the curtains, she said to my brother, so I can see the trees. In fact, she died the following week.
>
> On my birthdays as a child, it was my father rather than she who gave me memorable presents. She was too thrifty. Her moments of generosity were at the table, offering what she had bought and prepared and cooked and served to whoever came into the house. Otherwise she was thrifty. Nor did she ever explain. She was secretive, she kept things to herself. Not for her own pleasure, but because the world would not forgive spontaneity, the world was mean. I must make that clearer. She didn't believe life was mean – it was generous – but she had learnt from her own childhood that survival was hard. She was the opposite of quixotic – for she was not born a knight and her father was a warehouse foreman in Lambeth. She pursed her lips together, knitted her brows, as she calculated and thought things out and carried on with an unspoken determination. She never asked favours of anyone. Nothing shocked her. From whatever she saw, she just drew the necessary conclusions so as to survive and to be dependent on nobody.
>
> When I was in my thirties, she told me for the first time that ever since I was born she had hoped I would be a writer. ... a writer was a person familiar with the secrets. Perhaps in the end she didn't read my books so that they should remain more secret.
>
> If her hopes of my becoming a writer – and she said they began on the night after I was delivered – were eventually realised, it was not because there were many books in our house (there were few) but because there was so much that

was unsaid, so much that I had to discover the existence of on my own at an early age: death, poverty, pain (in others), sexuality. ...

These things were there to be discovered within the house or from its windows – until I left for good, more or less prepared for the outside world, at the age of eight. My mother never spoke of these things. She didn't hide the fact that she was aware of them. For her, however, they were wrapped secrets, to be lived with but never to be mentioned or opened. Superficially, this was a question of gentility, but profoundly, of a respect, a secret loyalty to the enigmatic. My rough and ready preparation for the world did not include a single explanation – it simply consisted of the principle that events carried more weight than the self.

Thus, she taught me very little – at least in the usual sense of the term; she a teacher about life, I a learner. By imitating her gestures I learnt how to roast meat in the oven, how to clean celery, how to cook rice, how to choose vegetables in a market. As a young woman she had been a vegetarian. Then she gave it up because she did not want to influence us children. Why were you a vegetarian? I once asked her, eating my Sunday roast, much later when I was first working as a journalist. Because I'm against killing. She would say no more. Either I understood or I didn't. There was nothing more to be said.

(Ibid., 47–9)

Mixed in with Berger's conversational tone is another note: 'don't expect me to tell you everything', which seems to have been learned from his mother, and, like her, he has no explanation for this natural reserve. The word 'secret' occurs at least nine times in the whole memoir. It's a matter of temperament. He is asking serious questions of himself about the role of writer, his chosen profession, just as he is of autobiography itself: 'a sense of being alone'. But if that's where it starts, it does not end there but with contacts, openings: 'the moments – which if I relate them well enough – will join countless others lived by people I do not personally know.' His aim, therefore, is to find those moments. But before he can do this he has to acknowledge, and perhaps therefore overcome, his natural reserve, especially when the subject here is so intimate. It was a reserve his mother herself would have understood. Is the writer's job to reveal secrets, or keep them? He doesn't know. Maybe the answer is both:

The last, the largest and most personally prepared wrapped secret was her own death. ... She lay in her bed, propped up by pillows, her head fallen forward, as if asleep.

On her bedside table was a tin of hand cream. I started to massage her left hand.

'Do you remember a photograph I once took of your hands? Working hands, you said.'

'No, I don't.'

'Would you like some more photos on your table?' Katya, her granddaughter, asked her.

She smiled at Katya and shook her head, her voice very slightly broken by a laugh. It would be so difficult, *so* difficult, wouldn't it, to choose.

She turned towards me. 'What exactly are you doing?'

'I'm massaging your hand. It's meant to be pleasurable.'

'To tell you the truth dear it doesn't make much difference. Which plane are you taking back?'

I mumbled, took her other hand.

'You are all worried,' she said, 'especially when there are several of you. I'm not. Maureen asked me the other day whether I wanted to be cremated or buried. Doesn't make one iota of difference to me. How could it?' She shut her eyes to think.

For the first time in her life and mine, she could openly place the wrapped enigma between us. She didn't watch me watching it, for we had the habits of a lifetime. Openly, she knew that in that moment her faith in a secret was bound to be stronger than any faith of mine in facts. With her eyes still shut, she fingered the Arab necklace I'd attached round her neck with a charm against the evil eye. I'd given her the necklace a few hours before. Perhaps for the first time I had offered her a secret and now her hand kept looking for it.

She opened her eyes. 'What time is it?'

'Quarter to four.'

'It's not very interesting talking to me, you know. I don't have any ideas any more. I've had a good life. Why don't you take a walk?'

Katya stayed with her.

'When you are very old,' she told Katya confidentially, 'there's one thing that's very, very difficult – it's very difficult to persuade other people that you're happy.'

She let her head go back on the pillow. As I came back in, she smiled.

In her right hand she held a crumpled paper handkerchief. With it she dabbed from time to time the corner of her mouth when

> she felt there was the slightest excess of spittle there. The gesture was reminiscent of one with which, many years before, she used to wipe her mouth after drinking Earl Grey tea and eating watercress sandwiches. Meanwhile, with her left hand she fingered the necklace, cushioned on her forgotten bosom.
>
> Love, my mother had the habit of saying, is the only thing that counts in this world. Real love, she would add, to avoid any factitious misunderstanding. But apart from that simple adjective, she never added anything more.
>
> (Ibid., 49–52)

Although we might think of this memoir as a portrait, it contains almost no physical description. How then does Berger succeed in bringing his mother's presence alive to us on the page? His method is to work with ideas: childhood, aloneness, contact, secrecy, love, and with illustrative speech, dialogue, voices. Through these, the ideas in his memoir spring to life. We experience his sense of his mother's reserve, its powerful attractions for him, the respect he gives her because of it. We hear those footsteps receding, and, when it comes to the death of a parent, the profound difference between a child's perspective and that of an adult. We also hear about things that lie at the centre of Berger's experience of his mother – her hands, the way she wipes her mouth, and these vivid physical details in the piece also help to balance and illuminate its ideas. It would be quite hard to imagine a memoir that did *not* deal with physical detail, with dialogue, with moments in close-up, with ideas. All are necessary to the delivery of this form of conversational drama.

Another interesting point is Katya's position. This is her grandmother. Unusual for a young person – she may be in her late teens or early twenties – to be present at what amounts to a deathbed scene. Many young people of her age choose to write about their experience of losing an elderly relative, though few witness the event at close quarters. John Berger's own record above begins with a reference to his grandmother. His detached account of the death of his mother, unsentimental, expressing reflection and insight rather than the obvious cliché emotions, could hold clues about how to handle the experience of bereavement in memoir form. As with all successful writing, we need to feel that the writer has taken us into a new space, allowing us to glimpse its secret reality.

Focus

The flamboyant dancer and eccentric Isadora Duncan, when asked to write her autobiography, almost lost her nerve at the suggestion.

'I confess that when it was first proposed to me I had a terror of writing this book. Not that my life had not been more interesting than any novel and more adventurous than any cinema and, if really well written, would not be an epoch-making recital, but there's the rub – the writing of it!' (Duncan, 1968:7). She admits that even given her interesting life (she obviously held few doubts about the height of its significance), something else is required, by which she meant the skill of transferring that sense of significance and excitement to her readers.

Your life may well be stocked with exceptional happenings, exotic voyages, famous or infamous friends, but if you spend the bulk of your time, as most of us do, within the realms of the ordinary, is anyone going to be interested in what you write? Asking this question is understandable but far from drawing a negative response the answer is: yes, they will. And they will because if you write in a way that will make people want to read and go on reading, it doesn't matter how interesting or dull you judge your experience. You will yourself discover where the interest lies, which is the point of personal narrative; you will have engaged your reader and yourself.

The idea of this chapter is to help you write something that people will read, not because your name is the epoch-making Isadora Duncan but because you have written it in a way that provokes and satisfies attention as John Berger's writing does. In personal narrative what counts is the writing, not the writer.

If you succeed in discovering the right words – 'relating it well' – you might then face the next set of questions that stumped Isadora: 'How can we write the truth about ourselves? Do we even know it?' But you have at least one advantage. No one is asking you for your whole life story from birth up to yesterday. Memoir writing is not the same thing as writing a complete autobiography. Memoir asks you to specialise and select, not to give the whole of the truth (even if that were possible), but to attend to one particular memory or set of incidents. As we shall see, there are many ways of doing this.

Even if you do decide to tell your life story, you will not be able to achieve it without focus, by which I mean close-up, rather than only wide-angle, shots. Ideally you need both, but without close detail and a sense of perspective your readers will feel less convinced that it is worth their while to look through the particular lens you have set up. I stress the idea of a camera deliberately. A wide-angle shot looks like this:

> I was born in 1968 and at the age of four attended a small primary school on the outskirts of Norwich, the largest town in

> East Anglia. My father is an architect and for two years was employed on rebuilding work to the cathedral. My sister worked in a bakery in the main street. My best friend lived outside the town at a pig farm near Taverham. When I was nine, my mother attended a WEA class on industrial archaeology.

Close-up shots prevent the slide from one piece of information to another by selecting a point of interest and holding it, thus:

> I am standing in the middle of a sweep of green. I stare at a point near the spire where a ladder perches and a tiny figure is climbing from rung to rung. Come on!' a voice calls, 'you'll be late, hurry up,' but I go on looking. The figure I can see, high up in the wind, is my father.

Something as simple as a voice calling – a small enough detail in itself – can add tension and generate involvement, but only if the focus has been adjusted down to that scale. Impact depends as much on minor effects as on broad strokes of background information, and this will be true whether or not the information is interesting, exotic, or concerns outrageous events and well-known people. Even where the events *are* outrageous, the small details count, as we shall see.

The skill in all memoir writing is finding a way of setting up the camera so that you can control the resulting shot, the one with appeal and maximum interest value. You do not have to worry too much about inventing the details since these are there already in your memory. You need to develop an accurate retrieval system, but the fact is that, as soon as you begin to aim your attention in one specific direction, you find you begin to remember more than you thought. You might begin with an actual photograph of a place or person of particular interest to you. At the back of your mind, what you thought of as nothing but a faint trickle or irrelevant source is in fact the whole reservoir; the more you attempt, the more you can recover.

Memory

In Chapter 1, I made a distinction between memory and imagination to highlight how certain events, images, scenes, become intensified, recalled in vividness, remembered whilst others subside into the unconscious mass of fragments it seems we have no use for. But if only it were that simple. The mind is not a filing system from which we can draw out an item of memory as fresh as the moment it was placed there. The system will have continued to absorb the item, digesting it, modifying it, and infecting it with numbers of other items. Storage is never pure or just automatic, a matter of canisters sealed with liquid ice; neither is memory retrieval pure.

It might help to think of memory as a function of the mind, not just an attribute or amusing side-issue, something to indulge in during long holiday weekends, looking at photographs, watching family videos. Its purpose could be considerably more dynamic. A peculiar, though common, feature of parenthood, for example, is the way adults focus on their children as they are and forget what they were like the previous year or the year before that. The protection and well-being of small children probably depends on this parental amnesia. The child as it is, in the present, encountering new dangers, learning new skills, demands every minute of our protective attention. Then, as children grow and become more reliably independent, parents stop forgetting and once more begin remembering. They tell you stories about yourself as a very small boy or girl – sometimes to your embarrassment. They start remembering to help build – possibly to challenge and therefore strengthen – your nascent identity. Like a growing community or a nation you need story, history, mythic traces, moments that stand out. You need images placed in a line of ascent to where you are now. In later life, when you pass through other changes, you might need these images or you might not. You might have to discard them, find others. It might be the present you need to concentrate on so, like your parents when you were small and vulnerable, you too enter a period of forgetting. Then, when that's over, memory might recharge itself again, enabling you to map the change and strengthen your new state. The point is that memory is a response reaction with a purpose – not just a store to be raided at will or ignored. The genuine task in memoir writing will be to understand your memory and work with it, and this means being honest about what you can and can't remember.

In the passage below, printed in full, Margaret Atwood decides that what she *can't* remember needed a whole paragraph.

> When I was five my brother and I made poison. We were living in a city then, but we probably would have made the poison anyway. We kept it in a paint can under somebody else's house and we put all the poisonous things into it that we could think of: toad-stools, dead mice, mountain ash berries which may not have been poisonous but looked it, piss which we saved up in order to add it to the paint can. By the time the can was full everything in it was poisonous.
>
> The problem was that once having made the poison we

couldn't just leave it there. We had to do something with it. We didn't want to put it into anyone's food, but we wanted an object, a completion. There was no one we hated enough, that was the difficulty.

I can't remember what we did with the poison in the end. Did we leave it under the corner of the house, which was made of wood and brownish yellow? Did we throw it at someone, some innocuous child? We wouldn't have dared an adult. Is this a true image I have, a small face streaming with tears and red berries, the sudden knowledge that the poison was really poisonous after all? Or did we throw it out, do I remember those red berries floating down a gutter, into a culvert, am I innocent?

Why did we make the poison in the first place? I can remember the glee with which we stirred and added, the sense of magic and accomplishment. Making poison is as much fun as making a cake. People like to make poison. If you don't understand this you will never understand anything.

(Atwood, 1994: 11)

This little story isn't something Atwood would have been told about by her parents. She is recalling all this by herself. Why this memory and not others? Perhaps this is her first encounter with magic – the power to rearrange the world so that you potentially control it – yet rather than weighted with explanations, the passage creates images we can share. She adopts a tone of tacit understanding towards her readers.

Her manner of enacting implies sharing, but with other children or with adults who vividly remember what childhood was like. This was extravagant, this was story, making the world strange, yet notice how simple the language is, straightforward, building the scene, repeating the words 'poison ... poisonous', asking direct questions she can't answer. Why is she recalling this memory? Does it have something to do with writing, being a writer? She doesn't say, yet we can feel its rhythm belongs to her present-day grown-up life. It has that intelligent, vivid force. This memory must have become necessary, also perhaps necessarily incomplete. What about her last two sentences? She hands the statement over to her readers – make of this what you will!

What we are told about ourselves, and what we remember, can merge together so that we can't distinguish the two. Doris Lessing makes this point at the start of the first volume of her autobiography, *Under My Skin:*

We make up our pasts. You can actually watch your mind doing it, taking a little fragment of fact and then spinning a tale out of

> it. No, I do not think this is only the fault of storytellers. A parent says, 'We took you to the seaside, and you built a sand-castle, don't you remember? – Look, here is the photo.' And at once the child builds from the words and the photograph a memory, which becomes hers. But there are moments, incidents, real memory, I do trust. This is partly because I spent a good deal of my childhood 'fixing' moments in my mind. Clearly, I had to fight to establish a reality of my own, against the insistence from the adults that I should accept theirs.
>
> (Lessing, 1995: 13)

Lessing's need to work on her memory, to fix moments, suggests her active participation in the dynamic of memory, a deliberate engagement with its processes. Sometimes like Lessing we are able to say, 'That was not just a memory but a signal; it showed the direction in which things were moving, only now I can see it'. It requires an effort to see and feel the underlying currents and shapes of time, and the recalled events she puts into her autobiography will be precisely those memories that indicate and detect a flow, measure a direction:

> The vividest early memory was – not the actual birth of my brother – but my introduction to the baby. I was two-and-a-half years old. The enormous room, lamplit, the ceiling shadowed and far above; the enormous bed, level with my head, on which my father lay, for he was ill again. ... 'It is your baby, Doris, and you must love it.' The baby I do not remember. I was in a flame of rage and resentment. It was not my baby. It was their baby. But I can hear now that persuasive lying voice...
>
> All you need is love. Love is all you need. A child should be governed by love, as my mother so often said, explaining her methods to us. She had not known love as a child, and was making sure we would not be similarly deprived. The trouble is, love is a word that has to be filled with the experience of love. What I remember is hard bundling hands, impatient arms and her voice telling me over and over again that she had not wanted a girl, she wanted a boy. I knew from the beginning she loved my little brother unconditionally, and she did not love me.
>
> (Ibid: 24)

To get back to the underlying drives of this memory, she has to re-inhabit it, climb right back into its skin. There are impressions; of what? Was this the moment when Lessing's lifetime resentment of her brother first took hold? She conceived no such resentment towards him. The real point of this memory, how it fits into her future development, is its sense of anger towards authority – especially towards authority figures (in this case her mother) who use words empty of actual experience, 'persuasive... lying', on and on, a hollowness she palpably detects. This mother's voice is the key – words and speech – more than the 'enormous room, lamplit'. As soon as memory reveals that voice, she hears it. From then on it starts to absorb almost all her attention. Lessing's aim in writing is not simply to evoke the moment but to go behind and beneath the memory, to relive its pressure in her mind, decode its signal.

Like Atwood's 'Making Poison', many passages in Lessing's autobiography *Under My Skin* reveal story-like experiences in her childhood. Memory has an attraction to such episodes. After the family's emigration to Africa, there was that secret region; the bush, close enough to the house to escape into: 'The bush was not then the domesticated bush it has become. It was full of dangerous noises, owls and nightjars, the crashing leaps of a disturbed buck, but above all, mysterious presences from our fairy-tales, released from the pages of books, and at large there all around us' (Lessing, 1995: 107) Running away there with her brother one night, the bush became Lessing's experience of story-world. Such places frequent the pages of memoirs and autobiographical fictions, especially when set in the writer's childhood. In one of her earliest stories, 'The Old Chief Mslangha' (Lessing, 2003: 13–25), she evokes the African bush as a place with its own narratives – those that belonged to the people indigenous to that world. She came to know and appreciate Africa as a child growing up – a child with only English and northern European fairy-tales informing her experience of landscape. Her change of country was a change of story world.

The life story of the gifted singer and actress Marianne Faithfull reminds us that one life can contain several episodes, in her case violently contrasting. Here's how her autobiography, *Faithfull,* begins:

> My earliest memory is a dream about my mother covered in armour, a coronet of snakes entwined around her head. I am three years old. I'm in my bed, in the little room with blue curtains. In the dream it is daytime, and sunlight is streaming through the curtains. Everything is blue, the blue of Ahmed's hashish and jewellery shop in Tangier. Blue curtains blowing in the wind. And beyond them a garden. The green green green of an English lawn. I hear a voice calling me, 'Come, Marianne, come.' I feel helpless. I have no choice.
>
> 'Marianne! Marianne! the voice calls again, so piercingly this time that I get out of bed. I float to the window the way Alice

> does, with her feet just off the ground. I open the curtains and fly down to the end of the garden, where my mother has planted an asparagus patch. I see a fantastic figure looming over me. It is my mother-as-goddess, wearing armlets, breastplates and greaves like the ancient warrior-queen Boadiccea. She is cooking, raking the coals with a pair of tongs. She lifts me in her arms and places me on the fire. The dream ends as I lie down and allow her to roast me on the grill.
>
> This happens night after night; again and again she arranges me on those hot coals. The dream always stops at that point. There is no pain, not really a nightmare at all, but rather a ritual that I obscurely recognise. A very Middle-European apparition – a proper, collective-consciousness dream about the mother, the goddess. Some form of training perhaps. It certainly prepared me for later life!
>
> (Faithfull, 1994: 1)

We don't need to know anything about the writer to sense the impact of this opening passage. Anyone could have written it. We don't need to know about her involvement with the Stones, Mick Jagger, drugs, or what her hit records in the 1960s were, or even how appropriate a beginning this is for a very bizarre and fascinating story. The passage is bizarre and fascinating in itself. The first sentence holds and provokes interest. A profoundly significant stereotype: the caring mother whose voice calls out our name so we come running and are lifted into her arms, has been altered into its opposite. The mother here is a female warrior of terrifying strength and size. If mothers traditionally provide food for their children and call them when it's ready, here is a child placed on a grill and cooked. The tone of almost hallucinatory extravagance changes what might be threatening and ominous to something quite comic, but not entirely so. The fact that we are reading a memoir must influence the questions this opening invites: Does the child accept her unusual treatment? Did her mother resemble this monstrous apparition in any way? If this is a test, will Marianne finally pass it and survive? What does it signify?

Note, too, the presence of exact reference: 'the blue of Ahmed's hashish and jewellery shop in Tangier. ... Alice ... with her feet just off the ground. ... the end of the garden, where my mother has planted an asparagus patch.' Once again, details endorse the claim of authentication, the feel of a world uniquely real to the writer; a lesser degree of exactness would simply mean less familiarity between writer and world. Without that sharp focus and personal knowledge writers are less convincing, and readers less convinced.

In the next passage, from 'Ocean 1212-W', the poet Sylvia Plath revisits the scene of her early childhood by the sea in North America. The memory itself and the style of language – textured, poetic, expressive – are both equally important to the impact she is creating. The territory here is well known to her, a physical place, but her sense of it is not just recalled but revived by the act of remembering. More and more comes back to her as she writes, but the focus stays firmly on the sea which appears like a living thing in a range of shapes.

> My childhood landscape was not the land but the end of the land – the cold, salt, running hills of the Atlantic. I sometimes think my vision of the sea is the clearest thing I own. I pick it up, exile that I am, like the purple 'lucky stones' I used to collect with a white ring all the way round, or the shell of a blue mussel with its rainbowy angel's fingernail interior; and in one wash of memory the colors deepen and gleam, the early world draws breath.

Sylvia Plath writes with anticipation and excitement. She has given herself complete permission to re-enter that world of her ocean childhood. She brings it to life: all of it. What will she discover? The sea is strange and obscure to her; alive, beautiful, dangerous. Her writing has touched that ambivalence of response, without loss of childlike curiosity:

> For a time I believed not in God nor Santa Claus, but in mermaids. They seemed as logical and possible to me as the brittle twig of a seahorse in the Zoo aquarium or the skates lugged up on the lines of cursing Sunday fishermen – skates the shape of old pillowslips with the full, coy lips of women.
>
> And I recall my mother, a sea-girl herself, reading to me and my brother ... from Matthew Arnold's '*Forsaken Merman*':
> Sand-strewn caverns, cool and deep,
>
> Where the winds are all asleep;
> Where the spent lights quiver and gleam;
> Where the salt weed sways in the stream;
> Where the sea-beasts rang'd all around
> Feed in the ooze of their pasture-ground;
> Where the sea-snakes coil and twine
> Dry their mail and bask in the brine;
> Where great whales come sailing by,
> Sail and sail with unshut eye,
> Round the world forever and aye.

> I saw the gooseflesh on my skin. I did not know what made it. I was not cold. Had a ghost passed over? No, it was the poetry. A spark flew off Arnold and shook me, like a chill. I wanted to cry; I felt very odd. I had fallen into a new way of being happy.

But would the sights and sounds of the sea, of any sea, anywhere, automatically produce the reactions she felt as a child? Her answer is no. It had to be that place on the Atlantic coast of North America: the sea by her grandmother's house. Living in England, 'in exile', she would be taken to the sea regularly as a cure for her nostalgia, but the cure never quite worked:

> The road I knew curved into the waves with the ocean on one side, the bay on the other; and my grandmother's house, half-way out, faced east, full of red sun and sea lights.
>
> To this day I remember her phone number: OCEAN 1212-W. I would repeat it to the operator, from my home on the quieter bayside, an incantation, a fine rhythm, half expecting the black earpiece to give me back, like a conch, the susurrus of the sea out there as well as my grandmother's Hello.

Only through writing could she revisit that atmosphere:

> The breath of the sea then. And then its lights. Was it some huge, radiant animal? Even with my eyes shut I could feel the glimmers off its bright mirrors spider over my lids. I lay in a watery cradle and sea gleams found the chinks in the dark green window blind, playing and dancing, or resting and trembling a little. At naptime I chinked my fingernail on the hollow brass bedstead for the music of it and once, in a fit of discovery and surprise, found the join in the new rose paper and with the same curious nail bared a great bald space of wall. I got scolded for this, spanked, too, and then my grandfather extracted me from the domestic furies for a long beachcombing stroll over mountains of rattling and cranking purple stones.
>
> (Plath, 1977:123–30)

In this last sentence, Sylvia Plath could easily have written 'then he took me for a long walk on the beach'. But the word 'walk' becomes 'a long beachcombing stroll' – so much more accurate – and the beach becomes 'mountains of rattling and cranking purple stones'. This refusal of the obvious, simple name for a thing, and instead revisiting the original sensations is what we see most frequently in poetry. Much of these passages by Plath reads like an artist's notebook; largely she is beachcombing for poems, trying out special images, connections, sounds, letting her mind drift where it wants to go.

One other thing to notice in these ocean passages: sensations, textures, colours and sounds have immediate meaning-quality and feed the writer's poetic, imaginative vision. Texture, colour (a shell's 'rainbowy angel's fingernail interior') merge, as a single substance; meaning clings to every shape and space (even a telephone number) because of its proximity to the sea.

But it isn't the sea anywhere. The drive of the writing is not to give us back what we already know, but to show us how meanings collect and store themselves and to show ways of raiding that store. Because of this, the place must be felt as wholly unique to the writer; it relates to no one but her; she to nowhere but exactly that positioning of the coast.

Travel

Memories of travel are often about excitement and anticipation – that moment when you wake up and know that in a matter of hours you will be in a plane crossing the Alps or the coastal forests of Eastern Canada in just as long as it takes to eat your breakfast. But as well as thinking about how to tap into all that anticipation, it might be useful to reflect on what travel has meant to us in the past. The idea of the journey occupies a central place in our creative literature, as if 'journey' and 'story' were synonymous. Almost all fairy-tales involve a journey: to grandmother's house, away on mysterious business with gifts brought back for the children, in a carriage which is also a pumpkin, into the forest escaping from a step-mother, bringing back impossible gifts and so winning the hand of the princess. There are the amazingly vast journeys performed by the hero of 'Finist the Falcon' a Russian fairy-tale that combines motifs from so many other tales. The journey as quest, also as pilgrimage, as proof of endurance or devotion, proof too – if you survive – of willingness to encounter, and overcome, whatever horror or obstacle is planted in your path. This, of course, will not be the experience we expect when travelling in present-day conditions.

Journey then, and diversion, distraction; but never journey *as* distraction, journey as pleasure. Chaucer, of course, allowed his pilgrims to toy with the idea of journey as pleasure, a new-fangled notion in the fourteenth century. Before that time, and for centuries afterwards, travel undertaken under precarious conditions betokened a purpose of the most serious sort: you come back changed – if you come back at all – and wiser. You lost your innocent sense that life was a spree. Even anecdotes relating what happened to us on this or that vacation get most attention according to how catastrophic they seemed. 'We only went to enjoy ourselves BUT ...', the story implies. Yet perhaps that wasn't the reason at all. Maybe the strange encounters, the unfamiliar food and plumbing arrangements were the point, after all. We get away from it all, 'it all' meaning not only drudgery and routine but also all that we count, and count on, as predictable. Not only that: when we come back, our ordinary world has, in our absence, acquired something of that tangible unfamiliarity belonging to elsewhere.

The visits to towns and countrysides of our past, old home places, are more obvious pilgrimages. But even the pure pleasure-seeking instinct we go into a travel agent's with might conceal some less obvious appetite – for *story* perhaps and, if so, what kind? Romance, adventure, danger, risk? What kind of journey is it we are making? Why does it stop at one place and not another? What are its turning-points? Are these the result of circumstances, cash running out, missed trains, or of more mysterious causes? Memoirs of travel become interesting, not just because what happens is being described in close-up, but when the motives of travelling are investigated. A pilgrimage? A quest? Initiation? What's it really all about?

What we are hinting at here is that journeys are metaphors. We often speak of other experiences as journeys – ones that have nothing to do with travel as such. Illnesses might be one such example, as in two recent autobiographies: *Out of Me* by Fiona Shaw and *Giving Up the Ghost* by Hilary Mantel. Some might think of long-term illness as a challenge, a struggle – you against it, so that your journey will be to overcome and triumph, be restored to the person you were before. We might call this a restorative journey. Your illness might be a quest (another type of journey) to discover what you can learn about yourself, about your relationship with yourself and with others as you begin to accept that your condition might be unalterable. Is it something that isolates you or enables connections with other sufferers? Always there is the undeniable need to be getting somewhere – without this, travel and journeys (and perhaps illnesses) can seem to have no point. But the endurance can be disruptive as well as highly pleasurable. In *A Walk in the Woods*, Bill Bryson, trekking over two thousand miles through Maine and the Appalachians, talks not just about mountains and hills but also heavens and hells:

> When, after ages and ages, you finally reach the tell-tale world of truly high ground, where the chilled air smells of pine-sap and the vegetation is gnarled and tough and wind-bent, and push

> through to the mountain's open pinnacle, you are, alas, past caring. You sprawl face down on a sloping pavement of gneiss, pressed to the rock by the weight of your pack, and lie there for some minutes, reflecting, in a distant, out-of-body way that you have never before looked this closely at lichen...
>
> (Bryson, 1997: 46)

Later, 'It was heaven. It's splendid, no question, but the thought you cannot escape is that you have to walk this view.' Later still: 'It was hell.' He knows what his readers might anticipate – the summit view, glow of achievement, happy exhaustion – then tells us what it was really like. Notice his use of 'you' in the passage, how it makes the experience both generalised and specific, as if he is dumping not just himself but us too – or anyone with these kinds of aspirations – on to that slab of rock.

Even without travelling there are ways of incorporating the collective experiences of travel into the writing of memoir so that you use its breadth of association to develop observation and insight. Bill Bryson's experience isn't one most of us have the opportunity to attempt, but we all will have visited places where travelling happens: rail stations, motorways services, wharves and docks, airports, the underground. Pub conversations about travel, depicted here by Bryson again, can be enough to illustrate *attitude* to it, in this case found only in England:

> If you mention in the pub that you intend to drive from, say, Surrey to Cornwall, a distance that most Americans would happily go to get a taco, your companions will puff their cheeks, look knowingly at each other, and blow out air as if to say, 'Well, now, that's a bit of a tall order', and then they'll launch into a lively and protracted discussion of whether it's better to take the A30 to Glastonbury via Shepton Mallet. Within minutes the conversation will plunge off into a level of detail that leaves you, as a foreigner, swivelling your head in quiet wonderment.
>
> 'You know that layby outside Warminster, the one with the grit box with the broken handle?' – one of them will say. 'You know, just past the turn-off for Little Puking before the B6029 mini-roundabout. By the dead sycamore.'
>
> At this point, you'll find you are the only person in the group not nodding vigorously.
>
> (Bryson, 1995:15–16)

As a master of detail, Bryson's grip on the point is tightened by these exaggerations. And the Underground: 'There's something surreal about plunging into the bowels of the earth to catch a train. ... And it all happens in such orderly quiet: all these thousands of people passing on stairs and escalators, stepping on and off crowded trains, sliding off into the darkness with wobbling heads, and never speaking, like characters from *Night of the Living Dead*.' (Bryson, Ibid.: 35)

Doris Lessing catches a moment when such order and quiet suddenly unravels: in seasonal terms the Underground's version of spring:

> Charing Cross and everyone gets out. At the exit machine a girl appears running up from the deeper levels, and she is chirping like an alarm. The girl is a fey creature, blonde locks flying around a flushed face. She is laughing dizzily, and racing a flight or flock of young things coming into the West End for an evening's adventure, all of them already crazed with pleasure, and in another dimension of speed and lightness, like sparks speeding up and out. She and two girls push in their tickets and flee along a tunnel to the upper world, but three youths vault over, with cries of triumph, and their state of being young is such a claim on us all that the attendant decides not to notice, for it would be as mad as swatting butterflies.
>
> (Phillips, ed., 1997: 102)

Not just platforms but seasons, even a hint of the myth of Persephone escaping the underworld, 'crazed with pleasure'. Again we find the writer building worlds, producing images, making time eventful and extraordinary in words that seem to be passing through the moment, shaped by its energy. We feel the privilege of having been there too. All good writing achieves this, and memoir writing is about 'being there', even if 'there' happened to be your climb to the summit of a mountain in America, your first meeting with your new baby brother, hearing your mother talking about 'love' – in Lessing's case very differently from Berger's. The writing moves among spaces, people and objects; the world is present sensuously, heard, seen and felt, and the writer is also thinking, exploring early sources of later attitude, curious about experience. Journeys are not just periods of transit between one point and another. For some even an arrival at a tube station one evening will be an adventure.

Travel writing started long before Kerouac's *On the Road* was published in 1960, yet this book, still widely read and deeply enjoyed, celebrates travel as initiation. Into what? The writer isn't sure, which is part of its charm. Here is Kerouac describing how it feels to be lying on the floor of a car travelling at high speed and driven by your friend with the asphalt inches away from your face.

The road is an image, dangerous, accessible, with an unknown future: travel and time transformed into speed and energy. Notice the mixture of long and short sentences:

> One of the boys jumped in front for the fun. Great horrors that we were going to crash this very morning took hold of me and I got down on the floor and closed my eyes and tried to go to sleep. As a seaman I used to think of the waves rushing beneath the shell of the ship and the bottomless deeps thereunder – now I could feel the road some twenty inches beneath me, unfurling and flying and hissing at incredible speeds across the groaning continent with that mad Ahab at the wheel. When I closed my eyes all I could see was the road unwinding into me. When I opened them I saw flashing shadows of trees vibrating on the floor of the car. There was no escaping it. I resigned myself to all. And still Dean drove, he had no thought of sleeping till we got to Chicago.
>
> (Kerouac, 1991: 234)

The next extract in this section, a piece of unpublished personal narrative, 'Permanent Nights, Winter 81/82', by Eric Jackson, also involves dangerous driving. Here, too, the writing is sensational, made so by the uncomfortable extremes packed into it:

> *1.45 a.m.*
>
> Sometimes I'd be half-asleep and it was difficult to tell how much was real and how much was just hanging behind my eyes. The alarm tearing into my dreams: a cold clenched fist in my stomach. Everyone else would be sleeping, Dad snoring in the next room. I'd sleep with most of my clothes on, slump out of bed – fatigue and resentment a single emotion – and do as much as I could in darkness.
>
> Black coffee to scour a clogged throat, woke me up as if there were some purpose to this. Kid myself. In the bathroom I'd put the light on. Sting my eyes like shampoo does when you're a child. In the mirror always the same vampire face, the matted hair, red eyes, pale skin. So tired, so incredibly tired and fighting against it.
>
> I'd tip cups of water, cold, over my head. A shock like toothache to bring me alive. After the coffee go outside shivering to try and start the van. Freezing in scarf, gloves, hat, everything. Often I'd fill hot water bottles and wear them inside my coat across the small of my back. The heater in the van didn't work and there were gaps around all the windows. Once

I'd started the engine I'd have to get out again and clear the ice from the wind-screen. There'd be snow in the driveway and the cat's footprints over the roof of the van.

The drive to work. A roller coaster of left-over dream images and sudden black bends. Trees and walls leaping out of nothingness directly into my path. The line between sleep and wakefulness as blurred as the hedgerows rushing past. Reaching the outskirts of town – a flood of orange lights, the odd police car; cats and lovers hurrying home down some side-street; the warehouse.

Sometimes there'd be thick, bitter tea in unwashed cups. A treat if it was the foreman's night off. There'd be nothing to say. I'd be looking at their dead white faces, tanned by neon and touched by moonlight more than sun, thinking: 'Is that me? Do I look like that?' Like defeat and acceptance and long since abandoned bitterness.

The machine would rattle and hum and my fingers, the skin, too colourless to bleed, would crack on the strapping as the parcels piled up. In the yard, wagons shunted and lumbered ('Left hand down') spewing carbon monoxide into the loading bay, gears grinding and grating on my nerves. As far back as I could remember; as far forward as I could see.

They'd give me forty five minutes to do the deliveries, because they thought it was impossible. I'd do it in thirty five. Stack the parcels properly in the back, that was the key, then alter the brain to sleep while reactions took over.

I'd leave the yard with tyres spinning gravel and the door still half-open. Leave the window down to hear the engine, the screaming rubber, to flood the van with night.

Never cruising. Always accelerating madly or breaking desperately, blocking out the times, a dozen a night, when I'd leave the tarmac and lose control. Just for a second but long enough careering down unlit country lanes on the wrong side of the road, the rush of fear was the one spark of life in this robot existence.

Still in darkness I'd tear past the milk floats back into town, ignoring red lights, one way systems, pavements. ('If it's flat you can drive over it.') And the metal of the van would screech in protest, remembering its twisted frame and buckled wheels and shattered glass not so many nights ago on a road exactly like this.

All this to possess those last ten minutes and say, 'These are mine'. To park on the road along the beach and hear the engine ticking as it cooled, and outside hear the surf and the gulls. I could watch the sea and watch the sunrise, watch the birds with marble eyes scavenging the empty chip bags, coca cola tins, rubbish stacks. See the first light paint the sky and glint across steel grey waves and the aluminium doors of Gilly's Fun Palace, Big Prize Bingo, and the Original Gypsy Rose Lee's Palmistry Stall with its faded pictures of Des O'Connor, Les Dawson, and Frankie Vaughan.

I didn't need her magic.

I saw my future and my past: a hall of mirrors reflecting to infinity in all directions with me at the centre, staring through the filthy windows of a Ford transit, watching the sea and shivering inside.

(unpublished)

What do we know about this writer's feelings? From the last image he clearly feels trapped. His sense of relief is transitory, but we are not told this explicitly; we feel it without the need for direct comment. He could, for instance, have begun his piece with a list of explanatory details: 'Two years ago I was working shifts driving a van in Redcar for a transport company. I hated the job but needed money for a trip to Peru', etc... Would more data have benefited? The only information of this type is the merest: '*1.45 a.m.*'

By being real to the writer as he writes, this experience becomes real to the reader. Much of it consists of things which exercise physical rather than mental reactions, but even those parts which do reflect on the experience go a step further: 'Do I look like that? Like defeat and acceptance and long since abandoned bitterness.' The writer assumes that given this particular set of conditions, most of us would respond as he is doing. That moment of freedom and peace at the end is one we can each relate to. 'All this to possess those last ten minutes and say, 'These are mine'.' The statement is both anonymous and personal, and succeeds in saying something about work and its squalid demands. Given that is the issue, the finer and more detailed the exactness, the stronger the bridge between writer and reader. Instead of explaining: 'Then we drank some tea', he almost chokes us with it; we can taste it. We feel we have experienced what he knows. We feel this because of the strong dominant viewpoint, but also because the writing is like a magnetic field; every detail points in the same direction. It has rhythm. It speeds. It drives impressions home, phrase after phrase. The rhythm changes for the final paragraphs: 'All this to possess...' The sentences tick over like the engine; they are longer and slower than the stabbing rhythms. They reflect on what has happened, but without losing touch with the new circumstances: the litter and the gulls and the sea itself. And this rhythm is just as important for their meaning as what the words actually say. In this passage, although Redcar might not be Chicago or Acapulco, in its momentum, tumbled thoughts, fullness of world, sudden glimpses of close-up and wider perspective, it revives some of the same qualities of perception and enactment as Kerouac's *On the Road.*

Finally, at another extreme, travel can lead to encounters with people whose ways of life differ profoundly from ours. The result casts deep shafts of enquiry into the traveller's mind, so that we feel we have almost left travel writing behind and crossed a border into philosophy. The Arctic explorer Barry Lopez writes:

> What did Columbus, sailing Zaiton, the great port of Cathay, think of the reach of the Western Atlantic? How did Coronado assess the Staked Plain of Texas, the rawest space he ever knew, on his way to Quivera? Or Mungo Park the landscape of Africa in search of the Niger? What one thinks of any region, while travelling through, is the result of at least three things: what one knows, what one imagines, and how one is disposed.
>
> (Lopez, 1987: 243)

> Eskimos do not maintain this intimacy with nature without paying a certain price. When I have thought about the ways in which they differ from people in my own culture, I have realised that they are more afraid than we are. On a day-to-day basis, they have more fear. Not of being dumped into cold water from an umiac, not a debilitating fear. They are afraid because they accept fully what is violent and tragic in nature. It is a fear tied to their knowledge that sudden, cataclysmic events are as much a part of life, of really living, as the moments when one pauses to look at something beautiful. A Central Eskimo shaman named Aua, queried by Knud Rasmussen about Eskimo beliefs, answered: 'We do not believe. We fear.'
>
> (Ibid.: 180)

Later on he talks of tribal warfare among the Eskimos, 'families shattered by alcohol, drugs and ambition'. But he knows, vaguely, yet conclusively, that 'the land, in a certain, very real way, compels the minds of [these] people'. This attitude, very unlike our own civilised distance from the natural world, could have been left deliberately unaddressed, but Lopez does not choose this direction. All he has are his own culture's methods of enquiry, questions about being and practical life. These are his means of approach:

> In moments when I felt perplexed that I was dealing with an order outside my own, I discovered and put to use a part of my own culture's wisdom, the formal divisions of Western philos-

ophy – metaphysics, epistemology, ethics, aesthetics, and logic – which pose, in order, the following questions: What is real? What can we understand? How should we behave? What is beautiful? What are the patterns that we can rely upon?

As I traveled, I would say to myself, What do my companions see where I see death? Is the sunlight beautiful to them, the way it sparkles on the water? Which for the Eskimo hunter are the patterns to be trusted? The patterns, I know, could be different from ones I imagined were before us. There could be other, remarkably different insights.

Those days on Ilingnorak Ridge, when I saw tundra grizzly tearing up the earth looking for ground squirrels, and watched wolves hunting, and a horned lark sitting so resolutely on her nest, and caribou crossing the river and shaking off the spray like diamonds before the evening sun, I was satisfied only to watch. This was the great drift and pause of life. These were the arrangements that made the land ring with integrity. Somewhere downriver, I remembered, a scientist named Edward Sable had paused on a trek in 1947 to stare at a Folsom spear point, a perfectly fluted object of black chert resting on a sandstone ledge. People moving, over the land.

(Ibid: 180–2)

The Personal and the Collective

There's no reason why personal narrative should mean writing entirely about yourself; it's also striking how often and to what good purpose the writing of a memoir includes other people, portraits, comments on social life. To take this idea one step further, it can also be fruitful, and interesting, to explore the personal narratives within a group or community, showing contrasting perspectives, shared perceptions, difference and coincidence. The example below, written by a demonstrator against nuclear weapons in 1975, shows how memoir can weave together the personal and collective:

I set off to Greenham as a critic – not as a critic of the issue of nuclear war/weapons – but as a critic of what I expected would happen: of the long and passionate speeches, full of clichés, and 'guilt-tripping' statements about what we should all be doing. Basically I was tired of emerging middle-class leaders in the peace movement making careers out of telling us what we should be doing and how we should be doing it! As a working class woman I've felt alienated from the peace movement and, worse still, guilty that the problems of surviving as a single

> parent meant I had little energy left to direct into any campaigning – no matter how important I felt that campaign to be. Nuclear disarmament is the ultimate issue of the day and so I've always made a point of attending most of the local and national demonstrations. In terms of the media, numbers are important, and so I was content to be a 'head to be counted'! However, after a while, this can be a demoralizing and tedious way of making a protest – you come away feeling tired, anonymous, and with a feeling that the demonstration would have gone on quite well without you.
>
> On December the 12th at Greenham it was different. All my own criticisms, based on previous experiences, disappeared within reaching a hundred yards of the fence. I don't think it was the day, the event, or the common cause which was responsible for making every woman present feel a vital part of the day – it was the fence itself.
>
> (Bretton Women's Book Fund, 1983: 14–16)

Collections of personal narrative can open doors on the experiences people share, at school, in a college, a town, a workplace, a community. Each generation will produce different narratives, will develop its own attitudes and idioms. You may be able to develop a project reflecting in vivid and accurate detail the kinds of experience that distinguish your generation as it develops from childhood and on through the various stages that follow.

You will need to focus on experiences shared by people in a group.

Summary

Autobiography and memoir are forms of personal narrative. Autobiography is a complete personal narrative covering at least several years in duration, while memoir enables you to focus on a comparatively short period of experience lasting days, even hours or minutes. You are telling a story about yourself. But it can, of course, be one that involves other people and groups. One of its strengths is its conversational tone, as seen in the extracts above, and the way it opens up a discussion with its readers.

Personal narratives need ideas and themes and also dramatic illustration, moments captured through description, dialogue, close-up, angle and focus. But sometimes writers start off not knowing what they are going to discover. In this approach, all they have is the sense that this or that experience is real to them in some important way. The writer aims to find out why it matters. He or she unearths the ideas as they go along, and reaches an understanding during the process. The writing develops a tone of reflectiveness, leading to a new sense of the importance of a memory and its place in the story of the self. The piece by Eric Jackson is a good example of writing as discovery.

Personal narratives often occur in clusters round basic themes. In the extracts I have included examples of writing about memory, travel, and collective narratives. These branch out into a range of topics, closely related but offering a wider scope. Always think about what your chosen topic might branch out into. For example, the idea of a journey might include the experience of illness or disability, or the sense of a quest or a re-visiting. Memory can get you thinking about why you remember this or that particular event, or why you might have forgotten certain things. Work with your memory. Write to show, illustrate, dramatise your experiences as well as to explore them. Try to discover more than you thought you knew.

Suggestions for Writing

Aim to make your experiences vivid and real to your readers. See where you can use close-up focus, finding the angle and approach that will reveal places and events in detail, moment by moment. Look again at how Sylvia Plath and Jack Kerouac focus on sensation in their writing, yet still need ideas to give it direction. Try to avoid taking your reader somewhere they already know. Take them to new places, emotionally, in terms of response, thoughts and ideas. This means being careful to avoid clichés and any sentimental reactions – the predictable. However moving your experience was to you, your readers will not appreciate this without the sense that your writing has opened doors, shown something new, fresh and surprising about the real world of our experience. Refuse the obvious. Take that extra step towards the real.

1 *Writing about childhood.* Think about memory, using focus and close-up. Build your writing around a starting point: an object, a person, a place, an encounter or event. You could choose something unusual, or quite ordinary and familiar. You must aim to make this person, object, event or place interesting to your readers, using narrative, dialogue (if appropriate), vividness of detail, and other features. A particular combination of sensations – sounds, smells, colours, voices – may be a useful trigger for your writing, a stimulus to your memory, a way into a forgotten experience. The experiences you describe here could be useful for fiction, but you need to approach your experience first as an adult looking back.

2 *Ideas and Issues*. All good personal narrative includes ideas; it's a way of making contact with your readers and holding their attention. Investigate one particular issue – local, national, global – that has affected you personally. The issue could involve gender politics, sexuality, or education, health issues, the law, social reform. It might involve solutions to a practical problem: housing, social benefits, traffic, pollution. You will need to describe your own experience, your story, in a way that illustrates the issue for your readers. You may need to do some research or to interview people with a similar (or slightly different) experience to your own. (See a related exercise in Chapter 6, Number 8, page 226.)

3 *Turning Points*. Explore a period of transition in your life. It may involve physical changes such as moving house, living in a different city or country, meeting new friends or losing old ones. You might tell the story of how you felt about a loss or bereavement, the end of a love affair, or the beginning of a new relationship. Again, you will need to develop insights, offer ideas, illustrate them with close-up detail, narrative and focus. To stimulate your writing you might make use of a still photograph or moving image film of a person or group. What was happening before and after? Who were you then? Who is no longer part of the group?

4 *Journeys*. Tell your story of an actual journey, short or long distance. It could be anywhere. (Eric Jackson's dawn rush happened near Redcar.) Or it could be a metaphorical journey – back to health, a readjustment of your sense of identity, reaching or failing to reach some goal that preoccupied you. Think about the meaning of this journey – not only for you but for any other people involved, your attitude, theirs. Write so that your readers will get to feel a sense of involvement.

5 *Plural narratives*. The main difference between this approach and the others listed above is that these are the stories put together by a group of people who share similar goals, values, ways of speaking and thinking, yet who might not see eye to eye about everything. What holds them together? What threatens to drive them apart? There's an opportunity here for comic and serious writing, social insight, recording of experience common to your contemporaries. This could be a group project, using research, interviews, sound and video recordings to reflect the experiences of friends, family, community, workforce, a team or a group sharing in one activity at a certain time and place: a gap-year experience of travelling together might be one example. The aim is to build a selected narrative record.

As you begin to develop your memoir, it may be that some of your ways of showing and illustrating your experience provide you with creative ideas for a short story, poem, or a piece of drama. Personal narrative can provide a good jumping-off point for working in other creative genres.

Revision and Editing

Look back at your whole piece. Have you made use of detailed focus, reality-effects? Have you used other ways of 'relating things well'? For example, speech and dialogue (if and when appropriate), vividness, the sense of a story being told, an appropriate tone – possibly like conversation but in well-written form with clear, strong sentence structure.

Does your writing contain ideas and themes, an attitude? If you achieve these it will mean that you and your readers are confident that your writing has found a forceful and definite aim: it is going somewhere.

Is your piece a narrative? Story-like qualities (events linked together – a reflection on a single, main event) will usually increase the impact of memoir writing. Does your piece lose touch with its narrative and, if so, can you revise and edit it to keep it on track?

One of your aims should be to get your readers to think, to have some new thoughts about an experience they may have shared. Keep them thinking right until the end of the final sentence.

CHAPTER 3

POETRY

Reading and Listening

William Carlos Williams described a poem as 'a machine made of words', and in the first part of this chapter I want to look closely at some of these machines of words to discover how they are put together, how they perform as they do and why they are able to attract the attention of readers. As writers we need to learn how poems can be made by looking at certain examples of finished poems, finding out what kind of pleasure they aim to provide and how our imagination is being engaged. One peculiarity about poems is that they can exist in two places: on the printed or hand-written page; and in the air, as sound.

We hear poetry aloud at a live reading, on radio or television, as poetic drama on stage, or very occasionally as part of a film sound-track. It can also be read aloud by readers in private. If a poem is read silently on a page, the reader can read at his or her own pace; he or she controls the reading and can repeat it or go back over passages within a poem. Most reading is of this backtracking sort, and many writers would probably hold that if this is the case then a vital link is missing: the link that connects poetry with the sound of a speaking voice. If the reading is controlled by an outside source – the actor or speaker reading to an audience – the audience is subjected to that control, and must listen or lose out. To read a poem aloud from the page enables it to come across as uninterrupted sound, and this at least is preferable to silent reading. Even silent reading can be *voiced*, but only if the reader is able to make the conversion from print to voice quality and to enjoy the words for their rhythms and echoes as well as for the shapes of lines on a page. Poetry offers both these forms of pleasure: its shaped figure and its voice.

Several writers have drawn attention to the quality of voice in poetry. Seamus Heaney writes about his work as rooted in the speech of his own region. D. H. Lawrence wrote poems reproducing the speech of his childhood background in north-east Nottinghamshire. The poet and dramatist Tony Harrison has experimented with poems which include phonetic symbols in the written text of his work, and which therefore demand that readers distinguish between forms of pronunciation. Printed, they look awkward; they challenge the whole idea of *book* poetry which Harrison was taught at school. Asking him to read Keats aloud in class, his teacher at Leeds Grammar School ridiculed Harrison's schoolboy Yorkshire dialect: 'stuffed with glottals, great lumps'. On the one hand Harrison was fortunate in having a teacher who did insist on the reading and hearing of poetry aloud, but on the other unfortunate in that his teacher also believed that a proper delivery required 'proper speech': *enunciation*, not dialect. It may be unfair to cite Harrison's teacher as an example of a common mistake, but in the minds of many people poetry has come to be associated with high culture, excessive formality and with making its first appeal to the trained intellect. Otherwise, it is slushy, sentimental, pretentious, self-pitying. Either way, the words of Sam Weller in Dickens's novel spring to mind: 'Poetry's unnat'ral'.

Of course it is quite possible to write poems that sound formal or sentimental, but those are qualities most contemporary poets and readers of poetry would denounce. There is also some cause for identifying poetic language as the very opposite of intellect and abstraction. Writers often prefer the notion of poetry as unrefined and primitive: the kind of language you learn before you learn how to reason and think in abstract concepts. The psychologist D. W. Harding wrote about conceptual thought as having an origin and infancy; it does not appear fully-grown from the start; the language of poetry deals with thoughts as they are 'in their dumb cradles' – that is, in their earlier stages of growth. The language as learned in childhood, language close to its dialect origin, therefore, exhibits more substance and stronger emotional power. Poetic language has a basic *physicality*; its sound-quality and sharply focused attention on what is immediate in the physical surroundings guarantees an appeal first to sensation. Poetic language offers language itself as a sensation; it makes language into texture and musical sound structure. Writing in dialect is one of the methods of drawing attention to the texture, and away from the abstracted meaning or message of a poem. Instead of the usual question 'What does it *mean*?', the preferred question should be 'How does it *speak*?'

We need to be sure of one basic point, however. Poetry is for everybody to hear, and for everybody to write. To enjoy reading Harrison or Heaney we do not have to do it with an accent.

Fortunately, it is not necessary to have an Ulster background or use Harrison's awkward-looking phonetic symbols in order to write for the voice. Nor is 'voice' the only means of enjoyment. As we shall discover, not all poems *are* written for the voice; some writers deliberately choose to shape their poems for the page; some choose to let their poems inhabit both these dimensions.

To insist on the voice is a partial but important and neglected truth. Here is a piece from *Macbeth:*

> – Now o'er the one half-world
> Nature seems dead, and wicked dreams abuse
> The curtain'd sleep: witchcraft celebrates
> Pale Hecate's offerings: and wither'd Murder,
> Alarum'd by his sentinel, the wolf,
> Whose howl's his watch, thus with his stealthy pace,
> With Tarquin's ravishing strides, towards his design
> Moves like a ghost. Thou sure and firm-set earth,
> Hear not my steps, which way they walk.
> (Shakespeare, *Macbeth*, Act II scene 1)

At this moment I am typing Shakespeare's text into a word processor. Until printed it only exists on a screen, but clearly this space is not the same as the one within our minds as we hear it happening. To retrieve it from being just writing inside a book you will need to read the piece from *Macbeth* aloud and let it come into being inside your thoughts: it gathers pace, builds, rushes forward. The page is flat, screenlike and uneventful, but the space of thought twists and shapes writing to an active image; it acts like skin to touch; it has that kind of surface. Words merely printed or on a screen cannot realise the impact and effect of words read aloud and heard.

One of the skills involved in writing poems is to discover what will re-occupy that screen of imagination. How does Shakespeare do it? Clearly some words extracted from the text will create big difficulties: Who was Hecate? Tarquin? What was meant by 'sentinel', 'alarum'd'? But imagination does not hear this passage in terms of such problems of isolated meaning. Instead, it watches with a sense of events swept forward by murder's approach. Whatever the word 'sentinel' means in a dictionary, it contributes to, and is joined with, a flow of voice that cannot be stopped. Equally we sense, because these words are spoken by Macbeth himself, that what they produce is also imagined by him, and helplessly; he, too, is swept along. Against his better judgement he aims to convince himself that he can kill. Night is not just the shadow side of the earth, but a place where things, including Macbeth's words, arrange themselves for atrocity. The verb-phrase 'Moves like a ghost' at the end of this quotation makes all previous phrases its tributaries; the murder must happen. The commentary is delivered in a horrified whisper, the whisper becomes a torrent, and nothing can convince like the inevitable.

I once had an argument with a friend about football and poetry: which offered the more aesthetic experience? With scholarly enthusiasm he said football, of course. But it strikes me that the first response on hearing this piece from *Macbeth* is to punch the air and shout, *Yes that's it!* – not to stop and wonder who Tarquin was. Response first, replay and tactics later.

In Milton's poem *Paradise Lost,* the angels find Satan whispering into Eve's ear:

> Him there they found
> Squat like a toad close to the ear of Eve,
> Assaying by his devilish art to reach
> The organs of her fancy, and with them forge
> Illusions, as he list, phantasms and dreams.
>
> (Milton *Paradise Lost*, Book IV)

These passages from Shakespeare and Milton imply that the power of language can indeed be fearful: something more than just words when judged for effect. These writers correctly acknowledge the power that lies in their hands, not just in the hands of their villainous counterparts. The ultimate aim of Milton's poem is to whisper things conceived as a force for good, but the power of the whisper is the same: a transforming power, it gets inside the feelings and inclinations; close to the ear, it forges illusions and dreams. At this level, language is not just a series of acquired message-producing codes but an event in the mind before the rational angels intervene. By means of unusually strong voice rhythms, it suspends judgement and the reasoning faculties in favour of what T. S. Eliot called the 'auditory imagination'.

The idea that poetry can do this more than any other of the verbal arts accounts for the belief that it carries high risk responsibility. Something out of the ordinary is implicated: the poet is a special kind of person, a legitimate trespasser on the sacred, someone whose own ear has been whispered into by powerful, devilish or divine messengers. It is not my aim to argue either for or against this view. The relationship between a poet and his or her community does not have to involve a tiny select minority of eminent writers and a large amorphous majority of non-writers. In certain communities everyone writes, not only the specialist. But in all communities where poetry has a presence, the belief holds that within the mind a space exists for words to generate meanings that will transform. In other words, imagination is real; hearing Milton or Shakespeare can still awaken it; it can be awakened with or without their methods and constructions of the world, and new forms of awakening can be found.

Acts of Attention

Writing that seduces, persuades, argues, comforts, contradicts, writing resembling speech but speech with impact – poetry can display all these tones in its register. It aims to throw a charge between two points, the first being the subject, topic, piece of the world, and the second the reader's responsive imagination: the space in the mind that responds to sound and image. It makes use of rhythm and other forms of sound quality with that imagination primarily in view. It aims to root itself there so that, like Eve, we become unwarily entangled. This would seem at first to require either very susceptible readers or very heavy methods of literary technology, neither of which we can count on. But fortunately, one aspect of poetry is surprise: a sense that things in the world about us are surprising and that words, even obvious and simple words, can be organised to enhance surprise. A word often used to describe this effect of surprise is *de-familiarisation,* a 'making strange' of the things we usually think of as familiar and not worth a second look. The focus of a poem is so sharp that it de-familiarises; it does make things worth looking at twice, as in the poem below by William Carlos Williams. As we shall see, the language is straightforward; clever and elaborate metaphor is not necessary.

> *'Proletarian Portrait'*
>
> A big young bareheaded woman
> in an apron
>
> Her hair slicked back standing
> on the street
>
> One stockinged foot toeing
> the sidewalk
>
> Her shoe in her hand. Looking
> intently into it
>
> She pulls out the paper insole
> to find the nail
>
> That has been hurting her
>
> (Williams, 1968: 63)

The art of this poem (as in the passage from *Macbeth)* is its organisation. It could have moved straight from the subject of the sentence ('A big young bareheaded woman') to the rest of the main clause ('pulls out the paper insole/ to find the nail'), but the intervening phrases delay the verb and all the information it supplies. Why? The poem needs to place this information at the point where it will surprise us. The structure prolongs our attention in the same way and for the same length of time as the poet's attention is prolonged by what he is seeing. He becomes absorbed, temporarily, in someone else's absorption. We witness a sudden act of concentration: the woman's, and the poet's, and even though the event described might happen any day anywhere, something we might not normally notice has been brought close to our attention and valued.

A common question is how to define the way poetry differs from prose, especially when faced with a piece like the one above. Its language seems too ordinary to be in a poem, and the subject itself far too commonplace for the elevated treatment we expect. But really the word 'poem' implies a space, and as with the space on a theatre stage, what you put into it can be just what you decide you will put into it. One way of filling that space is to think of a poem as a form of drama where words in conjunction create settings, generate voices, enact moments of tension, crisis and possible illumination. Prose fiction and memoir build up worlds where characters and ideas circulate, conflicts develop and may be resolved. Stage plays use music, lighting, the physical stage space. The difference is that, in comparison with other genres, poems produce such effects with unusual swiftness. Words have to do what technicians, designers, musicians and actors accomplish, and this can be done only because language, both spoken and written, possesses an amazing versatility. Poets know this and can write in a way that moves us, even though the poem's space amounts to less than half of a book page. Here are the first two lines of Ted Hughes's short poem *'Full Moon and Little Frieda':*

> A cool small evening shrunk to a dog bark and the clank of a
> bucket –
>
> And you listening.
>
> (Hughes, 2004: 182)

With these few words Ted Hughes has invented a way of giving us setting, sound, time, event and atmosphere in the space of a mere twenty-one syllables. Just as the evening seems to respond to a dog bark and the clank of a bucket, so the little girl responds – at the end of the poem – to the moon, pointing at it and shouting out 'Moon! Moon!'. Hughes's whole concentration is focused on a moment when sensitiveness of response-reactions reaches maximum intensity, in the poem's own words like 'a spider's web, tense for the dew's touch'. But the poem has impact not only for that reason. Suddenly the world's enormous presence has appeared to a child who points and expresses her amazement – perhaps for the first time. In twelve lines Hughes captures the drama of consciousness finding itself alive.

The poet is mixing a sense of the world with a sense of language, and doing it so they are mixed inextricably. That world only exists in those lines, yet it seems as real or more real, more present, than the actual evening where I sit typing these words in this book. Just as what happens on stage becomes more real and occupies more of our attention than the part of the theatre where we happen to be sitting, so the world of a poem can draw us into its sphere, can in a sense *remove* us from ourselves. For a second we are elsewhere – by that river, in that house. To write poems involves being able to take people with you into that other space, so that they sway with the crowd in the tube, walk with Sandra Lee Scheuer in the poem by Geddes (see p. 10), feel the smallness and also the expanse of that evening where a child points at the moon and shouts 'Moon!'

Because words in poems can achieve much in a comparatively small space, our attention is sharpened, our alertness adjusts itself into a state of preparedness, and the poem therefore must aim to reward us and not let us down. Reading a new poem by a poet whose work has moved you or excited you in the past, and from whom you anticipate new events in language, can make you remember that moment when a child finishes counting, with eyes shut, then opens them wide and runs to find her hidden friends. To read a poem we choose a time when we can concentrate, give it all our attention, and exactly the same, of course, applies to the experience of writing. A first draft might not get within range of a finished poem, but it will often contain those first valuable indications that a poem is there to be discovered, that we can move forward, find ways to dramatise the sense of an encounter or conflict, a moment of illumination. The obvious way to proceed is scene first, then action. A voice might be heard, or voices. Parts of the scene might stand out as an image. The drama of the poem might depend on the sense of a turning-point, a moment of transition, a speaking voice delivering some news, some warning, a challenge, an invitation. The following poem by the American poet Anita Wilkins dramatises one such turning-point:

'Cherries'

After his aorta ruptured
early in December
and after weeks in Intensive

Care, my father
longed to go north, following
the cherries as they ripened,
those small dark hearts,

and to pick them
himself, in the green orchards,
moving from tree to tree,
his blood (channeled now
through Dacron tubing)
beating strong again in his chest,

while overhead the blue northern sky
stares down, intent
as a surgeon's great solemn
scrutinizing eye –
under the hot floodlights of spring.

(Wilkins, 1982: 38)

The cherries ripen under a hot blue sky, and healing seems a natural process, but the last lines correct that impression. The process involves the heavy engineering of the operating room with its overhead power-lamps. The poem brings the mechanical and natural together in one stunning metaphor: 'the hot floodlights of spring'. Despite their gradual convergence we experience this final conjunction as a shock. Just at the moment when we thought of spring as the healing force, we are reminded of the surgeon's eye. However strong the recovery was, a sense of being assailed still continues. The poem couldn't produce this insight without details of setting or world, without image (the way colours impinge with forceful clarity), and story – from illness to recovery. We hear of recovery, also of persistent exposure, a turning-point that doesn't quite make the turn, of green orchards, also Dacron tubing. A dramatic tension holds these impressions together.

Transmitters

But something else is important here and that is the poem's relationship with its world. In this poem the cherries aren't there just to provide realistic touches and therefore credulity, not used just to brighten its colour spectrum. They are performing a central function in this particular machine of words. More than objects, they appear as transmitters of meaning, become *signals* of colour, an awakened sensuousness, sought for as an affective supply of life. What sort of cherries, how many, how red, etc? Just to describe them statically in terms of size and shape, along with everything else, is not the point. By *transmitter*, what I mean is that a particular object doesn't just receive special attention, it galvanises the rest of the poem's world, generates a force field, a polarisation of energy. If you describe it you will be doing more than just representing an object in words. Its signals seem to steer the attention we give to the poem as a whole, and to a wider meaning as we read. A transmitter can be a person or an object, animate or inanimate, a street sign, something in a landscape. If poems are dramatisations of experience, then one way of enhancing that drama will be to think not of static scenes but of shaping energy.

Examples of transmitter poems include *'The Tyre'* by Simon Armitage, many of Sylvia Plath's poems, particularly 'Tulips' from Ariel, 'A Disused Shed in County Wexford' by Derek Mahon, is another. The following poem by Daniel Weissbort, a poet well-known for his publishing of modern poetry in translation, shows how objects – in this case flowers – transmit a whole series of meanings. Notice how he doesn't describe them statically; instead he shows what they do:

'Peonies Again'

The peonies are on the march again.
There's no more room for them underground.
Spearpoints break surface,
Specks of colour in the crumbling dirt.
I stop to examine this upthrust
at the bottom of the garden,
this promise of future order in a wasteland,
order and organization, as though someone
sat and planned it all in a notebook,
this rising straight up from the ground,
the sap busy in them.
And the tight promise of these tips,
swelling to cupolas,
rounding into globes,
tight fistfuls, bunched, bales,
packed like golfballs.
And the stems starting to tilt.
And then the black ants come to these oozing earths,
make passes across them as though urging them on,
milking them, milking them,
until their resolve snaps! They split apart, unfurl.
Like a great sigh.
The stems sink lower, lower,
as rank on rank of petals unpack themselves...

> Not this year.
> They are building a parking strip there,
> at the bottom of the garden.
> I stoop and easily spot them,
> only their tips showing among great clods,
> cans, boxes, brittle scraps of paper from the alley.
> 'We're back again!' they are saying.
> 'We'll soon get things straightened out here.'!
> And you can almost feel the earth tremble from their upthrust.
> But this year it's not like other years.
> This year diggers and concrete-layers will bring order,
> cars with their snouts and staring eyes
> will assemble where peonies gave their colour to the air.
> (Weissbort, 1986: 98)

For a moment, as we read, the world becomes centred on these flowers growing in what sounds like a rubbish dump: 'In a wasteland' in the first part of the poem, 'among great clods, cans, boxes' in the second. This is an urban poem set in the northern United States where the poet now lives. Far from being portrayed in a static position, as in some vase or still life painting – every petal given in beautiful detail – these flowers are not being admired for any decorative qualities they may have, but for something we don't usually associate with plants – their *organising* power, their promise of plans, of order, almost like a military campaign. But then the dramatic change occurs. This year, order is supplied by other means. If you have been reading the first part as a kind of celebration of action and energy, the second part shocks you out of that. Nevertheless the peonies persist. 'We'll soon get things straightened out here!' We hear this line with a sense of dramatic irony – or, worse, pity, or fearfulness. The plot has changed. Notice how the poet introduces voices, makes a line stand out by using a capital letter: 'Like a great sigh' splits the poem into two stanzas; 'Not this year.' creates metaphors for cars which make us see them as brainless destroyers. All these are forms of *dramatic* effects in poetry, generating surprise, impact, and, ultimately, emotion. We can say this poem has point of view, action, consequences, crisis, a type of story – the features we recognise more easily in other genres, simply because we expect them to be there. But they exist in poems as well.

Seeing certain objects as transmitters causes us to view the world in unfamiliar terms, so that as we read, as we write about them, sets of rearrangements start to occur, new force-fields; old polarities subside. You can try this by looking around at your present surroundings, seeing what might be a transmitter. What is it about that object, that place, which attracts your attention?

Almost every word in Daniel Weissbort's poem – adjective, noun, verb, participle – serves a *forward* movement. By contrast, the transmitter in the following poem by Sharon Olds develops *enfolding* qualities. It might seem from our story-directed position that dramatisation must be forward-oriented, involving words such as 'upthrust ... promise of future ... sap busy', but that isn't so here:

'The Hand'

After he falls, and his elbow is turned backwards,
our son's hand wastes away,
and we learn to know his left hand
as it is now, muscles atrophied,
fingers decurved. I try not to envision it
healed, it seems somehow disloyal;
I consider careers he can have with one-and-a-
half hands. When the doctor has stuck
the needles into his forearm and unloosed
the current, there is a crackling on the monitor,
a scribble of activity on the screen, my throat
thickens as I hear the life of the nerve,
and the doctor says, A healthy nerve
doesn't sound like this at all,
this nerve is dead. For a second I had pictured
the muscle at the base of his thumb, flexor
pollucis brevis, and the heel of his hand,
risen again, like dough under
a doubling-cloth. Years later,
I saw him in the album, holding his weak hand
in his strong one, the way he used to hold it,
as if carrying a sleeping marmoset,
it was eighteen months after the accident,
we did not know if the hand would come back or not –
that was the way we talked, then,
as if the hand were on a journey,
we chatted about the dead nerve,
the tendon transplant they'd try later
if the hand did not come back. All year he seemed happy,
a boy with one hand curled up
like a day-old day lily. What did he think of
at night? He had no God, he had
himself, a hand like a mouse to take care of,
the way he took care of Cowboy and Tiger,
cosying them against his clavicle.
He had what the day had brought him – as when he was

a newborn he never cried, my mother
wondered if he was alright, the way he always smiled.
Even before he was fully born, when he
looked around him, he seemed content,
I saw him in the little birth-room mirror,
his bluish head turning, his shoulders and
body inside my body, as if in this
new life, from the neck down
you wore your mother.
His eyes seemed even then to focus,
as if he knew this place, or had not
expected to know it.

(Olds, 1996: 49)

In Chapter 1 I emphasised how important it is to open doors in a piece of writing so that readers engage with its world. 'The Hand' tells of the poet's reaction to her son's injury, and his possible long-term disability, but as many new writers and teachers of writing are aware, intensity of emotional content is no guarantee of effectiveness. Questions to ask include: does your writing take you and your readers to new places within that emotional experience? Does it convince? Or merely lapse into sentimental clichés and generality? Sharon Olds's poem heads straight towards an especially dangerous emotional subject, but with no cliché in sight, just her straightforward attention to the specific, her determination to mould each line and cluster of lines as closely as she can around the experience, to expose it, not protect it from view.

Convergence

The way she takes us through the experience helps us to establish it as a story, one in full contact with objects, places, sounds. 'Fingers decurved ... A crackling on the monitor'.

The poem's form – a single block of lines of similar length – establishes it as a series of moments remembered as her mind reflects on the injury: what it looked like, what she thought, but she includes no words for how she felt – shocked, worried, frightened. Like any good writer, she concentrates on the details of place and scene that produced those feelings, and by this method enables us to engage with them at a deeper, more physical, level of experience. This way of writing effects a convergence between poet and reader. The accident, the monitor screen, the photograph years later: her mind moves back and forth over signs of recovery, of failure, of consequences, but reaches no generalised understanding. All is located in the specific. As readers we feel a creative process is taking place there right in front of us in this act of searching and remembering, and that we can share in each of its stages. She thinks about her son. The meditation leads her to ask:

> What did he think of
> at night?

with the following answer:

> He had no God, he had
> himself, a hand like a mouse to take care of ...
> He had what the day had brought him.

The poet has taken us with her on a journey, and in her thoughts about the question: 'What did he think of / at night?' has brought us to a new place in her experience. Her own journey is towards the centre of this experience, however painful it might be to remember. Because of the way she writes the poem – gradually moving through detailed scenes, presenting her moment-by-moment response to certain events – we are also there when she reaches its central meaning, its images of the single, protecting self.

The word 'poetry' has shifted some way from the time when lines such as those below formed our idea of it:

> Nature, and Nature's laws lay hid in night:
> God said, Let Newton be, and all was light.

Rhyme and regular metre lend authority to Pope's couplet from his poem *Essay On Man,* while in 'The Hand' we converge not with a shining, polished truth, but with the creative process as it happens.

Such convergence enables a closer acquaintance with the *process of making a poem* than we might gain from poems in other modes. Another type of reader-writer convergence comes about through the learning of poems, aided by a strong rhyme scheme and regular stress pattern, as in the style of Pope's couplet above. To recite from memory gives you control of all those amazing words. In free verse the sense of participation is achieved by other means, and one is by sharing the process of remembering exact thoughts and sensations, so that by travelling again with the experience you and your reader arrive simultaneously at the same point of insight.

Dramatisation

Earlier I referred to dramatic effects in poems, and it might be worth looking at this more closely. Certain thoughts produce fierce currents of verbal energy. These become visible first as speech. The speaker may be the poet, a persona, or a character in a poetic drama. Momentum develops from mind through voice to action. Thought itself produces such agitation of mind that serious consequences appear to be inevitable. In Shakespeare's *King Lear,* Edmund, bastard son of the Earl of Gloucester, meditates on the word 'illegitimate', and on 'Legitimate Edgar', his fortunate brother. He starts in a formal mode that soon deteriorates:

> Thou, Nature, art my goddess; to thy law
> My services are bound. Wherefore should I
> Stand in the plague of custom, and permit
> The curiosity of nations to deprive me,
> For that I am some twelve or fourteen moonshines
> Lag of a brother? Why bastard? Wherefore base?
> When my dimensions are as well compact,
> My mind as generous, and my shape as true,
> As honest madam's issue? Why brand they us
> With base? With baseness? Bastardy? Base? Base?
> Who, in the lusty stealth of nature, take
> More composition and fierce quality
> Than doth, with a dull, stale, tired bed,
> Go to creating a whole tribe of fops
> Got between sleep and wake? Well then,
> Legitimate Edgar, I must have your land.
> Our father's love is to the bastard Edmund
> As to th'legitimate. Fine word 'legitimate'.
> Well my legitimate, if this letter speed,
> And my invention thrive, Edmund the base
> Shall top th'legitimate. I grow. I prosper.
> Now, gods, stand up for bastards.
>
> (*King Lear*, Act I, Scene 2)

All this sounds like speech; moody, violent, sudden – as if he's having these thoughts for the first time. Thoughts simultaneous with their expression: this has been one of the vital springs of major dramatic poetry in our tradition. Once said aloud, thoughts *are* actions. Notice how voice qualities gather pace, how his speech bonds with the colloquial. The formal verse lines almost lose their structure. The closer we get to Edmund's *moment,* to his immediate excitement of thought, the more savagely he throws words about: 'base ... Bastardy ... Base ... Base'. The five-beat iambic verse virtually collapses. We hear his words banging against the hollow walls of restraint. He, too, will break out and spread chaos. Given this immediacy of utterance, thought travels out like a tidal wave. Imagine someone arguing for *legitimacy*: it would have nothing like the same active consequences.

This speech teaches us something about all poetry, not just poetic drama, for all poems have more or less the same capacity – to be dramatic, tell a story, make use of a persona or adopted voice. These devices are there if we choose to use them. Audiences, too, witness that moment when a chaotic energy first emerges. Convergence is nothing new – just in case we thought we had invented it. This speech also teaches us something about the power of language – the power to restrict but also release. Maybe that's one source of Edmund's frustration. His life is ruled (and almost ruled out) by other people's words. He struggles to get back his control of words. Speaking his thoughts points the way towards expressive action. His words now have consequences, and this threat has to be instantly audible to the audience. There's no time to argue for this or that interpretation. To write in this way we must acknowledge that poetry has been given a job to do. It has to cross the street, to communicate, and this, too, is a lesson for all poems.

Poetry and Story

Among genres, poetry is perhaps the least resolved in its relationship with its readers, in some ways the least confident. One reason for this might be that other genres deal explicitly with narrative, while poetry as publicly perceived does not. We might be able to correct this impression, but first we must ask whether people who read poems do so in the same way, and for the same reasons, as they watch a film or a play, or sit for long intermittent hours with a piece of extended prose fiction. I recently put this question to a group of experienced poets during a meeting of The Poetry Business Writing School in Huddersfield. In their view, an element of reading to see *what happens*, for suspense, takes over in all story-like writing, and poems are no exception.

Yet if a poem only *implies* a story or shows us only a few moments of it, doesn't this cramp our enjoyment, or is that the very thing we enjoy, that is, story fragmented, with time gaps and limited information? It's often suggested, and exactly for these reasons, that poems and short stories are the two genres that have most in common. So what is it that narrative poems do? Are there the usual rewards or special ones (or perhaps both) in this type of narrative? Here are some examples of poems as narratives, two from Thomas Hardy's '*Poems Dramatic and Personative*', and two by contemporary black British poets, Jean 'Binta' Breeze and Linton Kwesi Johnson.

Hardy's 'The Curate's Kindness' involves a just-retired curate and his wife who travel by wagon to the poorhouse, their new home. A hard end to a life of honest hard work, thinks the curate, but there is one compensation. In the poorhouse, husbands and wives are forced to live in separate wings, *'The rule of the Board'*. After forty dreary years of marriage (so he thinks), he'll be able to get away from his wife at last! But just at that moment a young parson arrives on the scene with the news that the rule has been changed: wives and husbands can be together after all! The poem begins with this stanza, repeated at the end:

> I thought there'd be strangers around me,
>   But she's to be there.
> Let me jump out o' wagon and go back and drown me
>   At Pumney or Ten Hatches Weir!
>
> (Hardy 1930: 194)

In Hardy's *'One Ralph Blossom Soliloquizes'* the story is reported in the Budmouth Borough minutes of 16__. One Ralph Blossom was asked to pay towards the upkeep of seven women 'who were mayds before they knew him'. But since, say the records, Ralph was 'dying of purple fever', no actual payments were requested. All this comes in an epigraph to the poem, which then begins with Ralph's own words just before his death. 'What will these seven women say to me?' Three show regret at what happened and blame him or themselves, but the four who speak after them show him kindness, genuine sexual gratitude:

> And Ann cries 'O the times were fair,
> So wherefore should you burn down there?
> There is a deed under the sun, my Love
> And that was ours. What's done is done...'
>
> (Ibid: 271)

Jean 'Binta' Breeze's *'Testament'* shows a black woman (the speaker of the poem) who has worked all her life in bad conditions in London bringing up her family, looking after her husband who works on the trains. Now her daughter is growing up, perhaps a little bit ashamed of her parents – the father who smells of train oil, the mother who speaks Creole (the language of the poem). The daughter has a high school education and her own set of friends, but is losing her connection with the family and its Caribbean experiences before emigration. The mother is proud of her past, proud of her daughter, but senses that their two worlds are growing to be incompatible. The mother-speaker refers to small important things like the weather, 'an de cole does bad tings / to mi knee'. She also talks about where she belongs:

we memories of back home
we regular Sunday church
in de back a de local hall
we is jus what we is
watching you grow
into dis place
an ah want yuh to know
dis is yuh own
we done bleed fi it
yuh born here
in de shadow a Big Ben
im strike one
as di waters break
an you come rushin troo.

(Breeze, 1992 :7–11)

The poem by Linton Kwesi Johnson, *'Sonny's Lettah'*, depicts a young black man who is arrested for the murder of a policeman in London. He tells the story to his mother, writing her a letter from Brixton prison. While waiting for a bus, he and his little brother Jim were accosted by three white policemen. They picked on Jim and accused him of theft. Jim backed away but the police attacked him and started beating him up. Sonny intervened to protect Jim and accidentally killed a policeman. Now he and Jim are both in gaol, one for murder, the other for obstruction.

Mama,
Ah jus' could'n' stan-up deh
An'noh dhu not'n:

so mi jook one in him eye
an' hi stated to cry
mi t'ump one in him mout'
an' him start to shout
mi kick one pan him shin
an' him start to spin
mi tump him pan him chin
an' him drap pan a bin

an' crash
an de'd…

(Johnson 1991: 25)

All narrative genres contain two elements; we might call one of these *narrative progression*, answering the questions 'what happened, to whom, when, where, with what consequences, and, finally, how did it all end?' The other, the *narrative image*, illustrates the *circumstances*, *prevailing conditions* under which the story develops. 'This is how these people live', it says. 'These problems are what they have to contend with, ones that will not necessarily change.' All three poets are interested in what happens and in what the consequences have been. But their narratives do not only engage us out of a need each time to follow everything through. Hardy's characters are left to wallow in the ironies of false marital loyalty and dreariness, or in the excitements of immorality – either way, we know their world is ruled by heavy restrictions, quasi-religious idealism, sexual dogmas designed to produce maximum unhappiness. From the other two poets we learn what it means to live in a culture where racial identity becomes a source of profound confusion and pain, even violence, and we learn about this not only through what they say but how they speak. To a community ruled by police racist intimidation, Sonny's vernacular would come across as almost a crime in itself. Hardy's voices have little say against sexual laws demanding fidelity under any circumstances. By showing us voices like these; marginal, ordinary, raw, yet full of urgency, a poem places less emphasis on narrative progression than is the case in the other genres. Instead we gain more of a sense of the cultural conditions illustrated by moments and predicaments, effects that relate to a *narrative image* of times and people.

The idea of *narrative image*, especially relevant to poetry's use of story, also has practical implications for the writing of prose fiction, drama and screenplay. All the poems so far included in this chapter could be described as 'dramatic' or 'narrative'. The difference from the other narrative genres is that poetry has is its own metabolism, converting living experience into images, compacting it instead of drawing it out, so that we quickly gain a sense of moments as turning points. Narrative image isn't the only effect poems can achieve. Matthew Sweeney's poem *'Tube Ride to Martha's'* (Sweeney, 2002: 37), describes some minutes in the life of one man travelling to meet his lover by tube. In the last few seconds 'as the smoke got thicker and blacker' he is caught up in an underground fire. Private lives, public catastrophes, moments when something irrevocable happens, or simply when things are not as they were; poetry can recreate such experiences, giving them meaning with dramatic impact.

Personae

In the introduction to his anthology *The Faber Book of Vernacular Verse*, Tom Paulin speaks of the 'vernacular imagination': 'Many of the voices here are disaffected and powerless. They know that in the public world polished speech issues orders and receives deference. It seeks to flatten out and obliterate all the varieties of spoken English and to substitute one accent for all the others' (Paulin, 1996: 262). Polished speech seeks to assimilate the kinds of vernacular Jean 'Binta' Breeze and Linton Kwesi Johnston use and keep in use. In each of their poems the speaker is a *persona* – a character in a narrative telling the story to someone else, or just telling it so that it gets heard. The use of personae allows writers access to a much wider range of experience, but it also, as in the above examples, enables them to dramatise, and thus preserve, experiences special to their cultural background. And there will be other advantages. Personae have been so widely used, especially in the poetry of the past and present century, that the reasons for its persistence might be very interesting to reflect on.

You, the writer, are imagining the voice of someone who could be a figure from history or myth, an animal, a stranger, a voice outside any of these categories, the voice of a member of your own cultural or ethnic group. In verse drama, the characters you invent will all be personae. The word 'mask' is often used to identify the voice style of a persona. Yeats speaks through the madwoman Crazy Jane; Geoffrey Hill speaks through the mask of Sebastian Arrurruz, Eliot in the voice of Alfred Prufrock. Elizabeth Bishop uses the strayed crab as a persona (see p. 37). The immensely popular Carol Ann Duffy's collection of poems *The World's Wife* has recently made another significant impact with personae.

Why has it been so useful? Writers often need to feel able to reach beyond their own personal experience. Your life-experience can be relevant to a whole range of cultural and social questions people ask. But if the aim is to widen out, to reach others, explore new perspectives, and to revive and re-examine old ones, then to write simply as 'I' – meaning yourself – could at some point become a restriction. Equally, you might choose to think through some aspect of your own life using a persona. You can become – for the duration – anyone or anything you choose. But there are restrictions here as well. Your chosen persona – human, object, animate or inanimate – must already carry some meaning for you and your readers. Even if you choose another real person – your Uncle Robbie for instance – then you will need to make him recognisable to your readers or listeners by making him in some way typical and significant. It is a fundamental fact that a poem, while it engages its readers, must also *disengage* them from asking 'Why should I care about this?', 'Why does this matter?'. Why it matters must be established implicitly, first by the way it is written, then by its connection – stated or otherwise – to our human experience. The use of personae offers a surer route to collective meaning, while not excluding the personal dimension of life we all recognise as a necessary route to that end. Like Adrienne Rich in her poem in Chapter 1 on p. 16, we listen to another living presence, another consciousness.

Surroundings

On the dingy edge of a Detroit suburb, a man aged about twenty-five crouches in his mother's caravan apartment. He's scribbling a poem, crossing lines out, writing, rewriting. Conditions seem miserable. He'll never make it. Next he's in an off-stage wash-room, vomiting. The audience won't wait. Someone else takes his place. Finally, he faces that audience. His name is Rabbit, an unknown, now taking the stage. Competition is fierce. All you can do is be honest, keep it real. He's terrified. 'He keeps forgettin / What he wrote down; the whole crowd goes so loud / He opens his mouth but the words won't come out.' But the words do come out; these are the lyrics of Eminem's 'Lose Yourself', in the film of his first performance, *8 Mile*.

How much do circumstances influence writing? How much should they? Of all genres, poetry responds to this influence the most, or it's assumed to. Raymond Carver in his poem '*Sunday Night*' not only shares this view but demonstrates it:

> Make use of the things around you.
> This light rain
> outside the window, for one.
> This cigarette between my fingers,
> These feet on the couch.
> The faint sound of rock and roll.
> The red Ferrari in my head.
> The woman bumping
> drunkenly around in the kitchen.
> Put it all in.
> Make use.
>
> (Carver 1997: 257)

Carver's poem does something more than give us good advice. It allows us a glimpse of the poet's surroundings, and shows us how these surroundings influence his writing. He makes us believe the conditions under which he is writing have entered the content of the poem, have become – in all their randomness – its subject. He causes us to imagine that while he is writing there actually is someone in the kitchen lurching around drunk, that it's raining outside, that he is smoking a cigarette. Can it be that the writer's outside world – not just the inner world of experience, or the abstract world of literary forms – becomes the factor in how poems are shaped? If you are writing in a crowded pub, are you more likely to write in free verse than in regular metre? Does writing a sonnet require solitude, while a rap lyric comes off best in the presence of a noisy audience? Many poems, perhaps the majority, show us a mind thinking, but thinking through response to some imagined or real object, person or event. Your poem will say something through its form – about its circumstances, about your sense of yourself as an artist, about your way of thinking in your world.

Poetic Forms

Rhyme, Metre and Stress Patterns

The four poems I have quoted from in the section *Poetry and Story* all make use of rhyme. They are also written (to emphasise the paradox) as speech. We might expect these two elements to be incompatible, but when we think about what makes these voices pleasurable, memorable, also direct and clear, it could be that very contrast between naturalness and artificiality. Tony Harrison's sonnets, his powerful poem '*v*', which imitates the slang speech of a skinhead, might also suggest that contrast, difference, clash of formal with vernacular registers, generate turbulent verbal energies. But this view – although it may contain a good deal of truth – will not put rhyme in its place for us. The speaker of '*Sonny Letta*' turns his speech into an agitated dance; rhyme as a desperate gesture. It indicates urgency. Jean 'Binta' Breeze's poem makes use of irregular rhyme patterns, words at the ends of lines rhyme with those within lines (internal rhyme) – 'memories ... is ... place' – while certain words – 'grow... know... too' – at the ends of lines show a typical irregularity: long spaces between rhymes set up an expectation of rhyme only to defer it. Rhyme, then, is not just an artificial device. It signals the link between poetry and music, poetry and its ancient oral roots (see Chapter 1, p. 25). New writers are often discouraged from using obvious rhyme, however, and there are some good reasons why. Rhyme needs to interact with other qualities in poems, with speech, with dramatisation, urgency, surprise, and with other aspects of form such as sentence lengths in poems. Rhyme on its own, rhyme without other qualities in poetry, can be dull, lifeless, and should be avoided.

Poems are written in lines of equal or unequal length. Regular metre counts the number of beats or stresses per line and keeps to a consistent number – five for iambic pentameter (as in Edmund's speech on p. 83 above), the most commonly found stress pattern in English metrical verse. Pope's couplet, from his 'Essay on Man', shows the pentameter in safer hands than Edmund's. Whenever we write or speak in English we make use of stress patterns. The word 'iambic' means that an unstressed / stressed pattern is operating, with stress falling on the second syllable, as follows:

> The bridge is wide. The Forth is deep.
> Iambic trains are made for sleep.
>
> (Bell, 1994: 16)

But speaking in regular metre would make us sound like daleks or metronomes. Even in instances of high regularity, as in the just-quoted couplet, the voice is only loosely attached to the beat. A breathing rhythm has its part to play as well. The heart is regular and beats involuntarily, but we can control our breathing. We can pause, slow down, speak rapidly, whilst still staying within the iambic range. In poetry the underlying sense of metre (like a heart-beat) is more pronounced than it is in ordinary speech, but only just. We can still hear it, as in this extract from a poem by Elizabeth Bishop:

> *from 'In the Waiting Room'*
>
> In Worcester, Massachusetts,
> I went with Aunt Consuelo
> to keep her dentist's appointment
> and sat and waited for her
> in the dentist's waiting room.
> It was winter. It got dark
> early. The waiting room
> was full of grown-up people,
> arctics and overcoats,
> lamps and magazines...
>
> (Bishop, 1991: 159)

This free verse retains a measure of regularity, with two or three stresses per line and some uncertainty about where they might fall. Notice, too, how the significant words occur at the ends of lines where we would expect to find rhymes, while 'to ... and ... in' come at the beginning. This effect is almost standard in free verse, though some poets, Sharon Olds among them, experiment with this feature by changing it about so that lines end with prepositions instead of with nouns and verbs: '... when he was / a newborn ... when he / looked ...' (see above p. 81).

Structure

The structure of Carver's '*Sunday Morning*', one of the simplest, is that of a list. This next poem by the Czech poet Miroslav Holub combines 'list' with 'narrative' in its structure:

'The Fly'

She sat on a willow-trunk
watching
part of the battle of Crécy,
the shouts,
the gasps,
the groans,
the tramping and the tumbling.

During the fourteenth charge
of the French cavalry
she mated
with a brown-eyed male fly

from Vadincourt.
She rubbed her legs together
as she sat on a disembowelled horse
meditating
on the immortality of flies.

With relief she alighted
on the blue tongue
of the Duke of Clervaux.

When silence settled
and only the whisper of decay
softly circled the bodies

and only
a few arms and legs
still twitched jerkily under the trees,

she began to lay her eggs
on the single eye
of Johann Uhr,
the Royal Armourer.

And it was thus
that she was eaten by a swift
fleeing
from the fires of Estrees.

(Holub, 1990: 52)

When referring to '*In The Waiting Room*' and '*The Fly*' as free verse, we don't mean that they are free of structure.

In free verse (where there are no rhymes or consistent metre), inner structure can completely displace surface regularity, and for a free verse poem to succeed, that inner structure needs to be strong and visible. It definitely is in Holub's '*The Fly*': 'She sat on a willow-trunk ... she mated ... She rubbed her legs together ... With relief she alighted ... She began to lay her eggs ... she was eaten...' Once a structure is established you can fit in the details and make them speak as you wish. The structure might appear to you before you write the poem, making you want to write it, just as a vague ghostly skeletal suggestion, but more animated, more definitely alive. Sometimes when we are reading a poem the structure doesn't seem to be very obvious; you have to search for it, especially if a poem exhibits a lot of surface regularity, as in the famous poem by W. H. Auden that was spoken by one of the characters in the film *Four Weddings and A Funeral*. The following is probably its most well-known stanza:

From 'Twelve Songs'

He was my North, my South, my East, my West,
My working week and my Sunday rest,
My noon, my midnight, my talk, my song.
I thought that love would last forever. I was wrong.

The last line above has six stresses. The rest have five and so keep the consistency intact. Yet rhythm and rhyme mark the strongest signifier here of regularity. If we look at this poem from a different angle we can see that it also has another kind of form that has nothing to do with surface regularity. It begins with a plea – to stop all the clocks, cut off the telephone, and then suggests that the policemen wear black cotton gloves. These details are not the same thing as dismantling the sun and pouring away the ocean, with which the poem ends. The poem moves from the small to the vast, away from the local towards the panoramic. To reverse that sequencing would alter the poem and destroy its emotional power. The sequencing is gradual but relentless, and we might describe this form as the poem's inner structure or architecture and identify it as a change of perspective or even a transformation.

So we need to be clear about these two kinds of form: *surface* patterning and *inner* patterning or *structure.* Why, then, does Auden's poem have both? Given that the inner structure is so obviously the more powerful, why have regularity? The answer is that the stress patterns and rhyme scheme act as a framework, a loom-like system into which odd and surprising details (the 'public doves' is a good example) are threaded. The poem creates a tension between expectation and surprise, and produces its extraordinary effects within the constant security of the rhyme. It is at once both predictable and unpredictable. The point of using regular form is to increase the reader's pleasure by combining reassurance with surprise, and thus to produce a heightened level of attention, or, as the American poet and critic Donald Hall expressed it, this type of form enables the poet and reader to feel 'the values of sameness against the improvisations of variety'.

We can easily see how Holub's *'The Fly'* follows a step-by-step narrative structure. Each encounter in the story is rendered stanza by stanza. Susan Burns's poem in Chapter 1, p. 32 shows a single main encounter followed by potential minor ones, and the stanza lengths have co-operated with this major-minor element to produce effectively one stanza surrounded by others less substantially developed. Olds's' 'The Hand', even though it refers to different episodes, is a single, unbroken act of thought. Its single extended stanza form is appropriate for following through to completion that process of thinking and remembering.

Free Verse Compact Treatment

The full text of Bishop's poem *'In the Waiting Room'* describes an encounter. What happens when things meet is still the question. The poet, within the poem and its autobiographical setting, needs time to reach her conclusions. The voice of considered careful exploration, therefore, leads towards the more open or extended treatment we find in Sharon Olds. But free verse can also be tightly arranged, formally exact, emphasising image rather than voice. The two poems below by Norman MacCaig combine a degree of formality – a clear visible shape – with a sense of the poet's speaking voice:

'February – Not Everywhere'

Such days, when trees run downwind,
their arms stretched before them.

Such days, when the sun's in a drawer
and the drawer locked.

When the meadow is dead, is a carpet,
thin and shabby, with no pattern.

and at bus stops people retract into collars
their faces like fists.

– And when, in a firelit room, mother looks
at her four seasons, at her little boy,

in the centre of everything, with still pools
of shadows and a fire throwing flowers.

(MacCaig, 1988: 47)

This poem is constructed from oppositions; the simple structure is stocked by brief details that are listed as opposites. One set of opposites doesn't replace the other; they coexist. But of course one has to come first, so that we do not experience this coexistence until the end. We are left with it; something was held in reserve. In their small space, the contrast injects vitality – cold to heat, unpleasant to pleasant. Imagine the sets placed in reverse order, beginning with:

> Such days, when in a firelit room, mother looks
> at her four seasons, at her little boy,
>
> in the centre of everything, with still pools
> of shadows and a fire throwing flowers.
>
> – And when trees run downwind,
> their arms stretched before them.
>
> Such days, when the sun's in a drawer
> and the drawer locked,
>
> and at bus stops people retract into collars
> their faces like fists.
>
> When the meadow is dead, is a carpet,
> thin and shabby, with no pattern.
>
> (MacCaig, 1988: 38)

The poem's meaning is in its vitality, and depends not just on contrasts but on the relative position of the scenes. In this version, the positive tone of the poem is lost completely. Which two-line stanza would make the most chilling ending?

In the following example by W. S. Graham, the poem's subject is a storm at sea where there have been casualties, but the treatment is to weave those details into a frieze, a monument, to emphasise metaphor and likeness in a design. In this way, too, the prevalent mood is one of readjustment:

> *'Gigha'*
>
> That firewood pale with salt and burning green
> Outfloats its men who waved with the sound of drowning
> Their saltcut hands over mazes of this rough bay.
>
> Quietly this morning beside the subsided herds
> of water I walk. The children wade in the shallows.
> The sun with long legs wades into the sea.
>
> (Graham, 1977: 68)

How extraordinary to make a scene out of such little detail, to make that detail stylised, formal, yet also very moving. But is the reader moved by the aesthetics or by the contents: a storm, death, no evidence, the beach and beams of sunlight indifferent to death? It becomes very difficult to know. Mazes, subsided herds, the sun with long legs – metaphors, formal devices – the very opposite of William Carlos Williams's treatment of the woman in the street removing a nail from her shoe (see above, p. 74). The objects and people in Graham's poem do not encounter each other or interact. Yet that is the point; that is the vision. You might have a preference for one poem over the other, but both kinds are available to use; both are examples of compact treatment. And it is by no means certain that the second example will fail to engage your attention, just because its treatment is impersonal, more literary, more self-consciously art-like and removed from natural speech.

Note how both stanzas in 'Gigha' are set to appeal to the eye, not to the voice. No one would ever *say* the sentence that begins 'Quietly this morning...' Rather than spoken it seems designed beforehand. But again that is the point – deliberate distortion, to evoke something familiar using unfamiliar language with peculiar sound qualities, to emphasise artifice, to discover new ways of constructing sentences, to find out what a sentence can do by inventing new sentences.

We have to say that poetry has the right to depart from speech just as free verse departs from regular verse, but we need to add that such departures are never quite total. All the free verse poems printed above carry vestiges of surface regularity. And all, when they do depart from speech, do so with a residual sense of words as spoken aloud. A trace is left; even the sentence from Graham makes reference to speech by reversing the usual order. It would have been more usual to say: 'I walk quietly this morning beside...' instead of 'Quietly this morning beside ... I walk.' Such departures sharpen the reader's response. In compact treatment the use of antithesis and the sound of a voice speaking in unspeech-like ways are two of the means whereby writers quicken our sense of the language of poetry and enable us to enjoy its inventiveness. In compact treatment the writer's and reader's imagination is responding to language as form invention with an obvious inner structure.

Syllabic poems

One of the most popular syllabic forms is the Haiku, a Japanese verse form of seventeen syllables in three lines of five, seven and five syllables. Less commonly known and practised is the Tanka, a form in lines of five/seven/five/seven/seven syllables. Examples can be found of syllabic form in more extended poems, such as Thom Gunn's 'My Sad Captains'. The point of syllabic form is that it produces a sense of tension and restraint without limiting surprise and freshness. But it's not necessary to keep to the traditional forms of syllabic poem to appreciate its dramatic possibilities.

I tried this method myself with two or three poems I wrote after watching children playing video games. I didn't like the effect of the games at all – life experience appeared to be a matter of zapping one adversary or problem after another; success was achieved when you finally zapped the lot. Alex Kidd was the name of the video character. Is success a matter of luck or skill? Could you repeat the performance, even if you finish as a winner? The syllabic effect seemed to fit this jerky, haphazard progress. The rule I invented for writing the poem was to use eight syllables per line in four-line stanzas.

'Alex Kidd in Miracle World'

Alex Kidd, he was devoured
by an eagle on a sea-cliff.
From side to side it moves across
the screen while Alex's little

ghost goes up and up and Alex
is back again with two more lives.
Skipping treacherous ledges he
drops in the sea, birds become fish,

swims down and along collecting
moneybags, and dodging the sharp
piranha. Where threat is he shifts
to reverse and negotiates

a greenish frog's killer bubbles,
a huge yo-yo fish. And this time
gets the hamburger. Lots of cheers,
but this is only zone one and

afterwards ten more. It's three he's
in now, waved at by a sucking
octopus. Another life lost.
Survival is miraculous

Alex, but where are all your friends?
Here they are and both on the safe
side, though in turn each one is you.
A skill they learn hazardously

gets you as far as you can go.
Now on a bouncy motorbike
then drowning in a lava lake
zone four is the limit so far,

Oh Alex Kidd, brave Alex Kidd,
so superiorly evolved,
see your punches coming easy.
Though in fine fettle, ghastlier

trials wait, and when you reach the
last zone, is your desired close
to know it's with a complete skill
you succeed, not from luck or by

accident? Can you be sure it
wasn't chance, impulse or a feint?
Go back Alex, try, and find you'll
defeat miracle world never.

(Mills, 1993: 70)

You may have noticed that in this poem I have broken the rule about ending each line with a significant word. The only rule for a line is to count the syllables.

Poetic Style

Metaphor

Metaphors are used in everyday speech. They find their way into common use even in more formal situations. Couples in therapy with relationship problems might be attempting to 'build bridges ... to embark on a journey of conciliation'. In such situations, exactness of expression is not essential; the context permits a margin of inaccuracy. If I say that common speech harbours dead metaphors, the word 'harbour' in this sentence is a dead metaphor applied to a dead metaphor. We need to be careful – especially when the context is a poem. Good style brings poems and comparisons to life. Faces don't just look miserable and cold; they are 'like fists'. In a recent poem by Simon Armitage, a coffee house waitress in an off-duty moment 'gives the kiss of life to a Silk Cut by the fire-escape', (*The North*, 2005, Vol 36, p 4).

To say faces look in that instant in the street 'like fists', is a response coloured with strong subjective feeling for which the poet offers no apology, no argument or proof. The metaphor itself is the proof and evidence. Only someone who felt things to be that way could say it that way. Metaphor, therefore, doesn't make things up. It is a feature of style based simply on the facts as they are seen and found to be. A guiding principle with using metaphor is that it might well exaggerate, yes, but along the line of feeling-response, so that it carries a sense of intent, of action and consequence, so that it *dramatises* the world. Charles Causley writes: 'An iron bowl sent out stiff rays of chrysanthemums. It / grew colder', (Causley, 1975: 155). We feel the cold of an iron and stiffened sun, as if the flowers emitted actual darkness. What could be seen as static objects – chrysanthemums in a bowl – are given animation and energy.

But we also need to acknowledge that the world of a poem can be made dramatic *without* metaphor. If a sense of action and story is one key to an effective style, it can be achieved by other means. Holub's poem, *'The Fly'* contains no metaphors, apart from the 'whisper of decay'. The following poem by Sujata Bhatt expresses a suspicion about metaphors. Here they are avoided, deliberately. This is a poem about writing poems. It shows us how the world of a poem can be made dramatic in other ways. The poet could have expressed her opening statement through metaphor – 'the green was the green of . . .' – but instead she chose not to, and for good reasons:

'Swami Anand'

In Kosbad during the monsoons
there are so many shades of green
your mind forgets other colors.

At that time
I am seventeen, and have just started
to wear a sari every day.
Swami Anand is eighty nine
  and almost blind.
His thick glasses don't seem to work,
they only magnify his cloudy eyes.
Mornings he summons me
  from the kitchen
and I read to him until lunch time.

One day he tells me
'you can read your poems now'.
I read a few, he is silent.
Thinking he's asleep, I stop.
But he says, 'continue'.
I begin a long one
in which the Himalayas rise
  as a metaphor.

Suddenly I am ashamed
to have used the Himalayas like this,
ashamed to speak of my imaginary mountains
to a man who walked through
the ice and snow of Gangotri
barefoot
a man who lived close to Kangchenjanga
and Everest clad only in summer cotton.
I pause to apologise
but he says, 'just continue'.

Later, climbing through
the slippery green hills of Kosbad,
Swami Anand does not need to lean
on my shoulder or his umbrella.
I prod him for suggestions,
ways to improve my poems.
He is silent a long while,
then, he says
'there's nothing I can tell you
except continue.'
(Sujata Bhatt, from 'The Reaper', 1987, No 16: 46)

In this poem each statement is definite; it says what it says clearly, without decoration. Excess literariness is stripped away. The effects of varying shades of green are simply stated as fact. Because it is a narrative the language of straight information is sufficient, everything becomes fact. Metaphor is questionable, and this mistrust is itself part of the narrative of the poem, the story of a process of thinking. The woman in the poem's own use of the Himalayas as a metaphor embarrasses her in relation to the old man's actual lived experience – she can't share that; she can't write from the centre of *his* experience, only from her own. A good style therefore bears the mark of truth. There is a flow of attention towards its world. It is simply a form of intelligent thinking, but with the facts of experience within range. Metaphor is one device among many for making us look and think again, for conveying that sense of a glimpse of something – a thought, maybe a fact – 'summer cotton'. But the advice the poet receives is of value too – we learn by doing. All you can do is continue.

Adjectives and Verbs

Basil Bunting's advice to student poets at Newcastle University in the 1970s was as follows:

1. Compose aloud; poetry is a sound.
2. Vary rhythm enough to stir the emotion you want but not so as to loose impetus.
3. Use spoken words and syntax.
4. Fear adjectives; they bleed nouns. Hate the passive.
5. Jettison ornament gaily but keep shape.

Put your poem away till you forget it. Then:

6. Cut out every word you dare.
7. Do it again a week later, and again.

Never explain. Your reader is as smart as you.

A useful list, but one that needs some comment. After you have worked on your own poems, revising and rewriting them, would you agree with Bunting's do's and don'ts? Cut every word you dare – yes, but be careful not to sacrifice number three in the process. Beginning writers can sometimes produce a clipped style they believe signifies 'poetry'. Number four is the main point here, though. A common warning: it can be read as '*All adjectives are bad, never use them*'. This advice is certainly familiar, and for the most part desirable. But what it most usually means is *use adjectives carefully* rather than not at all. To use no adjectives at all can indeed create great poetry. 'The tiger springs in the new year. / Us he devours.' (T. S. Eliot, Gerontion). Only one adjective ('new'), and the emphasis falling as it should on nouns and verbs, verbs particularly – 'springs ... devours'. But no adjectives ever? Where would Eliot have got to without the word 'dry'? We possibly do need to know about the snow in King Wenceslas – and more than the fact that it just 'lay round about'. Adjectives can only describe static states. The snow will always be deep and crisp and even. More important are the voices speaking and the word 'tread' which comes next. With adjectives, choose carefully. But, in preference, concentrate on action, use verbs.

Summary

Poetry makes language an experience – of rhythm and sound as well as form and shape. It also generates meaning, using effects we find in other creative genres, including the dramatic, the use of story, voices and personae.

Poems are about real things, people and places, and how these figure in our imaginative life. It deepens our need to find warmth, meaning and value in the world around us; at the same time it faces us with the facts, refreshes and enlivens our perception, makes the familiar strange.

Poetry discovers connections between meaning and physical sensation. It shifts from the general to the specific, makes the creative process more accessible, emphasises the moment and the local.

It serves difference, fights assimilation, but is also interested in the typical, the collective, in what binds people together.

Suggestions for Writing

1 *Topics*. Poetry anthologies often list poems under separate headings. (For example, *Staying Alive*, edited by Neil Astley, includes '*Roads and Journeys*', '*Growing Up*'.) Compile a list of poems under a heading of your choice, then write your own poems on this topic. If the heading were 'Home', for example, you might find the following instructions helpful:

Home could be a house, a city, a neighbourhood, a country or a continent. It could be home in the past or the present. Homes you have known. A house inhabited by somebody else but which you can enter into imaginatively. Start off by writing notes on the following, then develop your poem around the thoughts, scenes and details that interest you most. Focus on a place you call home *now*, or have called home before now. Picture the place you are writing about, from the outside – a building, a street. Describe this place in terms of an action – something happening to it. Or what it does to you or other people. Show a person you connect with this place: a parent, child, brother, sister, fellow student, tenant. The person is doing something, indoors or outside. What is he or she doing? Someone is speaking, saying something about this place.

Make a note of which of the examples above appeals to you (some, all, none, which).

Think of a place that is different from home. Write an impression of why this other place is better, or worse, than home.

When a visitor/friend enters, what do you hope he or she will notice, and will not notice?

Describe a very messy area of home – focus closely on the objects there (under the sink, down the settee, etc). Write down exactly what you find.

Write a poem about 'Home', using one of the notes above as your starting-point. Develop the poem making use of the other notes you have made, rejecting some, including some, building up a set of images of 'home'. You may have gathered ideas on this subject already from the previous chapter's suggestions for writing.

Deciding on your own topic will bring you into contact with the work of other writers, as you find examples of how the topic has been treated by others. In this way you will develop a sense of the variety of styles, forms, approaches and tones of voice within contemporary poetry. Don't worry if you can't find very much written on your topic; write about it anyway. Topics you might try: the sea, the weather, the city, living abroad, disability; death or loss, the body, work, voices, technologies, art (painting, sculpture) or music.

2 *Personae.* Write in the voice of another person living or dead, real or imagined. Another term for this form is dramatic monologue. (Examples are: Carol Ann Duffy, '*Warming Her Pearls*'; U. A. Fanthorpe, '*Deus versus Adam and A. N. Other*'; Robert Browning, '*My Last Duchess*'.) You will find many other examples. Look around, read for ideas. The persona you choose may mean you need to do some research, about the character, his or her background, place in history (if appropriate), culture. The following instructions might help you to get started:

Write about what interests the persona you have chosen has. Enter his or her world, way of thinking and speaking. Listen to what he or she has to say, and write it down.

Who is he or she speaking to?

Your persona is remembering something – an event, long ago or recently, that had a great impact on him or her. He or she describes it, reflects on it, and remembers it in close detail, again with an attitude. What happened?

Now your persona is looking into the future. What does he or she fear, hope for, believe will happen?

Explore some or all of these directions in a poem that catches the rhythms of this person's voice.

Note: an exercise involving Browning's poem appears in Rob Pope's *Textual Intervention,* (Pope, 1995: 15–30) as follows: 'Translate the whole poem into a conversational idiom with which you are familiar, presenting the results on a page or at a live reading.' You might also experiment by changing the circumstances, class, role, age and relationship of the speaker with his 'duchess'. For other suggested ideas about interventions see Chapter 4, Exercise 3 and Chapter 6, Exercise 9.

3 *Narratives*. You can tell a whole story, or you can just reveal important moments in someone's life and link them together. (Examples are: Sylvia Plath, '*The Rabbit Catcher*'; Elizabeth Bishop, '*The Burglar of Babylon*', Tony Harrison, '*Long Distance*'.)

If you wish, use some of the following ideas to get started:

Tell the story of a person who lived in the past and who may not be very well known. Research a turning-point in his or her life. Write a poem that goes into detail and aims to re-create and visualise the events and states of mind he or she is experiencing. Tell a story of a person (real or imaginary) who is known to your readers. Choose a moment in his or her life and show what happens; for example, when Little Red Riding Hood catches sight of the wolf. Angela Carter's 'The Company of Wolves', in her collection of stories *The Bloody Chamber*, gives her version of this encounter. See if you can catch a sense of the girl's attitude in poem form.

4 *Transmitters*. The idea of this exercise is by focus and concentration to bring to light new sensations and perceptions about the world, perceptions influenced by your unconscious fears, desires and dreams. (Examples are: Ted Hughes, '*Pike*'; Sylvia Plath, '*Cut*'; Thom Gunn, '*Hampstead, The Horse Chestnut Trees*'.) The aim might be simply to describe something – an object or scene through the window or inside a room. Try various approaches – use a voice for the thing you describe, for example. It may be that your poem is about something else altogether – the object you chose has become a metaphor.

5 *Portraits*. (Examples are: U. A. Fanthorpe, '*Olive*'; Philip Larkin, '*Mr Bleaney*'; Jean 'Binta' Breeze, '*Grandfather's Dreams*'.) Some of the following might be points for development:

Describe a real or imagined meeting between you and the person concerned.

Think of an object you associate with this person. Describe this object as if it were him or her.

Think of something he or she often says/used to say.

Imagine some of the things he or she doesn't talk to you (or anyone else) about.

What settings do you associate with this person?

Ask him or her a question important to you, (one you might actually ask, or one you would never ask). What is the question? How does he or she reply?

6 *Experiments with form*. Re-read the poem in the section *syllabic poems* (p. 97) above. In eight or ten stanzas of four lines each, write a poem where each line contains eight syllables. If you have written eight syllables, go on to the next line. Choose your subject first. It could be an event, a portrait of a person, a setting with an encounter involving one person, yourself, or a group. It could refer to something in the present or the past, and you could use either tense. Don't worry about rhyming or sound patterns. These can happen without your having to think about them, and even if they don't, it doesn't matter; you will have written a poem. Simply keep to the four-line stanza, eight-syllable rule.

Try writing poems in more elaborate forms, including rhyming poems. As an example look at Elizabeth Bishop's sestina, '*One Art*' and also examples of the sonnet form by the contemporary poet Edwin Morgan in his *New Selected Poems*, (2000: 130).

7 *Surroundings and circumstances*. Write a poem in response to the pressure of circumstances (real or invented). One of Peter Sansom's poems, for example, begins:

> Come home, if you can.
> You don't need to explain
> anything to anyone.
> Come home alive.
>
> (Sansom, 2000:12)

Write a poem beginning with the line: 'I'm writing this …' referring to your immediate surroundings: on a bus, in a street. You are standing among a crowd at a wedding. Write a poem to the bride or the groom.

Revision and Editing

When you read your poem aloud, does it have a strong rhythmical delivery that will hold people's attention all the way through?

Will listening to it be a memorable experience?

Check the lengths of the sentences in your poem. See if shortening or lengthening a sentence will strengthen its rhythmical delivery.

Are there any superfluous words – or even whole lines – that are causing interruptions to the flow of the poem? The ideas you want to convey may be complex and difficult to express, but the poem should still be as simple and clear as you can make it.

Good poems develop a strong sense of contact with real or imagined worlds. Have you put enough 'world' into your poem, enough physical detail, vividness and sense impressions?

Is your poem a monotone, lacking idioms, actual speech or references to speech, use of the voice? If so, can you find ways of introducing voice qualities?

Writing free verse can be a way to experiment with form. As well as sentence length, experiment with where to make line-breaks. A line-break is a type of punctuation; it alters the spoken delivery of a poem. See how line-breaks affect your experience of reading. Do this too with stanza forms; four-, five- and six-line stanzas all sound slightly different. Do you want regular stanza lengths? See how to control your poem's appearance as writing. By experimenting in this way you will find your intuitive preference and discover for yourself how the look and sound of a poem alters its impact.

CHAPTER 4

FICTION

A New Genre: The Story of Modern Fiction

Imagine you were born at the beginning of the eighteenth century in England. You've just heard of a book called *Robinson Crusoe.* Having received instruction in grammar and music until the age of fourteen, you take an interest, but almost every story you've heard about, or read, or memorised, has come from the Bible or, like *Pilgrim's Progress*, has upheld a tradition, based on Christian principles, of preferring Truth and Virtue over Vice and Folly. You are also familiar with Greek and Roman mythology. You've heard of Helen of Troy, King Priam, Paris and Hector, Achilles and the Greeks. Your father, a local tradesman and cousin of a bookseller in London, has recently delivered a copy of a book of fairy-tales to the great country house whose parkland stretches beyond your market town, but these stories – *The Arabian Nights* – were not like Rumpelstiltskin or Cinderella, stories you'd heard from your grandmother as a child, or the story of the Patron Saint of England, St George. And even more terrifying than tales of dwarves and dragons was the story of a local witch, Agatha, who, fed up with being gossiped about in the town, caused a whole wedding party to be attacked by wolves.

Your narrative consciousness, like everybody else's in your village, also contains tales of triumphant battles at sea, and, before these, of wars about religion in England and on the continent. As for current affairs, you might occasionally see a copy of a newspaper, or even *The Spectator*, but all these histories, anecdotes, rumours, folklore, fables and parables, myths and news, share something in common: none of them have an author, nobody made them up. They seem just to have come about without any identifiable origin, or because they were believed to be facts. *Robinson Crusoe,* however, does have an author, and, what's more, this author – Daniel Defoe – claims he is the editor of a personal narrative written by this same Crusoe. His books are full of other people's words, and, more confusing, of other people's worlds: remote islands, tropical seas, savages and survivors. And yet it all sounds as if it could have happened just as it was, exactly as described. It's like reading a letter from someone you know.

You believe the Greek myths because nobody could have invented them out of nothing, because they are the first stories that speak about the relation of men and gods; Bible stories because they are the word of God; *Pilgrim's Progress* because its purpose is moral instruction, not historical record or myth; folk-tales because everyone has been told them for generations, and the latest news simply because it's the latest news. Scandal and ruin from the country estates is usually entertaining. All these stories, authenticated by gossip, by an oral or religious tradition, or by virtue of being historical fact, don't have to *convince* you that the events in them could actually happen. You assume they did, here or elsewhere. But why should anyone read a novel? As you read the novels of Daniel Defoe or Samuel Richardson, you realise their stories are authentic in quite a new way. They have to be. Such novels and novels like them are going to take you on a journey through new tracts of experience; they are going to show you the modern world. The future generations of your family are going to have to live in a state of upheaval in a world dominated increasingly by science, by new forms of religious dissent, by travel, empire, trade and exchange, by challenges to the very things that novels challenge: authority, rank and tradition. All of this is going to transform your point of view of the Bible, scandals, celebrations, saints and myths. In future you will see yourself and people like you in the novels you read, and their settings will be the spreading industrial cities, the growth of ironworks, mines, foundries; their subjects will be marriage, education, family divisions, money, ambition and class.

Your experience is already shaped by stories, real and imaginary, traditional and local. Like all human beings of the past, present and future, you have what we all have: a narrative culture. But it is changing. This new genre, the novel, will show you how people think, inwardly, when they are alone, as well as how they behave in the company of others. It will do what no other type of narrative before has ever needed to do. It will start to try and show you the way people think and act when their circumstances change for the better or worse, and what it's like for them moment by moment, hour by hour, sometimes month by month, but always with *time* as the prevailing wind. All this is authenticated not by any traditional authority, or by oral anonymity, but by being grounded in actual-seeming conditions and circumstances, by the telling of detail.

In our own time, in reading about the history of the novel we are likely to encounter certain descriptive terms, perspectives on its place in literary history, opinions about what modern fiction can do, why it came into existence, and even whether it might disappear in the near or distant future. Among such terms will be *realism,* a key feature that separates this type of fiction from earlier ways of telling a story. Modern fiction stands closer to personal narrative, closer to the experience of living people, recreated for us as we read. It insists that experience leads, conditions are fraught, justice is temperamental and that personal progress is far from guaranteed. And yet the possibility of a reformed world, re-educated by popular movements – the rights of women, an end to slavery, the rapid expansion of literacy and press freedom – also coincides with the increased reading and writing of new fictions, authored stories whose powers of influence rest on their being convincing. It's no accident, therefore, that novels came to be written in the form of long correspondences, diaries, personal records, real-seeming accounts of made-up events.

But do writers need to know anything about the rise of modern fiction? Does it help with the process of putting together a story or novel for their present day readers? Aspects of its early history might have bearings on its later developments. It might help us to grasp the point about what readers once looked for in fiction, what they gained from it. More than that, it could suggest actual topics for writing, links between how it was and how it is. The novel itself is a fascinating subject, not least to novelists in our time. What fiction is, what it can do, and how it managed to come into existence are subjects of continuing critical debate, and among the many perspectives on its development is the comment below by David Skilton. He points out that the author of *Robinson Crusoe,* published in 1719, had already written several novels before the one we now remember him by:

> Defoe's novels are all *first-person accounts.* Social deviants, criminals, adventurers, in their old age reformed and supposedly repentant, his protagonists tell their stories with unconcealed gusto, interspersing their accounts with bouts of moralizing. They relate their lives mainly in terms of changes in their social status, financial condition and states of their souls or consciences. Character and behaviour are to a great degree controlled by environment, not by the laws of immutable 'human nature'.
>
> (Skilton, 1977: 12)

The criminal, the deviant – territories of fiction present-day writers are themselves equally keen to explore, minus the moralising, perhaps – together with social status, social change, financial conditions, hazards of circumstance, background and environment, these, too, are themes we recognise. In choosing these areas of experience, the novelist selects in favour of *instability*, of the unpredictable as reality. Worlds of encounter in which it becomes difficult to hold a sense of moral coherence or integrity are shown to us in close-up as personal narrative. To make plausible, to convince, the novelist places herself inside the mind and being of her characters, in their skin, also in their consciousness. In modern fiction we hear the stories people tell *themselves* about their lives, we can tune in to their intimate, private monologues, a state of continuous response, remembering, reflection (stream of consciousness), or go deeper, enter an underground of feeling beyond conscious reach, a stream of *un*consciousness.

Realism as Topic and Technique

The notion of realism meaning 'every day ... familiar ... a picture of real life' is only one of its uses; we might call this *topic realism*, realism of reference. Topic realism accounts for the large majority of works of fiction published over the past two centuries. A typical example of this type of realism is D. H. Lawrence's novel *Sons and Lovers*, published in 1914. In the passage below, Gertrude and Walter Morel confront each other in the family's tiny kitchen. The focus is on encounter, action and circumstances, just as much as on emotion and feeling-response. The level of emotion in the encounter depends directly on actualised circumstances detailed here in the scene:

> The kitchen was full of the scent of boiled herbs and hops. On the hob a large black saucepan steamed slowly. Mrs Morel took a panchion, a great bowl of thick red earth, streamed a heap of white sugar into the bottom, and then, straining herself to the weight, was pouring in the liquor.
>
> Just then Morel came in. He had been very jolly in the Nelson, but coming home had grown irritable. He had not quite got over the feeling of irritability and pain, after having slept on the ground when he was so hot; and a bad conscience afflicted him as he neared the house. He did not know he was angry. But when the garden-gate resisted his attempts to open it, he kicked it and broke the latch. He entered just as Mrs Morel was pouring the infusion of herbs out of the saucepan. Swaying slightly, he lurched against the table. The boiling liquor pitched,

Mrs Morel started back.

'Good gracious,' she cried, 'coming home in his drunkenness!'

'Comin' home in his what?' he snarled, his hat over his eye.

(Lawrence, 1913: 32)

Because we see them in action and in the circumstances, we can sense here how the different rhythms of husband and wife clash.

This passage also provides a good example of the second meaning of realism – *as technique*. 'Get the important details present to the eye,' Lawrence once told one of his young correspondents asking for advice about fiction writing. But what are the important details? Realist technique does not mean recording each and every detail regardless, but, as we saw in Chapter 1, finding those objects, sights, sounds and scents that allow readers to inhabit the scene for themselves. *These will be the details of importance to the characters.* Building up a fictional world requires not just a *Where* and a *When* but a *Who* – at least one living, reactive-responding consciousness actively present in the scene you are describing. As a technique, realism therefore uses objects dramatically, includes only what it needs, arranges them for impact, wastes nothing.

But realist technique isn't found only in topic realism. With her prose narrative *Achilles* – a classical subject not in the least every day or familiar – Elizabeth Cook evokes the destruction of Troy by its Greek invaders:

Throughout the city the throats of sleepers are cut.

Then the dogs start up their rumpus.

Mothers who run out into the street with their babies are met by dark-clothed soldiers with knives and clubs and ropes. Some attempt to hide their babies – in chests, in the jars where bread is stored, up chimneys. One tells her child to hide in the well she'd often forbidden him to climb down. There is a little shelf, a sort of chamber down the well-shaft where he's crouched many times, hiding from friends. He stays there, shivering, listening to the dogs and the screams, seeing the bright gleam of the moon reflected in the water below him. After many hours the silver of moon is replaced by the gold of flame.

It is ten years since these Greek men have seen the families they left. Mothers and fathers have died in that time. Wives given birth to other men's children. Now they show what it has been like; the harm that's been done to them. Listen to the little sigh a child's body makes when you pierce it. See the mother's expression as you rape her with your hand, your penis, your spear, in the presence of her dead or dying child.

> The palace is like another city; so many dwellings and quarters, linked by passages instead of streets. Halls instead of market places. And while soldiers whose names we'll never know give vent to their injured lust and imagination to murder, loot, rape, and torch the citizens of Troy whose names are also forgotten, the Greek commanders – the celebrated warriors – do much the same amongst the palace's royal inhabitants. There are only so many parts you can slice or hack from a man or a woman: only so many holes and crevices you can fuck.
>
> (Cook, 2001: 80–1)

This passage generates the same vividness as Lawrence, accomplishes, in Henry James's phrase a 'solidity of specification' that makes the realist style. Realist writing, as a technique, can take us into worlds beyond the ordinary and familiar. There seems no limit. Stories and scenes once designated as remote, sealed off as classical, fabulous, mythic or as folklore are now open and waiting to be revisited. We enter the mythic history of the Greeks at Troy, but more than that. We are with the Trojans in their city, also with the Greek soldiers invading. The imagination hovers over the scene, plunges down to merge with one then the other, stays with the experience of both, meditates on the horror of the encounter. We find with a shock that our present-day narrative culture also harbours images of populations slaughtered, street fighting and unprotected children. But because of that immediacy of scene, close-up moment-by-moment sense of experience, access has been widened, images held at the back of our minds start to grasp our attention and move forward.

Where, When and Who

If realist technique needs Where and When, does a consciousness have to be there, a Who? Can it be left out? Virginia Woolf's novel *To the Lighthouse* includes a section in the middle part of the book 'Time Passes'. Woolf here attempts the removal of all human characters from the scene, leaving behind only a deserted setting. But it's hard for Woolf to avoid putting in some reference to conscious beings – either the erstwhile children, or 'the prying of the wind, and the soft nose of the chimney sea airs, rubbing, snuffling, iterating, and reiterating their questions'.

It's just possible, with difficulty, to cut down on Who, but even then we have the author's voice. Occasionally a writer will make the mistake of bringing into a story a vast quantity of his or her own research into time and place. The case, then, is that of the novelist who knows an enormous amount of detail about New York in the

1950s, for instance – the cafés, bars, favourite dives, the furniture, even the confectionery – and forgets that these need to have meaning primarily *for the characters*, not just the research-bound writer. Over-researched writing, for example, too much When and Where but not enough Who, occurs here and there in Sebastian Faulks's novel *On Green Dolphin Street.* But suppose we try to obliterate When and Where and cut out immediacy, the specific, the very features that distinguish realist style? In the following example, Margaret Atwood tries to do just that. Here the scene is person-dominated, while detail of place, minute-by-minute vividness, are taken out of the picture altogether. Whenever I show students the following passage, questions come up: is it actually a story? What is a story?

> John and Mary fall in love and get married. They both have worthwhile and remunerative jobs which they find stimulating and challenging. They buy a charming house. Real estate values go up. Eventually, when they can afford live-in help, they have two children to whom they are devoted. The children turn out well. John and Mary have a stimulating and challenging sex life and worthwhile friends. They go on fun vacations together. They retire. They both have hobbies which they find stimulating and challenging. Eventually they die. This is the end of the story.
>
> (Atwood, in Lee, ed., 1985: 370)

Readers may disagree, but most will probably notice that if this passage is a story it lacks certain, if not all, fundamental story-like features. It has a beginning – 'John and Mary fall in love' – and an end – 'Eventually they die'. It contains characters, shows the passage of time, and offers a hint, though this is debatable, that the recurring phrase 'stimulating and challenging' is typical of the characters' own way of speaking about themselves; in other words it suggests their private opinions about their lives. But unfortunately, as Margaret Atwood no doubt calculated, the passage amounts to little more than a latter-day version of the formulaic story ending: 'And they all lived happily ever after.' This passage, in affluent societies, is what living 'happily ever after' means, or is supposed to mean, and most readers will recognise it as such, whether or not they privately think it desirable.

In modern fiction we hardly ever come across this style or type of approach – it is rare, and for very good reasons: it tells us almost nothing about its characters, and what it does tell us makes us feel disengaged from them – we don't really want to know anything much about them. Imagine reading long, detailed descriptions of John's hobbies, or of their endless vacations together! Realist style would simply be wasted on them, and on us – it would bore us to death. We need Where, When and Who, but we also need something else: a sense of danger, encounter, incident, disruption. Why this is the case is a mystery. Why aren't we happy reading about happiness? Why are we interested in people whose lives go wrong, who fail, whose high expectations come to nothing? It just seems that we are. Quoted in a recent film is the saying: 'If you want to make God laugh, tell him your plans.'

The John and Mary approach is rare because it abstracts these characters from a setting. Which isn't to say that sometimes readers need to hear an overview – a brief one – of a character's life story, and that writers can indulge in sketching a rapid summary. But when this occurs, if we are going to generate enough energy for close-up realisation in a story, if the wide-angle overview isn't going to stifle narrative potential, then *we must keep summaries to a minimum*. Equally, the opening paragraph of a story or a novel will hold that potential in readiness if it can manage the right combination of close-up and wide-angle, and if the overall impact creates the sense of something bound to change.

In the following examples of beginnings, notice how each writer combines close-up and wide-angle information, and introduces a sense of imminent story. Notice the phrase to 'search the inner room' in the first example. This is what fiction frequently aims to do, although here the protagonist speaker is interested in action and experience, not in thought and reflection:

1. My name is Karim Amir, and I am an Englishman born and bred, almost. I am often considered to be a funny kind of Englishman, a new breed as it were, having emerged from two old histories. But I don't care – Englishman I am (though not proud of it), from the South London suburbs and going somewhere. Perhaps it is the odd mixture of continents and blood, of here and there, of belonging and not, that makes me restless and easily bored. Or perhaps it was being brought up in the suburbs that did it. Anyway, why search the inner room when it's enough to say that I was looking for trouble, any kind of movement, action and sexual interest I could find, because things were so gloomy, so slow and heavy, in our family. I don't know why. Quite frankly, it was getting me down and I was ready for anything.

   Then one day everything changed. In the morning things were one way and by bedtime another. I was seventeen.

   On this day my father hurried home from work not in a gloomy mood. His mood was high, for him. I could smell the train on him as he put his briefcase away behind the front door and took off his raincoat, chucking it over the bottom of the banisters.

   (Kureishi, 1990: 3)

2. I had been making the rounds of the Sacrifice Poles the day we heard my brother had escaped. I already knew something was going to happen: the Factory told me.

   At the north end of the island, near the tumbled remains of the slip where the handle of the rusty winch still creaks in an easterly wind, I had two Poles on the far face of the last dune. One of the Poles held a rat head with two dragonflies, the other a seagull and two mice. I was just sticking one of the mouse heads back on when the birds went up into the evening air, kaw-calling and screaming, wheeling over the path through the dunes where it went near their nests. I made sure the head was secure, then clambered to the top of the dune to watch with my binoculars.

   Diggs, the policeman from the town, was coming down the path on his bike.

   (Banks, 1990: 7)

3. A man stood upon a railroad bridge in Northern Alabama, looking down into the swift water twenty feet below. The man's hands were behind his back, the wrists bound with a cord. A rope closely encircled his neck. It was attached to a stout cross-timber above his head and the slack fell to the level of his knees. Some loose boards laid upon the sleepers supporting the metals of the railway supplied a footing for him and his executioners – two private soldiers of the Federal army, directed by a sergeant who in civilian life might have been a deputy sheriff.

   (Bierce, in Bohner, 2002: 150)

4. It is very seldom, that mere ordinary people like John and myself secure ancestral halls for the summer.

   A colonial mansion, a hereditary estate, I would say a haunted house and reach the height of romantic felicity – but that would be asking too much of fate!

   Still I will proudly declare that there is something queer about it.

   Else, why should it be let so cheaply? And why have stood so long untenanted?

   (Gilman: 1981: 9)

5. The madness of an autumn prairie cold front coming through. You could feel it: something terrible was going to happen. The sun low in the sky, a minor light, a cooling star. Gust after gust of disorder. Trees restless, temperatures falling, the whole northern religion of things coming to an end. No children in the yards

> here. Shadows lengthened on yellow zoysia. Red oaks and pin oaks and swamp white oaks rained acorns on houses with no mortgage. Storm windows shuddered in the empty bedrooms. And the drone and hiccup of a clothes dryer, the nasal contention of a leaf-blower, the ripening of local apples in a paper bag, the smell of the gasoline with which Alfred Lambert had cleaned the paintbrush from his morning painting of the wicker love-seat.
>
> Three in the afternoon was a time of danger in these gerontocratic suburbs of St Jude. Alfred had awakened in the great blue chair in which he'd been sleeping since lunch.
>
> (Franzen, 2002: 1)

In each of these extracts, a writer is not just beginning a story but starting to get a feel for the story's atmosphere, its potential, for what will be a defining image. Setting will have something to do with this: a type of house and household interior, a father in a suburb smelling of diesel, a certain messiness of damp paint in the hands of a somewhat testy Alfred Lambert. Finding its strangeness, 'something queer about it' can be a vital process in the making of a story. And so it's important to find characters whose own mental and physical states will enhance that strangeness, respond to it, be in continuous touch with its vibrations.

Extreme Realism

The scene is a slum district in Rio, Brazil. Two small boys are crouching against the concrete wall of a shack. Seconds ago they were part of a gang racing the alleys, but now the group has split and a third boy, just a bit older, hovers in front of them aware of their fear. A fourth stands above them, draws a gun, points it at their two faces. Everybody knows what's going to happen, but not quite how it will happen – or there just might be a chance to escape. 'Shall I shoot you in the hand or the foot?' he asks the two crouching boys. Both are just old enough to know what a bullet does to a hand or a foot, and that this guy means what he says. Nobody else speaks. One little boy holds out his hand. 'This hand? You want this?' There's a pause, then he shoots both boys in the foot. It hurts. Their dirty, bewildered faces are smeared with tears. It goes on hurting. The top of one boy's trainer is holed with blood. The big kid turns to the eight-year-old boy by his side, gives him the gun. 'Choose one of them and shoot him. Let's see what you're made of.' The eight-year-old aims first at one then the other. 'Do it. I haven't got all day!' He looks away, pulls the trigger. One of the boys is dead.

As some of you will recognise, this incident happens in the film *City of God*, directed by Fernando Meirelles in 2002. The story is based on a novel by the Brazilian writer Paolo Lins who grew up in the slum district of Rio, known to inhabitants as the 'City of God' where the film is set. The novel and film shock us because we know things happen that way, typify those conditions of living and remind us of their consequences. Instead of being a City of God this is the man-made city of drugs, punishment killings, threats, intimidation, youth power. It is realism at its harshest. The world it depicts is broken irrecoverably, and mocks the intention to deal it any promises. Watching the film we see the action in close-up, moment by moment. We share the point of view of each of the characters. The central viewing position, though, is that of the boy being handed the gun. He is the one we are forced to identify with. He acts without judgement, against his will. We feel *experience* taking the lead – nothing could have prepared him for this moment or ever enabled him to foresee it, yet it stays in keeping with the city's conditions and our impressions of these. Rapid action scenes, ground-level perspectives, enhance the *narrative image* within which such events become all too probable.

Fiction writing in our time doesn't lack qualities of extremity – that's clear enough if we think of Iain Banks (*The Wasp Factory, The Bridge*), Ian McEwan (*The Cement Garden*), Irvine Welsh (*Trainspotting, Marabou Stork Nightmares*), Margaret Atwood (*Bodily Harm*), Roddy Doyle (*The Woman Who Walked Into Doors*), J. G. Ballard (*Crash*), Brett Easton Ellis (*Less Than Zero, American Psycho*). While these novels keep within the bounds of the real world, they extend it by writing about extreme psychological states, forms of psychosis, deviancy, torture, obsession. Dostoyevsky becomes the novelist of choice. The emphasis is on the mind, on the disturbed, yet the underlying reality of *City of God*, political in its citation of poverty and drug culture as the circumstances of violence, finds an echo here in Welsh's *Marabou Stork Nightmares.* The narrator, Roy Strang, contemplates a return to his home city:

> I could see myself right back in the same life, the same school, the same scheme. I was gloomy in my resignation, only a sick anxiety brought on by the dread of leaving occasionally alleviating my depression. Edinburgh to me represented serfdom. I realised that it was exactly the same situation as Johannesburg; the difference was that the Kaffirs were whiter and called schemies or draftpaks. Back in Edinburgh, we would be Kaffirs; condemned to live out our lives in townships like Muirhouse ... self-contained camps with fuck all in them, miles fae the toon.

> Brought in tae dae the crap jobs that nae other cunt wanted tae dae, then hassled by the polis if we hung around at night in groups. Edinburgh had the same politics as Johannesburg: it had the same politics as any city.
>
> (Welsh, 1996: 80)

Here we find the equivalent in fiction (or somewhere close to it) of the *City of God.* One significant word is 'township', associated not just with South Africa but the Scotland of Welsh's (and Strang's) childhood. Instead of a physical description of place, Welsh gives us its image through vernacular. Language, especially spoken language, becomes another vehicle for realism. Roy Strang only needs to spend time thinking about Edinburgh, Niddrie and Muirhouse for these places to affect his speech, dragging it back to the way fourteen-year-olds talk whose aggression speaks for them. It's remarkable how, just by entering the voice of a speaker, Welsh recreates the impact of a locality. Solid specifications aren't always necessary, or in this case arrive in another form – through spoken inflexion, slang and attitude. A politics of exclusion is being addressed, and redressed, by the use of speech. One of the traits of extreme realism in fiction and other genres is its impatience with a literary audience, stripping them of their elite protection, attacking the cosy alliance of art and enlightenment.

Magic Realism

Lorna Sage, introducing her book about the novelist Angela Carter, writes how Carter's career began with 'a growing sense that realism and authenticity were somehow subtly false, threadbare, conformist even when they seemed not to be. The anti-novel, nouveau roman, fantastic tales, and satires on sincerity all gained ground, though there was ... no movement you could join' (Sage, 1994:7). The period in question was the late 1960s. At about the same time, David Lodge, himself a young novelist like Carter, wrote in his essay 'The Novelist at the Crossroads' (Lodge, in Bradbury, 1990:87) about the same shift away from realism. Lodge's word for this is *fabulation,* a term he borrows from a book by Robert Scholes on experimental fiction. *The Fabulators* are writers who abandon realism's traditional ground based on 'the individual experience of a common phenomenal world' and move towards fantasy, romance, folktale, even beyond these to the mythical. Realism or fabulism? The contemporary novelist, said Lodge, must now choose. As if to thwart this warning, however, Carter's fiction collapses these straightforward definitions.

In her book of short stories, *The Bloody Chamber*, Carter's fictional stance keeps both realist and fantasy settings in sight; she mixes them up. Petrol stations, bicycles, vampires, express trains, castle dungeons, animals that talk on the telephone, all cohere in a way that allows Carter the freedom she needs in bringing fairy-tale and folk-tale characters into contact with a sexually modern world, retrieving them from repression and gender stereotyping. The worlds she creates actually reduce the power of magic, except when sexual sensations take its place – desire, arousal, jealousy, possession.

> A witch from up the valley once turned an entire wedding party into wolves because the groom had settled on another girl. She used to order them to visit her, at night, from spite, and they would sit and howl around her cottage for her, serenading her with their misery.
>
> Not so very long ago, a young woman in our village married a man who vanished clean away on her wedding night. The bed was made with nice new sheets and the bride lay down in it. The groom said, he was going out to relieve himself, insisted on it, for the sake of decency, and she drew the coverlet up to her chin and she lay there. And she waited and she waited, and then she waited again – surely he'd been gone a long time? Until she jumps up in bed and shrieks to hear a howling coming on the wind from the forest.
>
> The long-drawn, wavering howl, has, for all its fearful resonance, some inherent sadness in it, as if the beasts would love to be less beastly if only they knew how and never cease to mourn their own condition.
>
> (Carter, 1995: 111–12)

Carter, however, still pursues some of the goals for which realism was originally invented. Her narrative style, grounded in detail, shows that experience means more than ideals. You learn more from life than from a pulpit. Fiction may be a product of the enlightenment, but order and reason are still under scrutiny, sometimes under attack, as they were first of all in Laurence Sterne's novel, *Tristram Shandy*, (1767). As a new genre, fiction is about experiment, indulges in playfulness, delights in difference, celebrates non-conformity, will not ignore the random and accidental.

In a more recent comment on magic realism Lodge refers to contemporary Latin-American writers, citing as an example the Columbian novelist Garcia Gabriel Marquez, as well as novelists from Europe – Gunter Grass and Milan Kundera. 'All those writers have lived through great historical convulsions, wrenching personal upheavals, which they feel cannot be adequately represented in a discourse of undisturbed realism' (Lodge, 1992: 114). Another example of fantasy effects – in this case the supernatural – is Toni Morrison's novel *Beloved*, about the aftershock of black slavery in America. Convulsion and upheaval create ghosts. From its beginnings, one of the goals of fiction has been to represent *unarticulated* experience, hence its fascination with the repressed, with sexuality, also, in a political sense, with marginality, exploitation, exclusion.

Experiments in Modern Fiction

Imagine a story in which narration and narrating become themselves the focus of the story, where a character telling his or her version of events – or perhaps failing to tell it – becomes an event within the story itself. Such fictional structures are not new. For example, Henry James uses such a device in his novella *The Turn of the Screw* (1898). Now the device is increasingly in use. Kurt Vonnegut's post-war novel *Slaughterhouse 5*, refers to the bombing of Dresden in 1945. The protagonist – who is the narrator – survived the air raid that killed more people than Hiroshima. In the first chapter of the novel he explains how he imagined telling the story of the firestorm engulfing the city on the night of the raid. It would appear as a straightforward sequence of events, and as a novelist he should be able to handle this with no problems:

> As a trafficker in climaxes and thrills and characterisation and wonderful dialogue and suspense and confrontations, I had outlined the Dresden story many times. The best outline I ever made, or anyway the prettiest one, was on the back of a role of wallpaper.
>
> I used my daughter's crayons, a different color for each main character. On the end of the wallpaper was the beginning of the story, and the other end was the end, and then there was the middle part, which was the middle. And the blue line met the red line and then the yellow line, and the yellow line stopped because the character represented by the yellow line was dead. And so on. The destruction of Dresden was represented by a vertical band of orange cross-hatching, and all the lines that were still alive passed through it, came out on the other side.
>
> (Vonnegut, 1969: 4)

This chart assumes you can follow through a person's life – even the fate of a whole city – in terms of a past, a present and a future, or beginning, middle and end – and for most of us, most of the time, it makes sense to see this assumption as reasonable. But one of the lessons of psychoanalytic thinking has been that individuals do not necessarily move on from one stage of growth to another in a way that defines certain experiences as 'past'. In *Slaughterhouse 5* the past is present, and together they do not provide a straightforward sequence leading from destruction to recovery, in Biblical terms, a modern form of Through-the-Red-Sea (in this case orange) experience. The hero of Vonnegut's novel – the one he actually wrote, having discarded this cross-hatched version – moves about from one part of his life to another, as if memory were a kind of time travel, so that past, present, and future become muddled up, fragmented, unsequenced.

A term for his condition might be post-traumatic shock, or even schizophrenia. But the other main issue for the writer was *representation*: how to make real what was surreal, outside, beneath or beyond our collective sense of a shared world. How to tell a story that isn't or will not become parcelled up as part of a finished past or a straightforward record of recovery and progress. The crosshatch representation is not just a story, a way of telling, but an evaluation. 'I'm telling you this because I want you to know that it's about recovery and restitution, a story of those who triumphed over a tragedy' is a typical Hollywood plot structure. Vonnegut had to find another way of representing Dresden, one that would carry a very different evaluation – 'I'm telling you this because I want you to know that it's not necessarily possible to survive the effects of war on this scale: although it might look like you come out of it at the end; you don't.'

In an essay on narrative discourse, Allan Bell defines evaluation as follows: 'Evaluation pre-empts the question, *so what?* It gives the reason why the narrator is claiming the floor and the audience's attention' ('The Discourse Reader',1999:237). In a significant amount of contemporary fiction, a recurring strategy has been to produce a deliberate *uncertainty of evaluation,* where one character might judge another as an unreliable narrator, where readers themselves might reach this conclusion about a first-person narrator in a novel or short story. As an example of this problem of narrative identity, Vernon Little in D. C. B. Pierre's novel *Vernon God Little* initially judges his own story to be so worthless and embarrassing that he deliberately avoids telling it to the authorities accusing him of mass murder. This is an evaluation that almost costs him his life.

In Patricia Highsmith's novel *The Talented Mr. Ripley*, we meet a character who creates a new identity for himself. He conceals the fact that he murdered his best friend. How? By becoming him. Tom Ripley checks into hotels in Venice as Dickie Greenleaf, draws money from his account, writes letters to the Greenleaf family back in the USA forging Dickie's signature. He then makes so-called Dickie 'disappear'. To Tom these letters and the little narratives they contain are tactics of survival. To those he deceives they are nice reassuring pieces of news from their son or nephew, saying that all is well here in Italy. And, of course, the more we read about Tom, the more we realise he is a novelist – an illusionist – a skilful one, too, and very convincing. Fiction is his business, one that pays.

The telling of stories is never neutral or innocent. A story is a telling, which also may include other tellings. These might be transparently sinister in motive. Stories can be told to exclude a listener, to intimidate, or deceive readers into a judgement based on lies, or can persuade us of truths others conceal. In Ian McEwan's novel *Atonement*, we read the story, then we hear it was written by one of the characters – one whose motives we are far from willing to trust. What evaluation does the text of the novel bring with it – for McEwan, for its 'author' Bryony, for the characters on whom she inflicted suffering, for ourselves? Is it possible for us to endorse the title of her novel: is it a real or a fake atonement?

In Meera Syal's novel *Anita and Me*, the narrator, Meena, a girl of 11, has a reputation for telling lies. In fact her aim isn't to deceive but to exaggerate, to elaborate somewhat on the facts to make them entertaining and dramatic – like fiction. She just wants to be in an exciting story. As with Tom Ripley, we enjoy Meena's skill with storytelling. What to her parents is 'telling lies' to her is a way of amusing herself, her friends, and us. As the novel's narrator she entertains us. Here, for example, is a hint of how Meena likes things to be exaggerated, how she evaluates stories. She's looking at a photograph of her parents in Delhi years before moving to England:

> Papa is leaning out of a steam train window in a brilliant white shirt, an overcoat slung over his waving arm. The smoke rises like cold-morning breath around his face. And he is backlit by a rising sun. He is smiling his gap-toothed smile, though his eyes are intense. Mama stands on the platform, the fingers of one hand slightly raised, as if she is afraid to wave him goodbye. She is impossibly young and utterly bereft, her long chiffon dupetta is frozen in mid-curl, lifted by the wind. Even in such a small photograph her longing is palpable, the way her fingers say what her mouth cannot.
>
> This was always one of my favourites, this image of my parents as epic, glamorous figures, touched by romantic tragedy. ... My parents in a love story! ... But when I confronted mama

> about her courtship adventures her face closed up like a fan. 'Don't be so silly!' she sniffed. 'We were introduced by an uncle. It was all done through the proper channels.' And that was that.
>
> (Syal, 1997: 31–2)

A love story or an arranged marriage? Meena experiences life in England as a clash of worlds: the world of her parents with the world of her friends in a village outside Birmingham:

> Our gang, which we named the Wenches Brigade, soon established a routine of sorts; we would begin with a leisurely meeting in an old pigsty, the one nearest the park, in which Anita and I would leaf through the current issue of *Jackie*, doing the quizzes on each other, How Do You Know If He Fancies You? ... Then we would do the rounds of our kingdom, Anita leading, me at her side, and the rest of the minions in a disorganised chattering crocodile behind us ... There Anita and I would find a space in the long grass clear of dog-shit and insects, and munch on sweets and talk, whilst our lackeys amused themselves with teasing the horses with ears of corn and conducting interesting experiments such as how far a two-day-old cow pat would travel when thrown by a small snotty-nosed child.
>
> (Ibid.: 138)

At the end of the novel, Meena is the witness of an incident. She must tell the truth to the police. Her strict Asian parents insist on it, but can they ever trust what they hear from her? Now she really is in a story, and for once she resists the temptation to exaggerate. To tell a story, to hear one, are events in the lives of the characters.

As a contemporary Asian writer, Syal's recreation of contrasting worlds depends on the techniques of realist fiction, but still leaves room for experiment. Meena's Indian family background and Midlands accent, her British teenage experience and sense of outsiderhood, enable her to take as yet unplotted tracks through our cultural life. For her, and for the novelist, the issue of representation, self, voice and identity will be a challenge, a new kind of complexity. The narrative culture Meena inherits mixes stories of British experience with those of her Indian grandmother's generation, stories of violence and genocide.

Uncertainties of narrative evaluation, of self and identity in fiction, surely figure in the new (or comparatively new) assessment of cultural shifts which the term *post-modern* addresses. The 'inner room' of the self is less a space where drives and needs converge or are in conflict as a place where products are on display.

Consumerism itself is a form of fiction-making. The narratives of advertising show people emotionally bound to the products that they use – whether to a Corvette car or a brand of powderball for a dishwasher. In Brett Easton Ellis's novel *Less Than Zero*, the self becomes both product and consumer. The novelist Umberto Eco has written about Disneyland (America's 'Sistine Chapel') with a fascination for its perfect fakes. Here is where we 'consume' the past, re-invent it as glamorous commodity. We enter Adventureland, the Pirates of the Caribbean:

> Each was devised by observing the expressions of a real actor, then building models, then developing skeletons of absolute precision, authentic computers in human form, to be dressed in 'flesh' and 'skin' made by craftsmen, whose command of realism is incredible. Each robot obeys a program, can synchronise the movements of mouth and eyes with the words and sounds of the audio, repeating, ad infinitum all day long his established part (a sentence, one or two gestures) and the visitor, caught off guard by the succession of events, obliged to see several things at once, to left and right and straight ahead, has not time to look back and observe that the robot he has just seen is already repeating his eternal scenario.
>
> (Eco, in Docherty, 1993: 204)

The Pirate scenario described here parodies that of fiction. A trafficker in illusions, the writer of fiction also creates worlds in authentic detail, a matter of craftsmanship, absolute precision, by observing the expressions of real people together in real settings. But as we have seen that makes up only a part of what fiction does. A text endlessly detailed and precision tooled like the 'authentic' wrought-iron balcony of a New Orleans coffee house (another of the Disneyland attractions), wouldn't produce the qualities of fiction people enjoy it for. They need a *Who*, a consciousness, a character participating. In the case of Disneyland, however, the only *Who* implied or actually present is a consumer.

Retellings

The retelling of existing fiction using new settings and characters is another way for writers to experiment with the narrative process. Writers make use of other stories by recasting them in a contemporary context. It is as if the books themselves are speaking to each other. An example of this method is Jackie Kay's short story 'Shell', from the same collection as 'Trout Friday' (see page 129). In 'Shell', the main character, a single parent living with her son Louis who is black, undergoes physical changes that appear to be connected with overweight and exhaustion. The narrator stays faithfully inside the main character's viewpoint and sensations, just as Kafka does with Gregor Samsa, the protagonist of his story *Metamorphosis*, when a man changes into a human-sized insect with a carapace. A similar change happens in 'Shell'; the stories are linked. 'Shell' is a working out of Kafka's story in a contemporary setting and with contemporary pre-judgements. Another example of *retelling* using an existing text as a basis for a new story is 'The Kugelmass Episode' by Woody Allen, based on Flaubert's novel *Madame Bovary*. In Woody Allen's story the invention of a time machine enables a frustrated Professor of Literature to make love to Flaubert's fictional character Emma Bovary, with catastrophic consequences. More obvious examples of fiction written in response to other fiction include J. M. Coetzee's *Foe*, based on *Robinson Crusoe*, and Jean Rhys's *Wide Sargasso Sea*, from *Jane Eyre*.

The Other

Reading through and comparing V. S. Pritchett's selection for the *Oxford Book of Short Stories* published in 1984 – his choice includes writers from Hawthorne to Hemingway and John Updike – with stories published more recently, we can notice a shift from third-person to first-person narration, and a parallel preference for character-speakers whose social roles have become less clearly defined. Characters tend not to be identified as groups of families or friends, or by their trades and professions. Personal identity, along with personal narrative, isolates the protagonists of stories written in the present day. In works by Jackie Kay, Ian McEwan, Will Self, Martin Amis, Raymond Carver and others, self is the new subject *apart* from others. Pritchett makes a similar point in his introduction. 'Particularly in the writers of this century we also notice the sense of people as strangers. People are left carrying the aftermath of their tale into a new day of which they can as yet know nothing' (Pritchett, 1984: xiv).

The increased popularity of the first-person voice, the continued growth of autobiographical fiction with its single protagonist-narrator, the ever closer attention to private life, marks a significant shift not only in terms of character and narration but also in the type of story told. Contemporary narrative produces a wide range of story forms, but one that recurs reveals the isolated self moving through experience with comparatively little anchor-drag (or support) from a class system or a community. If contemporary writers of fiction develop their stories around *one* major character, who might be the narrator (usually is) – or the focaliser if it's third person narration – then adjacent to this protagonist self is another character who acts as a major influence – positively or negatively – on him or her. This *other* character replaces the influence of that receding wider culture group. He or she might be a partner, husband/wife, or family member, close friend or even a stranger/intruder. McEwan's character Jed in *Enduring Love*, Nanzeen's lover Chanu in Moniza Ali's novel *Brick Lane,* Anita as Meena's Other in Syal's novel: the Other emerges from shadows cast by certainties in retreat, leaving the self exposed and in need. Sometimes The Other reflects the narrator's own sense of emptiness and betrayal, and so becomes another version of the self. In Carol Shields's novel *Unless,* the Other is Norah, the daughter of Shields' narrator-protagonist:

> I remember the look in her eyes as she sat at the kitchen table, and my thoughts become more and more reckless. It sometimes occurs to me that there is for Norah not too much but too little: a gaping absence, a near starvation. There is a bounteous feast going on, with music and richness and arabesques of language, but she has not been invited ... A deterioration has occurred in the fabric of the world, the world that does not belong to her as she has been told.
>
> (Shields, 2002: 89)

In D. B. C. Pierre's *Vernon God Little*, the teenage narrator – like Clay in Bret Easton Ellis's *Less Than Zero* – another update of Salinger's Holden Caulfield – travels by coach from Texas to Mexico to meet up with his (or so he hopes) girlfriend, Taylor Figueroa, the Other who inspires this journey and more:

> 'Drrrrrr' the motorcoach hits the road, and after nameless miles I hang suspended on the knife-edge of a doze, my brain like crystal grits. Then we pass a field of manure or something, the type of smeary tang your family pretends not to notice when you're in the car with them, and it suddenly floods my senses with Taylor Figueroa. Don't ask me why. I sense her in a field by the highway. She's down on all fours behind a bush, naked except for blue synthetic panties that strain hard into her thigh-vee, and glow dirty ripe. I'm there too. We're safe and comfortable, with time on our hands. I surf her upholstery with my nose, map her sticky heem along glimmering edges to the panty-leg, where the tang sharpens like slime-acid chocolate, stings, bounces me back from her poon. In my dream I bounce back too far. Then I see we're in a field of ass-fruit, and suddenly I don't know if it's Taylor's scent, or just the field I can smell. I

> scramble back to her cleft, but the edges have vanished. The forbidden odor dissolves into body-heat and aftershave of the bus. I wake up snorting air like crazy. She's gone. Empty distance rolls past the window.
>
> (Pierre, 2003: 149–50)

This passage superbly creates the transitory shock of desire. The Other is fleetingly glimpsed, intense, unreliable, but still driving Vernon. Yet it could be that with this sensational prose, this vividness of voice, the very qualities we admire themselves become a limitation, for something else is needed to make a fictional world plausible to its readers and that is a sense of how things happen in equally active fields of *public* experience – in law courts, office blocks, railway stations, pubs, police interview rooms, prisons, or even just school classrooms. Has the fictive imagination chosen to retreat from these public areas, as if we no longer know or trust what happens there? Public knowledge is an issue for Patricia Highsmith who has this advice for how a novelist might gain access to the working lives of characters through research:

> Varying the professions of a story's characters is one of the hardest things for a writer to do after three or four books, when he has used up the few he knows about. Not many writers have the chance to learn about new lines of work, once they become full-time writers. In a small town, where everybody knows everybody, a writer might have an easier time of it. The carpenter might let him come out on some jobs with him. A lawyer friend may let him sit in his office. I once took a job during Christmas rush at a department store in Manhattan. Here was a scene chaotic with detail, sounds, people, and a new tempo – pretty hectic – an unending stream of little dramas that one could observe in customers, fellow workers and the management. I used this new scene in my writing. A writer should seize upon every new scene that comes his way, take notes and turn it to account.
>
> (Highsmith, 1990: 96)

In Pierre's novel Vernon's version of events never gets heard by the jury, doesn't even seem to have been investigated. Can this be how the legal professions operate in Matirio? His is a trial by television – guilt equals the number of times your face appears on TV as prime suspect. And then, later, the jury having delivered its bogus verdict, prisoners on Death Row are eliminated by popular votes in a grim parody of reality television. Is Pierre attacking the US criminal justice system for the real faults within it, or for absurd, impossible ones? In one sense his hero complains about such liberties in films, suggesting that it matters how public worlds are represented:

> Where TV lets you down, I'm discovering, is not by convincing you how things really work in the world. Like, do buses stop anywhere along the road, to pick up any kind of asshole, or do you have to be at a regular bus stop? You see plenty of movies where some crusty dude stops a bus in the middle of a desert or something. But maybe that only applies in the middle of a desert. Or maybe only the drivers who saw the movies will stop.
>
> (Pierre, 2003: 148)

To raise this issue in the novel itself makes it a point of debate in the reading experience. Which comes first – the movies or life? Also, do bus stops matter? Or any real-world setting? Jonathan Franzen's novel *The Corrections* shows us love, work, illness, parenting, marriage, ageing, travel, fraud, homo- and heterosexual sex, in scenes that know about 'how things really work in the world'. This knowledge, once required of novelists, is rare among his contemporaries. McEwan's *Atonement* contains no trial scene, yet we are expected to believe that Briony's evidence at trial stands unquestioned – convenient for the story, but conceivable? It may be that fiction now takes us on excursions; all might seem comparatively familiar, but sooner or later we cross a threshold into the comic absurd, a world with no clues. As Vernon Little himself admits, 'I guess it's ironic, when someone passes off total bullshit as reality' (Pierre, 2003: 179). Few would describe either this novel or *Atonement* in such Vernon-like language, yet in contemporary fiction there is a debate about the idea of *passing something off*, at the expense of how things work in the world.

Close Encounters: Short Stories

About the short story, Nadine Gordimer wrote, 'how the characters will appear, think, behave, comprehend, tomorrow or at any other time in their lives, is irrelevant'. For writers, especially novelists like herself, the luxury of short story writing lies in its close attention to the moment, rather than to the continuous, complex life history. But shorter fiction can give a sense of significant change in the life-direction. What characters do afterwards will be affected by what happens to them on the day of the story. Because something has happened, they will be different, a trace will have been left, even though what has happened may be no more than a phone-call (or the lack of one), or an unopened letter.

The time period in short stories generally is shorter than in a novel, but we have to be clear what we mean by time and period and the treatment of time. With that and some other issues in mind I want to look closely at two short stories: 'Trout Friday' by Jackie Kay, from her collection *Why Don't You Stop Talking*, and 'Whoever was using this bed', from *Elephant* by Raymond Carver.

Kay's story contains almost no dialogue, while Carver's is built out of dialogue from the beginning. In spite of that 'Trout Friday' does have polyphonic qualities. In it we hear the voices of advertising, the popular media's self-help and personal health guides, internalised by its single protagonist Melanie, whose recent and distant family history is told to us by the third-person narration. This voice, though, and Melanie's (and the advice columns) overlap, so that we get a vivid example of free indirect speech (see Chapter 1, p. 6). Here is the opening of 'Trout Friday':

> If you want good teeth you must brush your gums as well. Gums cause more tooth loss than tooth decay. That's what the paper said. Melanie went straight to the chemist and bought a brand-new toothbrush. She'd lost too much already and she was only twenty-three and she didn't want to lose her teeth into the bargain. She lost her mother when she was nineteen. She lost her Uncle Barry. She lost a baby she was carrying. She liked it if she could read some fact and act on it. Like she read fish was good for your brain. So now she had salmon Monday, prawn Tuesday, cod Wednesday, haddock Thursday and trout Friday. Weekends she had fish-free because she only really needed her brain during the week. Weekends she splashes out and has takeaway: Peking duck with pancakes, lamb with spicy leaves and nan bread, or Kentucky Fried Chicken with large fries.
>
> (Kay, 2002: 67)

In Chapter 1 (*Story*, p. 27), I indicated how time is shaped for us by kinds of experience. Loss is an obvious one of these, but Melanie has her own way of putting time back in place, making it regular and routine. This story is about someone who *avoids* story. Bluntly speaking, a new toothbrush compensates her for the loss of her mother, even for the loss of her child. As we follow the unfolding narrative, these losses will be hardly mentioned, while the details of Melanie's routines – in particular her eating habits, but also her work at a travel agent – take up a huge proportion of page space. This is because they take up an equally huge proportion of Melanie's private thoughts. The writer introduces a gap between what Melanie does, and what is really significant in her life. We know she's avoiding several sources of pain; among the harshest is her mother's death. At moments her thoughts take a direction Melanie would probably have resisted, which is why Jackie Kay needs third-person narration for this story – to take us where the character herself won't go. Kay, whose ethnic background is part Nigerian, has chosen a character of mixed race, and this is another potently troublesome note:

> Her mother was from Ireland, County Mayo, and her father was from Trinidad and when she looked in the mirror, the pair of them were behind her, mixing themselves up in her face. [Her mother's teeth] had filled her with a nameless worry. A feeling of everything not being right in the world. A sense of unease. So that now the two were mixed up in her mind: her mother's stained teeth and her mother's dark death.
>
> (Ibid: 68–9)

Such excursions into her family past intensify our interest in this troubled character, while not quite fully arousing our sympathy, for Melanie's brittle determination to avoid the past trivialises a dull existence where she only functions as a consumer. Stories, as we know, usually begin with a *trigger event*, an *inciting incident* causing time to be shaped in a new way, and in Melanie's case this happens when she unexpectedly receives a letter which turns out to be from her father.

'She read somewhere that people who manage time well suffer less stress', and time in the story moves us through points in her routine day – from early shopping in a Hackney street market, to her office job. Here we have the only inclusion of dialogue – she with some clients and then with her female colleagues – but again the details are there to show us Melanie-type attitudes as they ordinarily recur. She, of course, relishes this ordinariness herself, occasionally spicing it with a treat, and trout on Friday will be the meal she cooks and eats alone at the end of each week. However, this particular Friday will be different. On the table as she cooks her trout the letter lies unopened and at this point she doesn't know (nor do we) who it's from. After performing her elaborate cooking ritual, (we hear about this in lavish detail) she opens it as she eats. It's from her father who left home when she was four years old – she hasn't seen or heard of him since – and who is living not in Trinidad as she imagined but some streets away, in Tottenham:

> The letter said he was sorry to hear her mother had died. Only just heard! Yet the news was four years old. He said he wanted to meet her and see what she had turned into and maybe she

> could cook him a nice meal. Melanie clapped her hands. 'Oh that's rich,' she said aloud. 'That's really rich.' She opened up her silver foil parcel. She was determined not to let the letter spoil her trout. She slid it out of the foil carefully and onto her plate. It was perfect, silver and pink and blue. ... 'Take a running jump,' she said, as she thoughtfully tasted her tomato and chilli salad.
>
> (Ibid: 80)

Her thoughts at this point are decisive, unrelenting:

> She took her last bit of trout. She struggled for a minute trying to imagine her father sitting opposite her eating dinner with her. Would he mind her having a glass of wine? In a way, the picture of Melanie and her father at dinner was quite romantic, but something made her shudder. Something repelled her. It was too late, somehow, to have dinner with her father. 'Nah', Melanie said to herself. Leave him like that. Leave it out.' She poured herself another glass of white wine. It was crisp, cold, elegant. She tried to think of more wine words she had read. Fruity. Buttery. Bold.
>
> (Ibid: 80)

This is how Jackie Kay ends her story. The trout and letter both have a meaning, each is attached to a separate series of events, and together they compete for Melanie's attention. But we as readers participate in the making of meaning here. Does the letter stand for contact, warmth, restoration, or for deception and betrayal? The words of the story deliver both options to us. And with the trout – does this suggest a trivial consumerism, spoilage ('A few bones stuck to the flesh. She picked them off one by one') or does it signify Melanie's boldness, feminine independence, her ability to spoil *herself*, and why not? Not just at the end, but all through, we've been drawn into the *story*, not into a position of abstract judgement.

This summary leaves out other successful effects: the travel agent's desk view of resorts, given in a exotic lists, along with the way people plan holidays and why; the more personal issue of global distance (Trinidad, Tottenham); the sense of the contemporary – family life and death, gender and independence, mixed-race origin, consumerism; the reader's sense of Melanie's *voice* through a third-person narrator. But most important of all from the viewpoint of writing is how the shaping of time in the story relates to its distribution of detail. The character – Melanie herself – seems to be the decisive factor here. We are, for its duration, in her consciousness. She is the *focaliser*; thus time appears to us as it does to her. Time reaches back to her earliest memory of her father, to her happy relationship with her mother. The father of the child she lost is referred to cursorily only once. The largest part of the narrative represents these memories and the events of a typical week, then a typical day in the life of Melanie. 'She thought of her father, once a month, on stuff-your-face Sunday because that was the day her mother told her he had left.' From years, months, weeks and days, as the story moves forward these time periods get shorter, so that in the concluding section we hear about only the trout and the letter, finally the wine, then nothing. These periods form the first sentences of paragraphs: 'Every Friday she bought a fresh trout at Ridley Road market, in the morning before work ... She came home with her fresh trout in her bag ... Now to the tomato and chilli salad.' Remembering the longer, earlier time periods meaning is compressed into one or two details: her father's hands, her mother's teeth, the behaviour of customers. These details figure more as *images* than as re-creation. In the shortest period of all – the forty-five minutes or thereabouts which it takes to prepare, cook and eat an average-sized trout – meaning develops through moment-by-moment realisation of considerable amounts of close-up detail. From entering her flat to the second glass of wine, the active, happening and present time of the story lasts just a bit less than one hour.

In Raymond Carver's 'Whoever was using this bed' (Carver, 1988: 27–44) the active time present continues for just under twenty-four hours, from the story's opening to its conclusion, with occasional memories intervening and at one point a recalled dream which becomes, almost, a narrative itself. The story is also written in the first person, delivered by a voice typical of many in Carver's work, male, middle-aged, white, slightly on the amiable side but also slightly upset, especially about women. Here's how it starts:

> The call comes in the middle of the night, three in the morning, and it nearly scares us to death.
>
> 'Answer it, answer it!' my wife cries. 'My God, who is it? Answer it!'
>
> I can't find the light, but I get to the other room, where the phone is, and pick it up after the fourth ring.
>
> 'Is Bud there?' this woman says, very drunk.
>
> 'Jesus, you have the wrong number,' I say, and hang up.
>
> I turn the light on, and go into the bathroom, and that's when I hear the phone start again.
>
> 'Answer that!' my wife screams from the bedroom. 'What in God's name do they want, Jack? I can't take any more.'
>
> (Carver, 1988: 27)

It is a strong, vivid opening with a wonderful sense of voice, and Carver's aim from this point on is to recreate the night-time conversation that keeps husband and wife awake until the next morning and resumes the following night after a shattered day at work. The narration remains with the husband, Jack, but Jack and Iris both have confessions to make – not, as readers might expect, about infidelities, but about illness, or their suspicions about it, their fears. By the following night Jack comments (to himself):

> I feel I've crossed some invisible line. I feel as if I've come to a place I never thought I'd have come to. And I don't know how I got here. It's a strange place. It's a place where a little harmless dreaming and then some sleepy, early-morning talk has led me into considerations of death and annihilation.
>
> The phone rings. We let go of each other, and I reach to answer it. 'Hello,' I say.
>
> 'Hello, there,' the woman says back.
>
> It's the same woman who called this morning...
>
> (Ibid: 43)

In terms of unease, this narrator has as much to fear as Melanie in 'Trout Friday' and – this is the point of the story – no way of avoiding it. Melanie has carefully planned strategies for giving story-like experience the slip. Jack has none, and his wife, Iris, drags him, out of paranoia (possibly) or genuine anxiety, to the point where he is facing illness, age, and either death or prolonged coma on a life-support machine. Why? Neither of them is ill; this is just talk. But she has a throbbing vein in her head and a history of strokes in her family; he has one of breathlessness and heart failure. The other point is, of course, the irrational nature of such night-time terrors: 'And I don't know how I got here.' The story's turning point has been reached before they even knew they were in a story-like situation, but they are. From now on time is shaped differently. They are not the same people. They have changed in a way that Melanie has not – though she was threatened, she resisted. The issue, then, is that in short stories an event triggers some potential change. When that change threatens, the characters experience crisis. But the crisis may or may not result in a turning point. For Jack it does. ('I feel I've crossed some invisible line.') For Melanie it doesn't.

Event, threat, crisis, turning point: these are the structural pressures compelling a piece of action, a stretch of experience, into story-like shape. What the characters in Carver's story want is serenely neutral sleep, no dreams, no phone-calls, but that's not going to happen. Both stories also share a similar narrative image:

the contemporary worlds of both produce anxiety, loss, fragility. People go missing – Bud, Uncle Barry, Melanie's mother and her child; man-woman relationships break down (Jack has been married before and who is Bud?); identities are confused: whoever was using this bed? And science, (especially medical health advice), and consumerism, two of our optimal escape routes, may or may not provide much of an answer. Because of this we feel these stories are definitely *about* something that concerns us. Both imitate or even pastiche the language of healthy eating, of life-style manuals, of the various commercialised modes of successful existence that dominate the interior worlds of these characters, their way of thinking and speaking.

Both also contain potential stories within stories. Jackie Kay could have allowed us to hear about Uncle Barry. Raymond Carver could have insisted on telling us about Bud. Unlikely, but in each case there are untried tangential characters and narratives. How can these be controlled? One answer is that the characters themselves, especially the focaliser or narrating character, control what they want to tell, consider, reflect on. Iris wants to share with Jack the story of a dream she was having that night. Stories within stories can be powerful, not least because, by introducing a new narrative voice, they add polyphonic qualities to a piece and so engage readers' attention. And in Carver's story an added tension arises because Jack does *not* want to listen to Iris's dream story at all. It arouses in him fears about the past, much as in the same way as Melanie's face in the mirror disturbs her fragile equilibrium, blocks off her escape routes, just as her father's letter threatens her self-indulgent pleasure on trout Friday.

Iris blocks Jack's retreat on several fronts. She barrages him with stories and images of life-support systems, hospital wards, her family's health record, scenes from newspapers:

> The covers are all over the place. She picks at something on the quilt, then she rubs her palm across whatever it is before she looks up. 'Did you see in the paper where that guy took a shotgun into an intensive-care unit and made the nurses take his father off the life-support machine? Did you read about that?' Iris says.
>
> 'I saw something about it on the news,' I say. 'But mostly they were talking about this nurse who unplugged six or eight people from their machines. At this point they don't know exactly how many she unplugged. She started off by unplugging her mother, then she went on from there. It was like a spree, I guess. She said she thought she was doing everyone a favour. She said she hoped somebody'd do it for her, if they cared about her.'
>
> (Ibid: 37)

These narratives are lifted from our current narrative culture about medical care gone wrong. Jack's story here acts as a new trigger, releasing Iris's own insistence that she should be 'unplugged' and that he would do it if he cared about her. It is this turn in the conversation that leads husband and wife to discuss an eventuality neither before has considered. Would they? Would they care enough? Jack's answer is straightforward: 'Don't unplug me. It's as simple as that.' Iris, however, makes the opposite request, which Jack reluctantly accepts:

> I'll do it for you. I'll pull the plug, or have it pulled, if I ever think it's necessary. But what I said about my plug still stands. Now I don't want to have to think about this stuff ever again. I don't even want to have to talk about it again. I think we've said all there is to say on the subject. We've exhausted every angle. I'm exhausted.'
>
> Iris grins. 'OK,' she says.
>
> (Ibid: 43)

The following night, while Jack answers the same wrong number yet again, Iris contents herself with unplugging the phone, though this word, so potent in the story, isn't used by Carver in its last lines:

> 'The gall of that woman,' Iris says.
>
> My hands are shaking. I think my voice is doing things. But while I'm trying to make myself understood, my wife moves quickly and bends over, and that's it. The line goes dead, and I can't hear anything.
>
> (Ibid: 44)

Switching off, unplugging, is the solution. This and only this will kill off the story: no more calls, no more conversation, no more woman wanting Bud, no more Bud, nothing.

Narrative Image and Progression in Longer Fiction

We can see how in the two short stories above, the active present where events unfold and reach a climax is supplemented by a background of other narrative, memory, dream-impressions, stories in newspapers, references to untold stories. In longer fiction readers are usually prepared to move through a good deal more of this supplementary narrative background. The central characters might be involved in various side-issues, minor but significant.

The point of this material is to create a pervasive image or impression of life as it is being lived in this particular region, city, culture or, group, under the usual conditions. The narrative image is made up of these supplements, each of which can be entertaining, colourful and suspenseful in their own right. But it's out of these, at some point, that the main story develops, moves to its crisis. A slowly narrowing vortex of action brings the main characters together, draws them out of their separate lives towards a position that will see those lives closely entwined. With escape routes cut off, confrontation follows. The aim of the writer will be to find a way of drawing his or her characters to this point of narrative progression, and one that is consistent with the overall narrative image, with the way life is being lived by people like this in this part of the world at this particular time. A major event: wedding, funeral, feast, reunion, or a departure of some kind, imposes a structure on the lives of the characters, forcing them to adopt a position towards it and each other. One of the best examples of this structure is Jonathan Franzen's novel *The Corrections,* where brothers and sisters meet for a last family Christmas together. It's also used by Roddy Doyle in *The Woman Who Walked Into Doors* and *Paddy Clark Ha Ha Ha*, a novel where progression is delayed, for good reasons, until quite late on in the story. In the stories by Kay and Carver, one character (Melanie's father, and the woman on the phone) have been removed completely from the scene, and the gap generates focus and interest. In Doyle's novel, Paddy Clark's story ends when his father returns, now separated from the family, for a visit. But Paddy's childhood has now come to an end, with a major shift of lives.

Fiction and Anecdote

Many writers draw on their own experience as sources for fiction, and there are clear parallels between fiction writing and personal narrative. But at some point we will need to acknowledge a distinction between fiction and other literary forms of narrative, as well as between these and non-literary forms such as the anecdote. Can we discuss these forms in terms of differences of content, or should we focus instead on their different techniques? Suppose, for example, that you have just failed your driving test for the third time and are telling your friends about it. If you then used this material in a short story, would you intend to shape the narrative differently, produce a more literary style, use third-person rather than first-person narrative? Or would your aim be to change the events themselves, add to them, subtract from them? What would you alter to make it sound like fiction?

My suspicion is that readers expecting a short story would not be wholly satisfied if they found themselves reading about your driving test, however brilliantly you expressed your version of events. The reasons behind my suspicion derive from the notion that narratives, like language itself, always operate within a social context. The social context of anecdote involves certain specific aims and conditions: the speaker is helping a known group of friends and associates to catch up on some recent information about his or her own life, on what has recently been happening to the speaker – the next installment, as it were. The context will also suggest that those listening could follow up with anecdotes of their own if they wanted to; the context implies continuity. With anecdotes, communication continues after the telling, just as it was already established before it. Both these conditions differ from those implied by fiction writing, where communication has not been established previously, will not continue afterwards, and does not rely on the listener's or reader's prior acquaintance with the settings and characters of the narrative.

The fiction writer will inevitably be more interested in developing the message or meaning of a piece for a general reader *unknown to her or him personally*. We are speaking here of a greater *degree* of emphasis on meaning general to all, rather than saying anecdotes have no emphasis of that kind whatsoever. In fiction writing we also expect the characters to exist to a degree independently of the teller and her or his audience of friends.

Camera Perspective

In the short story below by Anne Spillard, the teller or narrator moves around a group of characters, taking up a range of viewing positions. This technique immediately makes the story more fiction-like. We are enabled to see the characters from a distance, to hear their speech, to sense how a camera is moving in close to them, moving away, pausing on certain details. We visualise a scene. The story draws on the same techniques that we find in the visual media.

'No Legal Existence'

In the sluice, the nurses were looking at a mass of fibre and blood clots in a bowl behind the steriliser.

Phyllis peered over their shoulders, still holding the bedpan she had come to empty.

'What is it?' she asked, 'an abortion?' – It was just how she had imagined it would be, all that mess and blood. It didn't look a bit like a baby.

Jenny answered her: 'The afterbirth.' She went to the door and looked into the ward, to make sure no one was coming. The other nurse pulled Phyllis over to the urine-testing cupboard.

Dorothy took a crumpled white paper bag from the shelf underneath it, beside the plastic toothmugs.

'Look,' she said. She opened the bag and pulled a blue kidney dish from inside.

'A baby,' breathed Phyllis. Her eyes opened wider as she looked at the tiny foetus. Without moving her eyes she bent down and set the bedpan on the floor.

'It's perfect,' Dorothy said. They crowded round, looking at the perfection of the foetus, lying in the dish.

'Oh, look at its beautiful fingers, and its ears.'

Each fingernail was like a tiny pear, the ears waxen flaps pressed onto the skull by a hasty thumb as an afterthought. Only the eyes seemed too big. They were protuberant and staring, under lids you could see through. You could see the dark completeness of the liver through transparent skin. There was an awed pause.

'It's a girl,' said Jenny.

'Who's is it?' asked Phyllis.

'Miss Hayward's.' They all turned and looked through the window in the sluice door. Miss Hayward's bed was opposite. She was thumbing through a magazine.

'Dorothy's husband used to work with this man she'd been going out with,' said Jenny.

It was the usual story: he was going to marry her, when he'd got settled in Australia. But instead he'd sent her a letter…

It isn't a baby, thought Phyllis. Because a baby has to be there twenty-eight weeks. This perfect human shape is just a thing. It has no legal existence. It has never done anything, not moved or spoken, or seen anything, and no one except us will ever see it.

'What do you do with it?' she asked.

'Throw it away,' said Jenny. She made a face. 'You just wrap it up in the bag and put it in there.' She nodded her head towards the bin by the sink, with its rubber lid that didn't disturb the patients, and the white lining hanging untidily round its top.

(Stand Magazine, Vol 3, 1980: 63)

If we compare this passage with the John and Mary passage by Margaret Atwood (see p. 113), we can see that it does present sudden change. It breaks a routine. It lifts the character Phyllis (clearly a newcomer) out of her preconceptions, educates her, and educates its readers in the process. It is not anecdotal. We can't supplement the story with any prior knowledge about this hospital and these characters; we meet them independently. But we will have notions about how nurses behave, terminations, personal freedom, gender roles, women's independence; it will have *content* relevance for a wide range of readers, even to the point where some may object to the way it chooses to make its content relevant. What, for example, might Miss Hayward's version of events have been like? She presumably knows far more about the preceding situation than do the nurses, and could be in shock, even though their observation of her 'thumbing through a magazine' suggests otherwise. Her judgement of events is not available, and a more searching treatment might have presented her side of things. The characters are seen looking at the baby in the dish, and we focus wholly on them and on it: 'a girl'. In this way, the story aims to control our sympathy by leaving certain viewing positions vacant while emphasising others. Miss Hayward's story has been ignored.

But such objections imply that the story has force. What can we learn from it as regards technique? We need to know about some of the ways in which third-person narrative can work.

Narrators

In third-person narrative, an important decision you will need to make when shaping a story is to work out the position of the camera. Are you:

1. standing far away from the characters, seeing a large section of their life history in one panoramic shot (as in the John and Mary passage, see p. 113)?
2. standing very close to the characters, an eye-witness watching how they behave, where they stand, what they say, what they are doing from second to second?
3. standing right inside their heads, so that you are describing the world through their eyes and in their own words?

We call the first two positions *external narration,* and the third *internal narration.* An equivalent set of terms would describe (1) and (2) as *external focalisation* and (3) as *character focalisation.* Focalisation implies a camera position. As the writer, you have a choice. You can stand away from the characters and observe them as a group, move close to the characters, occupy their viewing positions, move back to a distance. Even third-person 'she/he/they narrative' can look through the eyes of a character and show us what they see. As readers, our sympathy is usually reserved for those characters whose viewing positions we are allowed to occupy, and withheld from those we are not. Hence the writer can manipulate the direction of our sympathy. In the story above it goes towards the nurses and the foetus, and away from Miss Hayward.

Phrases such as 'he/she saw/felt/wondered' begin the shift from straightforward external narration where the reader is addressed directly and given external information about scenes and characters. But when we hear a character's own reactions *in his or her own words*, we know that the shift is complete. Writers do not necessarily use these terms, but they do understand when a shift needs to occur.

In 'No Legal Existence' the first sentence shows us the nurses, while the second shows us Phyllis, each externally. The writer here is addressing the reader directly. But we soon realise that we are in the same position as Phyllis, that of a nurse 'peering over [the others'] shoulders'. We are not seeing what's there until Phyllis sees it, and, like her, we don't understand quite what it is we are looking at. When we get to: 'It didn't look a bit like a baby', this statement is clearly *Phyllis's* opinion, *and is addressed internally to herself.* These words are what Phyllis is actually thinking as she looks down at the placenta in the bowl. The shift is complete, and from then on we get her and the nurses' reactions, but mainly Phyllis's, in a second-by-second close-up record of response.

In the final seconds of the action, the closing shot pauses to outline the lid on the hospital bin. We know, now, why bins have soft lids. The story structure has moved from external narration to internal and finally back to external, and this device reinforces our sense that the story has reached a conclusion. The story is shaped partly by these switches in narrative position, and partly by the fact that the object of focus – the baby – has now disappeared.

In third-person narrative it is very important to realise that you do possess this cinema-like power of attention to a scene and its characters; you can make decisions about where you stand, what you see, what you choose not to see, or which character's vision to inhabit. You can therefore become the story's director, deciding the angles of shots, the degree of distance and close-up, and make use of pausing slow-motion effects, montage and flashback. Your readers will see what you decide to let them, and hear what you want them to hear.

If you decide to use a first-person 'I – narrator', then this 'I' will be occupying the same scene as the story characters and interacting with them. 'I' will be one of the characters.

But in some cases, the 'I' may not interact, and may observe without being part of the story. In the following passage by V. S. Pritchett, 'I' shows just enough hint of attitude to characterise him, but not enough to cause him to interfere:

> In a dead place like this town you always had to wait. I was waiting for a train, now I had to wait for a haircut. ...
>
> I picked up a newspaper. A man had murdered an old woman, a clergyman's sister was caught stealing gloves in a shop, a man who had identified the body of his wife at an inquest on a drowning fatality met her three days later on a pier. Ten miles from this town the skeletons of men killed in a battle eight centuries ago had been dug up on the Downs. Still, I put the paper down. I looked at the two men in the room.
>
> The shave had finished now, the barber was cutting the man's hair. It was glossy black hair and small curls of it fell on the floor. I could see the man in the mirror. He was in his thirties. ... The lashes were long too, and the lids when he blinked were pale.
>
> (Pritchett, 1993:130)

Like Scott Fitzgerald in his novel *The Great Gatsby,* Pritchett has used a narrator who is allowed to make independent judgments whilst maintaining a stance of distant but careful scrutiny. The external narrating camera eye has become a human 'I' witness, present but detached.

The hairdresser then tells the story that follows the 'I' narrator. It concerns the customer, in the above passage, who fell in love with the hairdresser's wife. The 'I' listens while the hairdresser tells him a story – an anecdote – about how the customer once tried to slit his own throat. (The swishing razor and a mark on the customer's neck feature strongly.) The whole piece has a framework that is larger than the anecdote itself, and distances us from it. The anecdote here is told by one complete stranger to another (the narrator is a newcomer to the town), which alters the sense from continuing friendly contact to one that is sharply and finally discontinued. Both these features bring the piece a degree closer to fiction.

Character Rhythm

This alternative approach can appear more attractive to writers because for one thing it doesn't so directly involve the technical business of narration change: external to internal, control over viewing position, visualisation. Though it can be visual, the approach here is more painterly, less photographic. Words move over the page like brush-strokes, and trace with their speed, slowness and adjustment the rhythm of a character's recurrent patterns of behaviour. The reader gets to know the character from the inside as well as from the outside, through the character's thoughts and processes of thought – which might turn into speech or stay unspoken – as well as from characteristics such as physical build, gesture, typical behaviour, even from smell, and certainly from the character's attitude.

In this approach, if you are using first-person 'I' narration, the narrator must be a character with strong presence. Opinions, prejudices, outrageous judgements can all be expressed by a speaker in the first person and it will be important, therefore, that the reader is able to recognise these characteristic attitudes and ways of speaking, and that these attitudes trigger the story's events. Character-rhythm holds clear implications for what happens in a story. It is because the characters are what they are that certain events happen to them while other events do not. Instead of writing *about* characters, the writer is producing their rhythm, and the characters' whole life will be present in that rhythm. With this approach, you really do have, in Ian McEwan's words, 'the opportunity to find out what it's like being someone else'.

A character's rhythm may change, be sometimes harmonious, sometimes discordant, and can be altered by circumstances. David Lodge's novel *Nice Work* opens with one of the main characters, Victor Wilcox, in a state of anxiety about work, a familiar enough experience especially on a Monday morning in the middle of January, which is when Victor wakes up. But Lodge does not merely give us information *about* Victor and his work; he shows it as it is happening *to* Victor. Reading this passage from the first and second paragraphs of the novel, it is not easy or even appropriate to describe it as internal or external narration, or to think of one type of narrative shifting into another. Somehow they are dubbed and become one style. The stance of the character and the style of the writer have become one thing, one substance. We see Victor lying in bed, but we also feel what it is like to be him and to have his thoughts. His actions, impressions and anxieties are stylistic features of the actual writing itself – flat, enervated; then a manic, frantic bombardment of images; muddled, fumbling reactions, all consistent with Victor's and his wife's half-wakeful state at this time in the morning:

> Monday, January 13th, 1986. Victor Wilcox lies awake, in the dark bedroom, waiting for his quartz alarm-clock to bleep. It is set to do this at 6.45. How long he has to wait he doesn't know. He could easily find out by groping for the clock, lifting it to his line of vision, and pressing the button that illuminates the digital display. But he would rather not know. Supposing it is only six o'clock? Or even five? It could be five. Whatever it is, he won't be able to get to sleep again. This has become a regular occurrence lately; lying awake in the dark, waiting for the alarm to bleep, worrying.

> Worries streak towards him like enemy spaceships in one of Gary's video-games. He flinches, dodges, zaps them with instant solutions, but the assault is endless: the Avco account, the Rawlinson account, the price of pig-iron, the value of the pound, the competition from Foundrax, the incompetence of his Marketing Director, the persistent breakdowns of the core blowers, the vandalising of the toilets in the fettling shop, the pressure from his divisional boss, last month's accounts, the quarterly forecast, the annual review...
>
> In an effort to escape this bombardment, perhaps even to doze awhile, he twists on to his side, burrows into the warm plump body of his wife, and throws an arm around her waist. Startled, but still asleep, drugged with Vallium, Marjorie swivels to face him. Their noses and foreheads bump against each other; there is a sudden flurry of limbs, an absurd pantomime struggle. Marjorie puts up her fists like a pugilist, groans and pushes him away. An object slides off the bed and falls to the floor with a thump. Vic knows what it is: a book entitled *Enjoy Your Menopause.*
>
> (Lodge, 1988: 13)

This passage is liberal with close-up and roots our reading response in the now of the characters – that list of worries in paragraph two. It also shows how they hit, how they act and what their effect is; the term 'effective', often applied to a successful piece of evocative writing, means that the novelist is following actions through, showing us results, causes and effects. And these effects are present within the style's mechanical urgency. If we ask, 'How do we know what we know about this character?' The answer is through the style and arrangements of words, in full, their rhythm. We also know it through the harsh references to finance accounts, pig iron, and the paraphernalia of items as they land plop on a desk and won't go away.

The whole rhythm of existence for Vic is determined by work and work's rhythms. And we know equally important things about Marjorie's rhythms, too; she engages in a somnambulist battle with Vic that is not actually aggressive, and we recognise the topic of her book. So if we ask another question: 'What is it about these characters that interests this writer? What is he trying to get at?', the answer is – to discover their rhythm, their style, their angle towards the world, themselves, and each other. Speech and dialogue happen as one more feature of character-rhythm. By changing their circumstances, their rhythms may change too, but not immediately. We might define fiction's style and purpose as an instrument for recording such changes, the equivalent in text of a seismic graph. At this point in *Nice Work* the fluctuations are small, but attention to detail and style will be there just as much as when a large event is occurring.

In the passage below from the beginning of V. S. Pritchett's story 'Handsome is as Handsome Does', again the writer is trying to find the rhythms of the characters:

> In the morning the Corams used to leave the Pension which was like a white box with a terra-cotta lid among the vines on the hill above the town, and walk through the dust and lavish shade to the beach. They were a couple in their forties.
>
> He had never been out of England before but she had spent half her youth in foreign countries. She used to wear shabby saffron beach pyjamas with a navy blue top which the sun had faded. She was a short, thin woman, ugly yet attractive. Her hair was going grey, her face was clay-coloured, her nose was big and long and she had long yellowish eyes. In this beach suit she looked rat-like, with that peculiar busyness, inquisitiveness, intelligence and even charm of rats. People always came and spoke to her and were amused by her conversation. They were startled by her ugly face and her shabbiness but they liked her lazy voice, her quick mind, her graceful good manners, the look of experience and good sense in her eyes.
>
> He was a year older. On the hottest days, when she lay bare-backed and drunk with sunlight, dozing or reading a book, he sat awkwardly beside her in a thick tweed jacket and a white hat pulled over his eyes. He was a thickset, ugly man; they were an ugly pair. Surly, blunt-speaking, big-boned, with stiff short fair hair that seemed to be struggling and alight in the sun, he sat frowning and glaring almost wistfully and tediously from his round blue eyes. He had big hands like a labourer's. When people came to speak to her, he first of all edged away. His instinct was to avoid all people. He wanted to sit there silently with her, alone. But if the people persisted then he was rude to them, rude, uncouth and quarrelsome. Then she had to smooth away his rudeness and distract attention from it.
>
> (Pritchett, 1993: 38)

If we look at the description of these two characters, our attention is drawn to physique, attitude, dress, way of speaking – separate features that together make up this man and this woman. Through expressions such as 'thickset', 'surly', 'blunt-speaking', 'stiff', 'short', 'struggling', 'frowning', 'glaring', 'big hands', 'edged away', 'instinct to avoid', 'sitting silently', 'quarrelsome', the writer is finding words for the slow-moving, clumsy, irritable temperament that forms in all its combined aspects this man and his life. His thick fingers matter as much as his thoughts. (Very often, inexperienced writers do not realise how powerful and important a character's size, appearance and build are.) The oddly combined, awkward rhythms of the man and the woman together will determine the direction of the story. At the end, will she still be smoothing away his rudeness? Will she have abandoned him? Which story-events will enable the writer to discover what binds her to him, or what might break the tie?

In suggesting these ideas about rhythm I suspect that I am only saying what most of us already know: characters in fiction are rhythm-like because living people are also like this. But fictional characters only exist in words. Finding a character means finding a style that fits his or her rhythm. The words that hit the page come with the same pace and spirit as the character who enters into being through the words – fast and sharp, or slow, warm, pleasing, cool and relaxed, sensual, ironic or irritable: character exists as style, and style as rhythm. One way to begin this type of writing is to try to get close to another person's living experience. John Berger, for example, in Chapter 2 reviews the obscure rhythm of his mother's life; and he does it so well that in his portrait we sense her whole life is there, even though we know little in the way of facts.

But a character is not a specimen in a bottle labelled ugly, handsome, large-boned or phlegmatic. The medieval theory of personality – that we are each mixtures of four humours, or of astrology – for example that Aries people like to get all the attention – are of little use to a writer unless the characters are set free into worlds of *action.* The question is not 'Who are they and what are their characteristics?' It is, rather, 'What will these particular characteristics make them do, make them say?' Fiction's research into character depends on style *and* action. Its aim is to find the style that drives action. After you have found out about your characters and recreated their rhythms, you will need to take them through an experience that may last, in shorter fiction, only a few minutes, hours or days. It's always tempting to build up a picture without actually doing the writing. But with character rhythm writing you can't do this for very long; you can only find out about your characters by placing them at the moving edge of time.

Rhythm and story structure are interdependent: one creates the other. Characters must interact with each other and the world; this or that style of action is how we know them. The writer arranges things so that they act. The writer has in mind some situation, some set of conditions, that will serve to produce the maximum revelation. If, in Melville's novel *Moby Dick,* the enraged, obsessive

Captain Ahab is placed in command of a ship, there is no way he will *not* eventually encounter the white whale.

Dialogue

Character-rhythm always moves along a central line that leads to dialogue, but may not reach it until circumstances make speech necessary. Dialogue occurs as one of the signs of characters interacting, so that if a short story begins, as it might, with dialogue and the interaction is stressful, then to show conflict the writer will be relying on dialogue alone. In Carver's story the dialogue opening succeeds in producing tension out of nowhere, because we all understand the annoyance of phones ringing in the middle of the night. No build-up is necessary. But if the opening dialogue illustrates a routine rather than a conflictual situation, the dialogue will still have to be significant, and this might present some difficulties. The touch of dialogue between Melanie and her colleagues in the travel agents shows a typical tension, a routine conflict, and so effectively illustrates her life in the office.

Character-rhythm needs to hold the possibility of speech; some characters find speech easy, others not. To some it will be naturally part of their rhythm; to others it only happens when rhythm is jarred. In a short story dialogue cannot be wasted; it is crucial, especially for conflict, but therefore the tension needs to build up *before* it can be felt through dialogue. Dialogue reserved for crisis points is usually more hard-hitting, for then the characters are likely to say something irrevocable.

In the conversation below, the writer restricts himself to only one means – telephone dialogue – for discovering the characters. Their rhythms *speak,* and as we read we know the characters, just as though we were hearing them described:

> 'Why haven't you called me? I've been worried to –'
>
> 'Mother, darling, don't yell at me. I can hear you beautifully,' said the girl. 'I called you twice last night. Once just after –'
>
> 'I *told* your father you'd probably call last night. But, no, he had to – Are you alright Muriel? Tell me the truth.'
>
> 'I'm fine. Stop asking me that, please.'
>
> 'When did you get there?'
>
> 'I don't know. Wednesday morning, early.'
>
> 'Who drove?'
>
> 'He did,' said the girl. 'And don't get excited. He drove very nicely. I was amazed.'
>
> '*He* drove? Muriel, you gave me your word of –'
>
> 'Mother,' the girl interrupted. 'I just told you. He drove *very*

nicely. Under fifty the whole way, as a matter of fact.'

'Did he try any of that funny business with the trees?'

'I *said* he drove very nicely, Mother. Now, please. I asked him to stay close to the white line, and all, and he knew what I meant, and he did. He was even trying not to look at the trees – you could tell. Did Daddy get the car fixed, incidentally?'

'Not yet. They want four hundred dollars just to –'

'Mother, Seymour *told* Daddy that he'd pay for it. There's no reason for –'

'Well, we'll see. How did he behave – the car and all?'

'Alright,' said the girl.

'Did he keep calling you that awful –'

'No. He has something new now.'

'What?'

'Oh, what's the difference, Mother?'

'Muriel I want to *know*. Your father ... talked to Dr. Sivenski.'

'Oh?' said the girl.

'He told him *everything*. ... The trees. That business with the window. Those horrible things he said to Granny about her plans for passing away. What he did with all those lovely pictures from Bermuda – everything.'

'Well?' said the girl.

(Salinger, 1986:2–3)

Just what was it with those trees? The telephone conversation also builds up suspense. The mother and daughter both know what their conversation is about, and we are forced to construct what we can from that alone. But the target here is precise: the worrying behaviour of Seymour. We are given the scattered jigsaw pieces of a narrative that possibly won't be complete until the end of the story: 'everything' must wait.

Delay and Suspense

Suspense is often associated with *genre* fiction: crime, thriller, mystery, especially with threats of violence or physical danger, but stories can still produce suspense without being classed as such. Writers can hold us in suspense for the whole of a novel's length, while delay is a narrative effect – a technique of writing that generates immediate suspense. Delay can focus attention by manipulating details that excite, but do not fulfil, our expectations. While reading the following passage from James Herbert's novel *Lair*, we already know from the blurb, the Prologue, the paperback cover picture and because this novel is a sequel, that the story depicts enormous voracious rats with a taste for blood. In a matter of time the rats will attack people, but when, how? The Prologue makes a definite suggestion about the existence of an outsized and hideously deformed white rat, so we read in expectation of its appearance:

> Woollard's weathered face was creased into deep trenches of anger as he turned the corner of an outbuilding, when suddenly he caught sight of a small white object lying in the mud. At first he thought it might be just a bird-feather, but the tinges of red along one edge aroused his curiosity. He squinted as he approached, deciding it wasn't a feather at all but a tiny, obviously dead animal. He was used to finding dead mice around the place, for the cats *usually* did their job well enough. This time, though, there was something odd about the furry corpse.
>
> Stooping to examine the body more closely, he suddenly drew in a sharp breath. He reached for the object he now knew was not a dead mouse. Blood had matted the fur at one end and two of the claws were missing. He dropped the cat's paw in disgust.
>
> (Herbert, 1979: 12)

Eight sentences pass and still no rat; several times we hear what the object is *not*. Only by the ninth sentence do we hear what it is – a cat slaughtered by 'something'. Delay works at the sentence level towards expectations strongly implanted. At the point of reading, our expectations make us guess, and guess wrong. The writing actually prevents the knowledge we desire, and then supplies something else. So we read on, hoping that maybe the next episode will supply what we anticipated.

As a device, delay cannot operate unless readers are given some goal, some target of expectation. If they are not, the withholding of facts will instead lead to obscurity. Delay will prevent readers from reaching the goal too quickly, but they must know beforehand what it is. Suspense writing operates by telling us what to expect, and finally supplying what we expect, but in ways we couldn't have imagined. The whole of *Lair* keeps us in suspense about the white rat. We know the end of the novel before we begin, but the pleasure is in getting there, in having the horrible details spilled out. The whole effect – since we are almost told the story beforehand – is eventually to offer us what we know, but in the precise, flavourful details, so that in the final stages of suspense we don't have to guess, just relish and enjoy. We know James Bond will always succeed; it is the *how* that matters, and this is suspense.

A more obvious but related type of suspense occurs when there is no actual delaying tactic but a momentary shock-effect. A door creaks, a window suddenly flies open, a potential victim is face to face with a maniac. What will happen? One event leads directly to another. But even here readers will need some target of expectation: the house is possessed; the vicar, we suspect, is a natural-born killer. Either we meet the monster and so can imagine the devastation about to happen, or we see the effects of the devastation without meeting the monster. In both cases something is withheld from us, but nevertheless it is something we anticipate. Beginning writers often assume that in order to keep readers interested some essential defining fact can be left till the end. But suspense needs to be felt *at the time.* Thus, in the 'it was all a dream' ending, readers may feel misled and resent the change of target expectations, and they won't explode with joy when the dull truth is revealed.

Delay, however, is a valued device, and not only useful in thriller writing. In the following passage from Kate Chopin's 'The Story Of An Hour' (written in 1894) the main character, Louise, has just received the news of her husband's death. She retreats to her room and sits by an upstairs window; we expect to hear her trying to come to terms with her sudden loss:

> She could see in the open square before her house the tops of trees that were all aquiver with the new spring life. The delicious breath of rain was in the air. In the Street below a peddler was crying his wares. The notes of a distant song which someone was singing reached her faintly, and countless sparrows were twittering in the eaves.
>
> There were patches of blue sky showing here and there through the clouds that had met and piled each above the other in the West facing her window.
>
> (Chopin, 1894, in Bohner, ed., 2002: 236)

The reader anticipates grief, only to be told about a view, and a surprisingly inappropriate one at that; we know what Louise is seeing, but not what she thinks or how she responds to these signs of spring life, or how these connect with her bereavement. Does she sense her exclusion from the life outside the window or an involvement with it? We are uncertain. The writer deliberately withholds the desired knowledge. Delay, in this story, raises questions about feeling, not action, and marks a difference between this type of story and the mystery or thriller-type narrative where close speculation about the characters' feelings (especially when these are half-formed or confused) is less likely to influence our attention. Though both types generate desire for an outcome, Kate Chopin's story truly does project us towards that unforeseen point where stock reactions are broken with and radically re-viewed. The woman finds herself alone with reactions she could never have predicted; instead of grief she uncovers a sense of excitement, freedom, power.

Foregrounding

All stories aim to achieve impact, and in longer stories there may be several points where impact occurs. It occurs when a speech, image or event is *foregrounded* for us; it stands out and becomes significant and memorable. In writing for children the degree of foregrounding will be of major importance to the technique of attracting and holding the interest of readers (see Chapter 5, p. 160). The writer wishes the reader to finish the story and carry away something: an image, a judgement, a face, a decisive speech. Writers need to imagine those points where the foregrounding will be memorable, and to keep such effects in mind. In the process of writing, new possibilities of foregrounding may suggest themselves. Foregrounding can serve to underline a story's basic motif, such as the *invitation* motif – a letter, a phone call, as in the Kay and Carver stories. But such emphasis is not all it can do. It can just be there for itself, and have nothing to do with the story's basic structure. A story may contain several foregrounded images, or just one: a colour, an object, a few seconds of elation or disappointment, a mistake, a face in a window. Beginnings and endings are the usual places to find them. In the passage below by Carson McCullers, the author begins her story 'The Ballad of the Sad Café' with an image:

> If you walk along the main street on an August afternoon there is nothing whatsoever to do. The largest building, in the very center of the town, is boarded up completely and leans so far to the right that it seems bound to collapse at any minute. The house is very old. There is about it a curious, cracked look that is very puzzling until you suddenly realize that at one time, and long ago, the right side of the front porch had been painted, and part of the wall – but the painting was left unfinished and one portion of the house is darker and dingier than the other. The building looks completely deserted. Nevertheless, on the second floor there is one window which is not boarded; sometimes in the late afternoon when the heat is at its worst a hand will slowly open the shutter and a face will look down on the town. It is a face like the terrible dim faces known in dreams – sexless and white, with two grey crossed eyes which are turned inwards so sharply that they seem to be exchanging with each

> other one long and secret gaze of grief. The face lingers at the window for an hour or so, then the shutters are closed once more, and as likely as not there will not be another soul to be seen along the main street.
>
> (McCullers, 1999: 7)

This is a bleak picture, but sharp and atmospheric; the story that follows is haunted by it: a wrecked house, a single, abandoned occupant, a sense of derelict, half-finished restoration, a secret gaze of grief. It constitutes one foreground in a story in which there are many. It somehow has to be just where it is and just as it is, and as we move through the passage we sense the writer is turning up the current gently, determinedly; the power-surge is slight but definite, the image not overstated. In this passage, foregrounding serves the underlying atmosphere; it shows us what connects the house, the street and the face; it shows us what habits link them. Each detail has a carryforward effect. Meaning here accumulates in the face: the decided point where atmosphere has reached its strongest expression, so that one detail counts for everything else. A rhythm is established. In this face the potential for change, for love, for contact, for a story, is dissipating, falling apart, and yet the potential is there, and in 'The Ballad of the Sad Cafe' the story that follows is about the attempt (the failed attempt) to establish a new atmosphere, new rhythms and rituals of behaviour.

Questions and Summary

Where should I start? You need to think about the Where, When, and Who, of your story. The most important element is Who – the characters. For stories and most novels you need a main character – the protagonist, and you need to know what he or she thinks of him/herself, other people, his or her life in general and own circumstances in particular. (See below, suggestions for writing, p. 153). Start by imagining your character in a setting (Where), and the passage of time as it is affecting him or her (When). Look at the examples of starts (on pp. 114–15, above). It's also useful to explore how another character or characters react to the protagonist, and/or if the protagonist has an *Other* (see p. 125).

Shall I use first-person or third-person narration? Character can be explored from the inside using both these types of narration. (Note the use of the third-person in *Nice Work.)* But the first-person can only show us what your main character thinks consciously, his or her choice of words, slang registers, expressed attitudes. This can be limiting, but you can also make such limits significant – as where Melanie (see above, p. 131) doesn't want to think about her father. 'I don't go there', she's saying. First-person narrative can indicate blocks, gaps, points of resistance – all useful devices, especially in short stories.

Third-person narrative can reach places the characters themselves cannot – can show both their conscious thoughts – through free indirect speech – and their hidden feelings and drives. In both types of narrative you need to get to sense your character's rhythm. Is your character a very expressive, talkative personality, or someone who finds speech difficult and avoids it? The type of main character might help determine the type of narration.

What about back story? Going back through your character's life story is a way of getting to know what matters to him or her, and finding out the direction in which he or she is going. When the story starts, there will already be a momentum, a rhythm. Back story is therefore important, but you must always think about what is important to him or her – to the character. This must always come first. You might include a short life history of your main character in your actual text, as Lodge is doing in the short extract below. It can be positioned within the consciousness of one of the characters, or within a specific place-and-time setting, as when Vic Wilcox looks in his bathroom mirror:

> Wilcox: Victor Eugene. Date of birth: 19 Oct. 1940 ... 1966–70, Senior Engineer, Vanguard Engineering ... [The list goes on] 1978–80, Manufacturing Director, Rumcol Castings; 1980–85, Managing Director, Rumcol Castings. Present position: Managing Director, J. Pringle and Sons Casting and General Engineering ...
>
> That's who I am.
>
> Vic grimaces at his own reflection, as if to say: come off it, no identity crisis, please. Somebody has to earn a living in this family.
>
> (Lodge, 1988: 17)

'As if to say: come off it...' The paragraph of facts sees Victor through a wide perspective, but in what follows we hear his voice and style, his rhythm.

How important are settings and circumstances? Setting is essential for fiction. Characters are in constant interaction with the material world, and are themselves part of it. Modern fiction was invented to explore real-world settings and circumstances, and to illustrate their impact in our day-by-day life experience. A change in circumstances can create the basic momentum for shorter and longer fiction, a trigger event that suddenly makes new demands on the characters. Researching your settings, going to the places where your action is set, can open up new story directions.

What about timing and events? Another reason for modern fiction's existence is its close-up record of moment by moment experience. But this experience needs to be shaped – by trigger events, crisis and (possibly) closure. In shorter fiction you need to choose a point when the story action begins; things might have been ticking over quite normally, then... At a crisis stage, the characters feel they have crossed an invisible line – no going back. It happens in Raymond Carver's story during the husband and wife's conversation. Closure implies that we know the line has been crossed and that the consequences have been made clear. In Carver's story the consequences aren't quite clear, whereas in 'Trout Friday' they are. Lack of closure leaves the outcome uncertain – a preferred option for some writers.

Suggestions for Writing

(See also Exercise 9 in Chapter 1, p. 39.)

1 *Finding a character.* Invent a character based on a photograph (of your own or from a magazine or newspaper). Write down answers to questions about this character, for example: name, age, sex, occupation, where he/she lives, who with or alone, one or two objects significant to this person, who or what he/she is afraid of losing, what annoys this character, what his/her relationship is to food, travel, animals, colours, his or her own body; what word he or she chooses to describe him/herself, what word friends and family choose, what he/she looks forward to each week, each day; what he/she wishes for. *Now make sure your character has some kind of irregularity or flaw – a preoccupation, maybe an impairment – physical or emotional – or an obsession.* Selecting from the above information, develop an idea for a piece of shorter or longer fiction with this person as your protagonist, then send the character through a significant three hours (or less) of experience. See what else you can discover about him or her.

2 The following story ideas can be used for discussion and/or for writing shorter or longer fiction. One point to discuss will be the potential development (very short/short/long) of each idea. Another will be to fill in the detail. Think about narrative image, progression, the use of time, also the tense, person (first/third), who the focaliser is, and whether the story reaches a turning point. Think of these suggestions as ideas for short stories, or as scenes from novels. How would the whole novel incorporate this story? How would you develop it as a story on its own? When you have worked on some of these, continue by inventing your own ideas.

A young woman leaves her baby in a push-chair outside a shop in the high street. When she comes out the baby has gone. She goes home to find her sister has taken the baby. Her sister is perhaps ill or…

A man reads a woman's diary and discovers something he'd rather not have known.

An old woman's husband has died. He is present in the house for the gathering of family and friends on the day of the funeral. She tries to keep him out of sight in the kitchen. Everyone is nice to him because he is dead.

Choose an issue out of the news. Develop a short story that sheds new light.

Write a one-page story using dialogue as in the Seymour extract (page 147).

Write a story about a character who is like you in only two of the following: age, gender, sexuality, race, social background. The story starts with this character getting ready to go out on a date.

Develop a narrative in which your main character is thinking about another character, his or her Other, obsessively. Something about the Other's behaviour isn't quite right, is disturbing even to someone very close.

3 Find a story you can retell using a new point of view, an added event or new circumstances. You could retell, for example, the ending of 'Trout Friday' so that Melanie calls her father. This may or may not lead to a satisfactory experience for the characters. Decide what your preferred ending is. Or, Miss Hayward (see p. 138) receives her letter. Write this story.

4 Flash Fiction. The aim here is to write a story in less than one thousand words. 'No Legal Existence' is a good example. Other well-known examples include 'The Story of an Hour' by Kate Chopin, 'A Very Short Story' by Ernest Hemingway.

You can get into practice with flash fiction by thinking about the following story. Here is its opening. How might it continue?

During the hot dry summer, the boy's mother told him he must only drink water from the tap or out of a bottle. On no account must he ever be tempted to drink water from the roadside ditches that irrigated the fields. It could well be poisonous, she told him, and filled with tiny snakes; if you take even a sip you could swallow a snake. On morning, she said, 'You might not even know whether you had swallowed a snake – not at first, not until it started to grow bigger and bigger in your inside. Then you would know, but by then it would be too late.'

The weather was hot and dry as the boy walked home from school with his friends that afternoon. They had been running so that when they stopped one look at the sky was enough to make them thirsty...

5 Stories within stories. Write a short story that involves one character telling a story to another character or to a group. What is the story? Why was it told? How was it intended to be received? How was it received?

Revision and Editing

Placing yourself wholly in the reader's position, see if your first paragraph gains and holds interest. Check this too by reading passages aloud. Go through your text looking for any passages that switch off your reader's attention, and find out why this is before you decide to cut or revise your writing.

Can you find ways to intensify your text's moment-by-moment re-creation. Will it have more impact if you changed the tense, or point of view or the focaliser? Have you avoided the obvious, and clichés, and allowed your reader to speculate, anticipate, make links? Be aware of your story's forward direction, its sense of the moving edge of time.

Have you thought what impact the ending of your story will have on your reader?

Are there important images you have foregrounded, impressions your readers will take away from the story – moments, faces, names, events?

Have you taken the chance to include *voices* in your text – through dialogue, references to speech, storytelling? Look at the use of speech and dialogue in examples of published fiction. How do these animate a story? Also, check their layout and punctuation.

Place an 'Author Keep Out' sign above your text. Your business is not to explain a scene or load the reader's mind with information. Be wary of showing how much you have researched. Your story should bring you close to the *characters*, their voices and their world.

CHAPTER 5

CHILDREN'S FICTION

Worlds and Voices

How can writers get close to the world of children's imagination? Is it possible to revisit our own childhoods? I argued in Chapter 1 that imagination selects its own subjects for writing, and we follow it, taking its promptings forward into research if we need to. For the writer, the world of children is itself such a subject, and sometimes the briefest glimpse into it can trigger a sense of its strangeness, its excitement. The sight of a group of children out of school crossing the road in twos, on their way to a show or event, suddenly allows us a sense of the curious energy of those voices. What are they thinking as they shout, sing, skip, make fun of each other? What kinds of things do they enjoy? What makes them afraid? What makes them real? What new forms of family life are they tied to? What do they think about adults? Do they see us as confident, mostly, or more often unsure about ourselves? Do they sense what worries us? Does what matters to us matter to them? In fiction, these questions can only be answered with regard to particular children, influenced as they are by age, ethnicity, gender and background. The main character, usually a good storyteller, brings us the individual child's experience realised in close-up.

Crossover Fiction

In recent years, several books published for children have widely appealed to both child and adult readers. The Harry Potter books and Philip Pullman's trilogy, *His Dark Materials*, are obvious examples of *crossover fiction*, which rightly challenges the notion that certain kinds of writing are suitable only for under-age readers. Can we clearly identify an area of writing as 'children's fiction' and, if so, how? Do we need a term such as crossover fiction, or does 'crossover' simply happen when readers of all ages become interested? The first part of this chapter addresses such questions, but not in an abstract way. As in earlier chapters my aim is to approach all the relevant issues through commentary based on responses to actual texts. In a section below, for example, (p. 163) I have commented on extracts from two pieces of written fiction. Roddy Doyle's *Paddy Clarke Ha Ha Ha* is a story spoken by a ten-year-old boy in a novel written for adults. Jaqueline Wilson's *How to Survive Summer Camp* is a story with a child narrator of the same age in a story for children. If all we had were the texts to go on, could we guess the implied age of their readers? Might Roddy Doyle's text be read as also written for children – a crossover novel? Might Jaqueline Wilson's be written for adults? Can children tell us why Roddy Doyle's novel doesn't fulfil their expectations of story (or does it?), and what are those expectations?

This chapter is written in the spirit of such an enquiry, and asks other questions about the process of writing children's fiction. In a recent article Mark Haddon, who began by writing books exclusively for children, and whose award-winning novel *The Curious Incident of the Dog in the Night-time* has been marketed for both adults and a young teenage readership, does see a difference between children's books and so-called crossover fiction. He uses the distinction between 'literary' and 'genre' fiction to explain it.

> Genre fiction says: 'Forget the gas bill. Forget the office politics. Pretend you're a spy. Pretend you're a courtesan. Pretend you're the owner of a crumbling gothic mansion on this worryingly foggy promontory.' Literary fiction says: 'Bad luck. You're stuck with who you are, just as these people are stuck with who they are...' I don't mean literary fiction is better than genre fiction ... nor that the distinction is a rigid one ... some of the best novels – *Jane Eyre, The Woman in White* – have a foot in both camps. ... When I was writing for children, I was writing genre fiction. It was like making a good chair. However beautiful it looked, it needed four legs of the same length, it had to be the right height, and it had to be comfortable. ... With *The Curious Incident* I was trying to do something different ... the book has a simple language, a carefully shaped plot and invites you to enter somebody else's life. And these, I think, are the aspects of the book that appeal to most younger readers.
>
> (Haddon, *Observer*, 11 April 2004)

Although the distinctions are not rigid ones, Mark Haddon does see *writing for children* as a special type of genre. It needed to do certain things writing for adults did not. *The Curious Incident* was something different from his previous books. While it invites you to share someone else's experience (an essential quality in all good fiction writing) and while it is written in simple language, he makes no apologies for its *adult* theme:

> It isn't entirely comfortable. It's about how little separates us from those we turn away from in the street. It's about how badly we communicate with one another. It's about accepting that every life is narrow and that our only escape from this is not to run away (to another country, another relationship, a slimmer, more confident self) but to learn to love the people we are and the world in which we find ourselves.
>
> (Ibid)

The truths the story delivers are harsh for adults – generally speaking these are adults interested in other relationships, slimmer selves. Christopher, aged fifteen, the main character of the novel, is in a position where adults and their understanding of the world could cause him very serious distress. How they see him and how he sees them is going to be decisive. In Philip Pullman's stories the same situation applies. Crossover fiction frequently points to a major crisis in child-adult relationships, which would explain its increasing appeal to both types of reader.

I shall come back to this point later, but let us start by thinking about what Haddon means by 'making a good chair'. Whether or not it appeals to adults, fiction written for children has to *work*, and its judges, its readers, have to agree; there can be no compromise. So it's therefore important that we reflect on what it is that goes into the making of a good story for children, one that stands up to the test of readability.

Reading for Pleasure

In fiction for children, a character's grasp of his or her own world in place and time is going to be the central issue for every young reader. Is this grasp strong and deliberate or weak? The characters' experience in a story must be imaginable *to those children who are reading,* must be part of a world they can inhabit. But that doesn't mean it has to be a known and familiar every-day form of reality. As we shall see, a great many children's books contain references to magic. (As another branch of its enquiry, the present chapter includes an extended section on that very subject.) But before we reach that point, we need to consider other basic issues. Writing for children (I mainly limit myself to the ten to fifteen age range) requires an understanding of how children read when they read for pleasure, what they look for, what is it they enjoy. As with other types of audience, the combination of expectation and surprise will serve as one useful measure of that enjoyment.

Writing for Younger Readers

In much new writing for younger readers we can already see how escape fantasy, the world of elsewhere, clashes with here and now, the world of the ordinary. Both have their markers (characters, objects, actions, events) as a fiction develops, and one of the signs of reading pleasure is recognising such narrative markers or counters in a story.

Some picture stories for very young children offer vivid examples. In Margaret Mahy's *The Lion in the Meadow*, a mother is coping with a restless youngster as well as a new baby. This is a very familiar situation for children – as well as for the adult storyteller-reader. It's also worth adding at this point that when a story is being read to a child, the adult storyteller's own interest is something every writer for children must cultivate. The adult reading the story aloud needs to be able to feel – and to show – his or her own sense of enjoyment. Children learn the feeling of pleasure by *hearing* it first in the reading voice.

So there has to be something in it for adults as well, as there is in *The Lion in the Meadow.* The little boy is telling his Mum that he's seen a lion in the meadow outside. She's busy with the baby and tries to distract him. Inside this matchbox, she tells him, is a tiny dragon. Take it outside and let it go. As it grows it will frighten the lion away. He does as she says, with the result that the frightened lion runs indoors and hides in the broom cupboard – a place that reminds us there are even more chores to be done – and stays there, eventually becoming a regular new member of the family. Now domesticated, the lion behaves more like a large, friendly cat. While the fantasy world's presence isn't denied, the pictures nevertheless show a typical cluttered kitchen, a house interior, pots and pans, untidiness.

The parent reader will see a child trying to attract attention to himself away from the new baby, and being successfully distracted. This reader will probably enjoy the story because its counters – matchbox, broom cupboard, kitchen – fit his or her understanding of how children need distracting games. The child's enjoyment, however, will unequivocally be based on the lion – large, but timid – and the dragon – even larger and not at all timid – and the broom cupboard – the lion's new home. The lion as a counter has been moved from outside to indoors, bringing the story to a neat, if rather bland, conclusion. The child in me, for example, would have preferred a much fiercer lion, somewhat less easy to accommodate.

This story needs 'wild' as well as domestic counters – counters from an ordinary world together with those from elsewhere. A similar story by John Burningham – again for a younger audience (many of whom might be too young to be 'readers') – is *Come Away from the Water Shirley*, where the child's flights of fancy are shown on the right-hand side of the open pages of a book, the ordinary real world on the left. This arrangement clearly opposes right-brain (imagination) with a left-brain (common-sense reason), with child on the right, adults on the left, so that both can enjoy the difference. Another example is Anthony Browne's story *Bear Hunt* where the bear, childlike, outwits his adult hunters by drawing pictures with a magic pencil that can turn the drawing of a bird into a real bird – the bear's rescuer. In this story 'drawing' becomes the main counter, growing in value as it helps the bear to escape.

Convincing worlds

Writers of fiction for older children also need to make use of narrative counters; these will become the currency of a story. But to establish that currency requires the skill of building convincing worlds – doing the same job with words that pictures would do for the younger audience. We can explore how this works by looking at two very different (or seemingly different) stories for children: Jacqueline Wilson's, *The Bed and Breakfast Star* (1995), and Stevenson's *Treasure Island*, written in 1881. Here are extracts from the first few paragraphs of each story:

> Squire Trelawney, Dr Livesey, and the rest of these gentlemen having asked me to write down the whole particulars about Treasure Island, from the beginning to the end, keeping nothing back but the bearings of the island, and that only because there is still treasure not lifted, I take up my pen in the year of grace 17..., and go back to the time when my father kept the 'Admiral Benbow' Inn, and the brown old seaman, with the sabre cut, first took up lodgings under our roof.
>
> I remember him as if it were yesterday, as he came plodding to the inn door, his sea-chest following behind him in a hand-barrow; a tall, strong, heavy, nut-brown man; his tarry pigtail falling over the shoulders of his soiled blue coat; his hands ragged and scarred, with black, broken nails; and the sabre cut across his cheek, a dirty, livid white.
>
> (Stevenson, 1994: 3)

> Do you know what everyone calls me now? *Bed and Breakfast*. That's what all the kids yell after me in the playground. Even the teachers do it. Well, they don't say it to my face. But I've heard them. 'Oh, yes, that's Elsa. She's one of the bed-and-breakfast children.' Honestly. It sounds like I've got a duvet for a dress, cornflake curls, two fried-egg eyes and a streaky-bacon smile.
>
> I don't look a bit like that. Well, I hope I don't! I'm Elsa.
>
> Do you like my name? I hope you do like it or Elsa'll get upset. Do you get the joke? I made it up myself. I'm always cracking jokes. People don't often laugh though.
>
> (Wilson, 1995: 5–6)

Both passages introduce key characters, the first as a frighteningly strange object complete with livid scar, the second as a friendly familiar voice. The first passage mentions secrets locked in the past – at least a hundred years before the story is written; the second offers an open, up-front introduction, actually a *Hello* – and a joke to match. My guess is that most children nowadays would find the first passage difficult, the second irresistible, but that's not to say that a writer for children can't learn something from both. To have a child's voice as narrator doesn't automatically mean a story will attract child readers. Children's stories without child protagonists are rare, but another factor seems to be necessary, too. The child readers of a narrative must be able to recognise its counters. They must recognise these first time through.

An example of a counter in *Treasure Island* would be the treasure map; another, the island itself; another, the scar. These are going to recur, to get moved about. While reading the story, our attention is focused on these, and children have to be able to understand that maps lead to treasure, eventually (though false maps and false trails are possible). They also have to understand that faraway islands can be dangerous, that struggles to possess both map and island are likely to cause conflict, and that such conflict will have violent effects – a 'livid scar'. The first encounter, however, is with the Admiral Benbow Inn, a place where men with old sea chests and secrets are likely to congregate. A gradually revealed secret, of course, is apt to make a good story.

Any counter or story marker must be aglow with interest for the characters – not just for readers. An object, a place, a person or people can all hold narrative energy. An action can be repeated. An event might only happen once but it can be referred to, remembered, even suppressed – it can be a narrative counter. As adult readers we can sense it too, but child readers wouldn't be able to if the story in question offered no image, voice, scene or world that triggered their feeling of recognition. Adult readers can wait for that sense of a trigger, children can't. While most adult readers *can* cope with narrative qualities that might seem comparatively lacking in shape, children need to form an impression of an available story element quickly and hang on to it. But how do they do this when, as in the case of Jacqueline Wilson's story, a term like 'bed and breakfast' applies? What is a 'Bed and Breakfast' star? On first hearing, the term doesn't make sense. Wilson realised *she needed to tell the full story* leading up to the bed and breakfast incidents in the narrative, or get her protagonist, Elsa, to tell it. Elsa does it very well. But when we actually reach the point when the family is made homeless and gets offered bed and breakfast accommodation at the 'Royal Hotel' ('it started to look a bit shabby the nearer we got') our need to recognise this counter requires close-up realist style at its most immediate:

> Mum was carrying Hank [Elsa's baby brother]. He got a bit squashed and started squawking. Pippa's mouth went wobbly and she tried to clutch at Mum too.
>
> 'I don't like this place, Mum,' she said. 'We don't have to go and live here, do we?'
>
> 'No, we don't, kids. We're not living in a dump like this,' said Mum. She kicked the litter in the driveway. An old Chinese takeaway leaked orange liquid all over her suede shoes.
>
> 'For heaven's sake,' Mum wept. 'Look at all this muck. There'll be rats. And if it's like this outside, what's it going to be like inside? Cockroaches. Fleas. I'm not taking my kids into a lousy dump like this.'
>
> (Ibid: 25)

More terrifying than pirate-infested islands is that Chinese takeaway on that shoe, a striking reality effect. The 'Hotel' might have no treasure, but does issue its own kind of challenge, and Jacqueline Wilson makes it seriously clear to her readers what 'bed and breakfast' actually means. Now established, this setting can be used repeatedly as a counter in the drama of the story. It had been held back, ready to be moved forward to hold our attention, as it does here with obvious impact. Another counter – Elsa's jokes – Wilson keeps in reserve.

A defining quality in Wilson's books is their structure. Her characters enter the story, move to a low point in it, then gradually start to ascend, usually as a result of a gift or talent they possess – something not valued, like Elsa's jokes – until circumstances change. Her jokes are a talent, like the ability to draw in *Bear Hunt*, though at first nobody values them very much. She tells jokes mostly to cheer herself up. The joke counter therefore must be held back. Though we are constantly treated to Elsa's wit as entertainment (and a lot of her jokes are genuinely funny), it doesn't start to function as a big advantage until much later. In fiction for children these basic story elements or counters are vital in the development of a plot, and readers of any age will need to sense them, to feel their importance, to know what they stand for in the overall picture the narrative generates. There must be no doubt about what 'bed and breakfast' signifies. The same is true for 'island', 'treasure', and 'map'. It's no accident that in each case the most powerful counters appear in the story's title.

A counter should be an encounter for its readers; we feel we have stumbled on something, have seen something placed in our way – a signal or signifier. As well as what maps or islands mean to us, or to the generation reading the story, the meaning exists foremost in the feeling-response of a character, someone who was really there and saw and felt, and then somehow put it all into words. Elsa reacts, also reacts to her mother's reaction, then records it, tells it to us. The whole scene above is filled with reactions. But at no point does the character say 'I felt depressed, angry, resentful, disappointed, upset, really horrified, fed up'. It's as if all the explaining general and obvious words were omitted, possibly even banned. The stamp of this writer is that she will not use them, but instead gives us the visual moment and image: 'orange liquid all over her suede shoes'. You can display such counters in the abstract – 'We were so upset. It was all such an incredible mess', or you can turn them back into an experience, through details, actions, speeches, moments, events. The reason this makes for good writing is that emotion and feeling are really rooted in a material world and in the arrangement of particular circumstances. Good writing reminds us this is the case.

The child narrator: how to survive Paddy Clarke

Roddy Doyle's Booker Prize winning *Paddy Clark Ha Ha Ha*, with its ten-year-old narrator, is an adult novel for adult readers. But how do we tell the difference between this story and a book for children also having a ten-year-old narrator? The difference should be obvious. By comparing the two we should be able to gain some sense of the elements of fiction child readers look for when they read. Sometimes there won't be a distinction. *Jane Eyre* and *David Copperfield*, both with child narrators, continue to bridge the gap by attracting readers of all ages. But when we compare Doyle's narrator with one of the same age in a Jaqueline Wilson story – the one I choose here is *How To Survive Summer Camp* – a considerable number of differences show up.

How to describe these differences is the problem. How would child readers describe them? We can, of course, ask them what they think by setting up an experiment. But equally useful would be our experience – as adults – of putting ourselves in their place. As it happens, the opening paragraphs of *Paddy Clarke* are typical of the book's style throughout:

> We were coming down our road. Kevin stopped at a gate and bashed it with his stick. It was Missis Quigley's gate; she was always looking out of the window but she never did anything
> — Quigley!
> — Quigley!
> — Quigley Quigley Quigley!
> Liam and Aidan turned down their cul-de-sac. We said nothing; they said nothing. Liam and Aidan had a dead mother, Missis O'Connell was her name.
> — It'd be brilliant, wouldn't it? I said.
> — Yeah, said Kevin. – Cool.
> We were talking about having a dead ma. Sinbad, my little brother, started crying. Liam was in my class in school. He dirtied his trousers one day – the smell of it rushed at us like the blast of heat when an oven door was opened – and the master did nothing. He didn't shout or slam his desk with his leather or anything. He told us to fold our arms and go asleep and when we did he carried Liam out of the class. He didn't come back for ages and Liam didn't come back at all.
> James O'Keefe whispered,
> — If I did a geek in me pants he'd kill me!
> — Yeah.
> — It's not fair, said James O'Keefe. — So it's not.
> The Master, Mister Hennessey, hated James O'Keefe. He'd be writing something on the board with his back to us and he'd say,
> — O'Keefe, I know you're up to something down there. Don't let me catch you. He said it one morning and James O'Keefe wasn't even in. He was at home with the mumps.
>
> (Doyle, 1995:1–2)

Teasing Mrs Quigley, Mr Hennessey's attitude to his pupils, Liam's toilet incident, James's aggrieved response – this passage offers several anecdotes, any of which might serve as a narrative sign, a counter that counts with readers of the story, a point of recurrence. But as we read on, their follow-up seems hardly perceptible, certainly not obvious. The text continues for almost half its length before even adult readers can reach any consensus about its direction. What we have is a holistic account or impression, a kind of *gestalt* of Paddy's childhood. The focus is on Paddy's attitude to himself, the world, other adults and children, and much of this experience is illegible to him as a whole; he can only see it in small pieces. He occupies separate episodes of it in turn but not in any order. To us, as we read the whole becomes visible gradually, to Paddy Clarke even more gradually. The idea of instant access markers or counters therefore doesn't apply in this kind of narrative and would be distinctly inappropriate. Adults as a rule cope with this partial visibility/invisibility, this gradualness in the process of reading. Child readers, however, are unlikely to.

In Wilson's story, *How to Survive Summer Camp*, the narrator is female, about the same age as Paddy Clarke, more clearly a story-teller, a teller, that is, of *one particular story* rather than a holder of anecdotes of childhood drawn out at random. Here is how it begins:

> I sat in the back of the car in my new T-shirt and my stiff new jeans and my pristine trainers and groaned. I kept dabbing at my new haircut. It felt terrible. Everyone would laugh at me. I thought about all these strange children at the summer camp. I peered down at the black lettering on my emerald green T-shirt. It said I LOVE EVERGREEN ADVENTURE HOLIDAYS. My new T-shirt was a liar.
>
> 'Are you all right, Stella?' Mum asked worriedly, turning round. 'Do you feel sick? You look a bit green.'
>
> 'To match my awful T-shirt,' I muttered, tugging at it.
>
> 'I think you look very fetching in your new outfit,' said Uncle Bill.
>
> I didn't answer. I just pulled a face at his back. I couldn't stick my Uncle Bill. Which was a great pity, because he'd married Mum that morning.
>
> I was the bridesmaid. Mum had bought me a very expensive blue dress with puff sleeves and a long flouncy skirt. It had its own white lace pinafore and with my plaits undone and combed out Mum said I looked like Alice in Wonderland.
>
> (Wilson, 1999:1)

Wilson assumes her readers will know – or be able to guess at least – what Alice in Wonderland looks like, and that Alice is part of their narrative culture. Writers cannot avoid these assumptions, and are mostly able to get them right. Alice belongs to the same culture as nursery rhyme figures:

> Only I didn't look like Alice at the wedding after all. I looked more like Humpty Dumpty, as bald as a boiled egg.

> It was all a terrible mistake. Mum said I could go to a posh hairdressers and have my hair properly cut and styled the week before the wedding. She wanted to come with me but she had to work. I said I could go by myself, I wasn't a baby.
>
> So I went after school and talked to this man called Kevin who looked like a rock star. He asked me how I wanted my hair cut. I decided I didn't want it too short. I measured a tiny amount with my thumb and finger. Kevin nodded and his scissors flashed. I screamed as they snipped. He hadn't understood. Before I could get away he'd snipped one side of my head to a stubble. He'd thought I wanted it that length!
>
> He couldn't leave it like that, half stubble, half flowing golden corn, so he sheered the rest off. Mum cried when she saw me. Uncle Bill said he thought I looked cute, but he was only pretending.
>
> (Ibid: 1–2)

The details here add up to a very clear message: 'I hate my appearance, and my step-dad, I'm unhappy, and I don't want to go to summer camp. I'm going, though, since I've got no choice. And what about the other children there?!' Hair-cut, step-dad, summer camp, other children – all these are strong counters *and established as such for the speaker, too.* For child readers they act as pointers in a forward narrative direction. As one reviewer of Wilson's fiction, herself a writer, points out: 'Wilson has the art of locating the really important details, often insignificant to adults, by which children navigate through their world.' The precise point is indeed navigation. The child reader feels he or she is entering charted waters, mapped with visible markers, but treacherous. The narrator, Stella, feels this too, and is trying to establish her own map of the probable dangers ahead. The young Paddy Clarke has no map – he doesn't yet feel he needs one. He navigates his bit of coast without realising until late in the story that there are life-changing currents, sunken reefs.

Counters in Adult Fiction

Doyle offers much more for the adult reader, even though his protagonist is a child. It frequently happens in adult fiction that *characters* are also *readers* of the text of reality. They make interpretations, generate stories, produce their own readings of the real. Adult readers of adult fiction will be able to identify the complexity and force of the counter 'Middlemarch' – the town and its culture, for example, by how characters themselves come to understand it as their stronger ambitions develop, by how they themselves encounter it in more ways than as a backdrop of scene or local colour. Adult fictions create a range of ever more complex counters, complex to the point where they seem not to be counters but something else. The father's Alzheimer's disease recurrently haunts Jonathan Franzen's *The Corrections*, but its gradualness, and the fact that the characters aren't willing to discuss it, means its visibility isn't at all obvious. We must decode the impairment carefully, marked as it is by the characters' own disgust and embarrassment, by their evasiveness and retreat, from a mass of deliberately confused signals. In this case, and to some degree in *Paddy Clark*, an avoidance tactic stands between characters and the truth. That kind of explicable confusion appeals to adult readers of adult fiction, whilst in children's fiction characters who mislead themselves and others have no place in the hearts of sympathetic readers. In books for children child characters need to be more definite, or to be able to ask definite questions. Counters assume that kind of character and opportunity. The world has to be instantly legible, or comparatively so, and the characters fully inclined to read its markers clearly.

Counters in *Curious Incident*

As an example of crossover fiction, how does Mark Haddon's novel operate? The narrator tells us he is writing a 'murder mystery novel' and also that it's about 'something that happened to him'. We suspect that it's a memoir-like record, a type of diary, but as fiction or as diary he is a narrator who reads signs, looks for clues, collects information, struggles to make sense of it. What counts with him are images and facts he can understand. Younger readers will respond to this deliberate search for clues going on whenever Christopher finds something unusual, something that captures his attention. Adult readers will also realise that Christopher is often getting it wrong – through no fault of his own – and that this obsessive attraction to data is a manifestation of his illness; Asperger's syndrome, a form of autism. The narrative markers are simple in one sense, complex in another.

Like Wilson, Haddon is writing in first person narration, and yet, like Doyle, this is a story whose counters are sometimes misread. The person we hear about most in the story misses the story. As adult readers we are in a better position to know what's going on than the person who tells it to us. The story is *not* just about a curious incident involving a dog – which Christopher thinks it is (to him, the dog killed in the night is a major counter: it counts with him). The story is about his mother and father, just as Paddy Clarke's story is really about his Ma and Da. But it starts off being the sort of story Christopher would have thoroughly enjoyed: one involving a puzzle, a proof, a solution. Like mathematics – his passion. Christopher reads his experience in terms of counters that will and can appeal *to him*, and to readers like himself or younger, while adult readers sense, of course, that the story is about much more than puzzles, incidents and solutions. In terms of its counters, it's as if Mark Haddon has given us a new kind of *Paddy Clarke* – one which children can read as well.

But Christopher isn't just a puzzle hacker. He possesses an extraordinarily strong grasp of what matters to him – a quality that is the key to his appeal. Younger readers don't ask their characters to be sensible. They can see that Christopher is very probably making mistakes, is too often thinking he's always right, is reading life for its solutions, but the problems aren't just inside Christopher's mind. The problems also exist out there in the world, in the way adults behave with each other, in their amazing attempts to deceive, in the clumsiness of their dealings with him. We know him as a person who deserves better. We also know the problems he causes his parents and his teachers. His disability sharpens his perception of the world, so that we see the chaos he sees – much of which comes from his parents' serious misunderstandings of him. Something terribly important has gone wrong. As I've already said, Haddon himself explains *The Curious Incident* as being 'about how badly we communicate with one another.'

Children and Power

In his book on the nineteenth century British novel, Peter Keating records how during the 1890s 'children were suddenly allowed to be themselves in fiction'. A major shift in social values had gradually started to change our view of the adult-child relationship. 'No longer were children praised for being pious, industrious, and well-mannered; instead the admired child was likely to be seen as imaginative, inventive, self-reliant and constantly in trouble' (Keating, 1991:220). This new viewpoint suggested that adults still exemplified all the virtues: piety, industry, good manners, but that increasingly children didn't need to follow their lead. Like Huck Finn in Mark Twain's novel, you could go off and do your own thing somewhere, find a raft and sail away downstream on the Mississippi. But a further shift was already happening. It's obvious, even in Twain's story, that adults are failing to represent higher values. Instead they are rapidly losing control. In worrying contrast to that of the child, their world is racist, violent, riddled with deceitfulness and revenge, a disaster compared with Huck's and Jim's on the river. In these conditions, children have no power and very little voice. Though they might express their opinions, all they can really do is keep their distance.

In recent years, the shift has reached even more dangerous proportions. A view of the world as secure in the hands of adults no longer holds. A place where adventures and rebellions are hatched in safety and at a distance has been largely abandoned in children's fiction. In recent books, a number of them written for adults *and* children, it is clear that parents cannot cope. Children have to step in and take up the position of authority for themselves. We can see this even in Wilson's books, filled as they are with adults whose laziness and stupidity ruin lives, especially those of the children in their care. In *Kiss File JC 110*, Linda Hoy's compelling novel for younger adults, parents and teachers make useless role models for the teenage protagonist existing on the fringes of alternative politics, exploring his sexuality, almost destroyed by deceit and ignorant neglect. During the post-war period in British fiction for children, adults seem to fare less and less well, and children struggle to take over adult responsibilities for themselves. Often they fail, and in consequence they too can enter the spiral of destruction.

While this almost happens in *Kiss File JC 110*, it happens quite explicitly in *Junk*, by Melvyn Burgess. In this story, a sixteen-year-old boy and girl leave home, join a band of travellers who beg on the streets and use the cash for crack cocaine, then heroin. They think they can stay in control of what happens to them, in control of junk, then of addiction. Even Paddy Clarke thinks he can control his parents, stop them arguing, and thus limit their power over him – a power that could wreck the security of his childhood. Parents' power to cause harm to their children may be unintentional, but it is nevertheless devastating. The young men and women who feature in crossover fiction are often seen confronting the adult world for the first time. Like refugees entering hostile territory, they are curious to learn about what goes on there, what the rules are, who is in charge – after all, their future, even their survival, might well depend on what they can find out. They rarely like what they see, it must be said. The peculiar drama of crossover fiction is that of crossover *experience*: *child to adult*.

Fiction for children is always discovering alternative worlds and spaces, as well as, in recent years, showing children forced to take control where adults have failed. In earlier stories they might have found some kind of other space – the den in the woods, the abandoned house, the derelict building site – where they could establish a safer world, a better understanding, even perhaps a more hopeful future. Publishers, however, reflecting the attitudes of anxious parents, can sometimes be wary of stories that allow children the freedom to stay away from home unsupervised. If that is the case, it is regrettable. Alternative space, in real-world fiction for children, operates as the magical does in fantasy. Like magic, it offers a redistribution of power.

Magic and Reality

If for over two centuries the growing preoccupation in fiction has been with real-world subjects and styles, with authored stories and written narrative, then children's fiction constantly reminds us that the separation between these and an earlier oral tradition is incomplete. In her introduction to the *Annotated Brothers Grimm*, A. S. Byatt makes a point that the power of fairy tales, folk tales, legends and divine stories, far from being abandoned by novelists, influenced the new genre. '*Mansfield Park* is 'Cinderella'. *Middlemarch* contrasts the diligent and lazy daughters. ... Witches and dwarves, ogres and wolves, lurk in Dickens and Hawthorne ...' She also refers to Angela Carter and Salman Rushdie, who 'claimed that there was more energy in the old tales than in the recent social realism'. (Byatt, Norton, 2004). An impulse towards experiment colours their writing, bringing a playful but fierce extravagance to the telling of old stories in new ways. As we have seen in stories for younger children (see p.159), a play with narrative can itself generate humour, intelligence, imaginative interest, and the strong participation of parents. Children can be involved in the making of meaning, not just in the reception of it ready-made. But in some contemporary fiction for children, magic takes its place alongside reality, as if to be believed – at least to be taken seriously by its audience, very possibly also by the novelist. We enter a world of transformations, shape-shifting, the mercurial, totem animals, daemons, other worlds. The wilderness period of human development suddenly stands close to us again, reminding us of how revelation, beauty, danger and terror were once everyday truths.

One point must be clear from the start: by 'magic' we don't mean sleight of hand, illusion or conjuring. It would certainly be possible to write an attractive and powerful story for children about a conjurer. But for the moment that's not our main line of enquiry. Let's assume that a magic element operates so widely in children's fiction that anyone writing stories for children will need to understand why it's there, how it works in a story, how it combines with a world of familiar reference where people prefer drinking water to dragon's blood. Let's also assume a range of readers in the years just before and during adolescence, and a story hero or heroine of the same age. What we can't assume is that all fictions that include magic will be of the same type or tone or approach; these will vary. What differences, for example, might we see between the Harry Potter stories and Philip Pullman's trilogy *His Dark Materials*, or between either of these and *Lord of the Rings*?

Compared with *His Dark Materials* and *Lord of the Rings,* some might see the Harry Potter stories more as a trip to the circus of magic than an experience of the magical. Similarly, Angela Carter's novels and stories might be described as experimental play rather than encounters with the wondrous. But even when doubts are expressed there is no doubting that the energy released has produced liberating results and that one of the releasing triggers has been escape from representations of the familiar. Student writers often express through their own work a similar need to escape. What can't be escaped, however, is realisation – the need, whatever subject or world you want to evoke, whether blood-sucking bats or school common-rooms, talking hats or Hampstead dinner-parties, to make that world real and habitable to its readers. As I have said repeatedly in this book, the key to good writing lies in a realist style as first practice, no matter how real or how far from the real the subject-matter, characters, scenes and settings are for your story. Whatever we mean by magic as such, the real magic occurs for readers in narrative realisation, the solid performance of an illusion before your very eyes and as you read, and in this sense the writer is involved in a kind of conjuring.

Characters in stories involving magic don't see its effects as take-it-or-leave-it forms of illusion or as entertainment. The consequences are often too overwhelming. Encounters with magic cause them to feel a sense of real evil, inexplicable good, and also to feel that these are forces in opposition. But how do we recognise the magical? In terms of stories, characters and events, what might be its manifestations? Below are summaries of stories for children, illustrating real-world and magic effects in a range of combinations.

Madame Doubtfire

Anne Fine's story about three children and their divorced parents includes a sixth character, Madame Doubtfire, who acts as a cook/home-help in their mother's house. Problems? While Dad is an out-of-work actor living alone, seeing his children briefly only once or twice a week, their mother has a successful job in business. When she advertises for assistance at home, Madame Doubtfire, who seems a perfect choice, fills the post. This lady, extravagantly dressed, but also highly efficient, a hit with the kids, turns out to be their father disguised in drag (as we might have guessed). The children realise this almost at once while their mother, at first too busy to notice, is outraged when she discovers the deception. A terrible argument between their estranged parents shocks the children. They finally stage-manage a truce, insist on a better understanding, and look forward to a more stable future. The story is at times harshly real; contemporary in its reference to divorce and family conflict. Nevertheless Madame Doubtfire brings relief of a kind indirectly associated with magic. Her name itself, mysterious, outlandish, derives from the pantomime season – a dame figure – where magic is stage entertainment, live performance. Lydia, however, the oldest child, whilst enchanted by her father as Doubtfire and her home kitchen transformed into a 'brightly lit stage' still prefers him as himself. She dislikes the illusion since it deprives her of his real presence. Behind her stated preference for the real lies the sense that she is growing up. Magic as entertainment (if that is what the story in part offers) now belongs firmly back in childhood. As children grow up they need to reason things out (the story implies), and take responsibility for what they themselves want.

The Sleeping Sword

This story by Michael Morpurgo, told from the point of view of a twelve-year-old boy permanently blind from a swimming accident, is set in the Scilly Isles west of Cornwall. The boy, whose name is Bun Bendle, finds a sword from Dark Age Britain unearthed from a field his father is ploughing with a tractor. Holding it by the hilt he feels a surge of power that seems both revelatory and dangerous. In a dream he grasps the sword again and finds himself in the company of Bedevere, one of King Arthur's knights. This was the King's sword Excalibur, which Bedevere had promised to throw into a lake just before Arthur's death. Now it's been found alongside the knight's bones. In a series of dreams Bun travels with Anna, the girl he loves, to an island that resembles the face of a sleeping warrior in profile. In a moonlit cavern he meets with the King and his knights. Arthur tells him to place the sword back in the stone from which it was first drawn. '*But how?*' I asked. '*How can I do it? It's impossible.*' The answer comes: '*Believe it will happen and it will.*' In a later dream Bun wakes and believes his eyes can see again. Bun dictates his story onto tape; Anna types it into her computer. It ends with the thought that his dreams have been prophetic, that contact with the sword has acted upon him with a healing force. The 'wonderful miracle' has been achieved by the presence of a magic object from myth acting through dreams to strengthen belief in the healing powers of the world. This is magic not as entertainment but as folklore, yet coexisting with a contemporary recognisable reality, relationships with friends, family, and the farming community of the islands. There's a sense that you are not the possessor but the instrument of powers synchronised with your hidden best interests – a sense derived from centuries of living in close touch with natural forces – here with the sea in particular on an outpost of land, closer perhaps than usual to wilderness. Bun resists having to attend a special school on the mainland. To stay with the people he knows and trusts is important to him; it places him in range of a healing power, a structure of favour, a Celtic notion of luck, not that he could explain it in such terms. The power remains a mystery, filtered through dreams.

Harry Potter and the Philosopher's Stone

Signed by his scar, Harry has to learn about good and evil, how sometimes they can seem indistinguishable. J. K. Rowling's first book in the series offers a perspective on growing up, a period of change, adventure, danger, discovery, signified by Harry's experience of his new school. The fact that this is Hogwarts, a school for wizards, doesn't mean that things will be that different from other schools on his first day. There's still the problem of making new friends, and enemies, learning who's who among the teachers, who's to be trusted, liked, disliked, given a wide berth. The fact that owls fetch and carry messages, dragons feed on chicken blood and brandy, ball games are played in the air by pupils on broomsticks, generates humour but hardly magic in any Celtic or Excalibur sense. We might, however, speculate about why certain animals and not others are judged as magical. The book is a catalogue of magic conventions, an inventory of occult paraphernalia, animate and inanimate, sometimes both: hats that talk, books that scream. Owls, bats, frogs, crows, cats are included but not pigs, donkeys, cows, sheep, swallows. Herd animals have little or no dealings with the supernatural, compared with those of the night, of winter, the wilderness, creatures that screech, croak, fly or swim in two worlds. This is the magic of the North European kind. Broomsticks resemble dead or leafless branches, fly in storms and skies lit by the moon. Harry has to learn the arcane signs, attend lessons in new and frightening subjects – potions, spells, alchemical formulae – get into trouble and out of it. The world of magic, wizards, ghosts, witches and their accomplices is in conflict with ordinary reality – the world of the Muggles – and we know which is the more adventurous, creative and witty. We also know that the world of magic contains a supreme evil – and Harry himself encounters it consciously just before the end. (He has encountered it before, unconsciously, as a child.) Harry bears several attributes of the hero of folklore. Separated from his birth parents, after an obscure upbringing, a rise to fame, a brush with death, he stands to gain a most prized reward – in this case, the Philosopher's Stone – the danger of which will always be that it falls in the wrong hands.

Skellig

Somewhere in a disused garage an old man lives on owl pellets and dead spiders. The boy – Michael – who discovers him, has a baby sister suffering from what could be a fatal illness. He has a friend called Mina who reads William Blake, who 'saw angels in his garden'. Michael and his family have just moved house. The house is falling to pieces, as is the garage and the garden they call a wilderness. The old man transforms into an angel; he can fly. Holding his hands, Michael and Mina are lifted from the floor by a flow of mysterious energy. Michael's mother dreams of an angel. The baby girl is taken to hospital where she has a heart operation. Michael remembers:

> I listened to the drone of the city outside, to the clatter of the hospital. I heard my own breathing, the scared quick breathing of my parents at my side. I heard them sniffing back their tears. I went on listening. I listened through all these noises, until I heard the baby, the gentle squeaking of her breath, tiny and distant as if it came from a different world. I closed my eyes and went on listening and listening. I listened deeper, until I believed I heard her beating heart. I told myself that if I listened hard enough her breathing and the beating of her heart would never be able to stop.
>
> (Almond, 1998: 91)

A few days later the baby recovers. The drift of the story from dereliction and hopelessness to strength and recovery is an experience structured around Skellig's transformation into an angel. Magic functions in this story by implying links between seemingly disconnected events. Such an archaic view of the world is especially relevant to major life happenings – illness, recovery, love, death – reviving our sense of the marvellous as real. David Almond's story not only brings us closer to Blake, however. It takes place in the world of school classrooms, biology lessons, football fixtures, Chinese takeaways, hospital wards, operating theatres. The archaic and modern coexist.

Writers can obviously write stories for children without making any reference whatsoever to magic or the supernatural. Given the presence of this element in so much of the fiction children read, however, it must be worth thinking about why a tradition supporting magic and the supernatural continues with interesting contemporary developments. Equally, perhaps, we should consider why so many books and stories for children contain animal characters, record the close contact of humans and animals, even show their interchangeable nature. A unique development has been Philip Pullman's trilogy. In these stories human beings and their animal daemons coexist in bonds whose dissolution is resisted by both to the point of death. Yet far from being a unique invention found only in children's fiction during the last few decades, this bonding of human and animal into a single spiritual identity has been occurring in human cultures for many thousands of years. To be deprived of one's totem animal leads to an essential atrophy of the spirit, a death of the soul of the kind that Pullman's girl hero Lyra fears and is threatened by in *Northern Lights*, his first novel of the series. It may be that children's fiction keeps alive a set of relationships that were considered of vital importance, not just for a flimsy aim such as happiness, but for survival. A daemon is another word for a person's bush soul, a 'spirit' that defends the human spirit against all forms of alienation. Magic was also a practical means of ensuring we acted cautiously when faced with inexplicable events; also a means of trying to ensure some control over powers that at times seemed to possess malevolent intentions, at other times to reward us with the miraculous.

It seems to follow, therefore, that anyone aiming to write for children – or, we should say, for children becoming adult, and/or children who are encouraged to develop intelligence, imagination, and an adventurous spirit – will have to put their minds in a new place, one where the world as we know it is still millennia away from the present. Yet each of the writers whose works have been quoted above, in dealing with the magical, does so whilst also respecting the ordinary in reality. Both worlds – magic and familiar – receive serious attention. This is especially true of *Skellig*, where the secret in the garage cannot be divulged to just anybody, and becomes known only to Michael and Mina. Michael has two school friends – Leakey and Coot. Both boys are suspicious of his growing friendship with Mina, the 'girl who lives in a tree', who stays at home to learn from her mother instead of attending school, who talks about William Blake. "Who's he?' said Coot. 'That bloke that's got the butcher's shop in town?' 'He said school drives all joy away,' I said. 'He was a painter and a poet.' They looked at each other and grinned' (Ibid: 100–1). Unless the story can be felt and appreciated by children from different backgrounds and with different types of intelligence, it won't work. It has to engage with a wide reality, not just Blake's and Skellig's, Michael's and Mina's. The central struggle within the story is to negotiate agreement between contrasting worlds. It has to be written, as it were, for Leakey and Coot: a salutary lesson for all writers for children. Towards the end, Michael himself registers a need to tell the story to those from whom he's previously kept it secret. For the duration, his friendship with Leakey has especially been neglected. – "It's like you've been miles and miles away' ... 'I know,' I said. 'Would you tell me about it?' he said. We paused and I looked at him and I knew he really wanted to know. 'Someday I'll tell you everything,' I said' (Ibid: 160).

Fiction as Record

Writing for children often shows how social problems bite into private experience. The damage caused by such problems can be harsh. Crossover fictions such as *Kiss* and *Junk*, also *The Curious Incident* and, to a significant degree, Jacqueline Wilson's stories, record not only the conditions but also the felt issues of recent history. The further back we look into the past, the more it appears that major events – a revolution, civil war, rule by some tyrant or mad monarch – loom up to dominate our perspective. We tend to see life only in their shadow. But in fact we often need to look away from these historical turning points. What else was going on? What was that like? Fiction for adults and children can supplement the official record of what happens in this or that decade, and tell us what we might not want to know.

Another type of children's writing deals with a major event in the past but explores beyond the familiar record so that fresh outlooks can be found. A historical event is, by definition, one that affects everybody – or enough of us at any one time or location to deserve special scrutiny, a search for understanding, dramatic and fictional representation, the generating of images. To look behind the cultural imaging, see the past in close-up, not just as wished for or subsequently received, has moved many writers for children to adopt the point of view of a young protagonist living through such events. Berlie Doherty chose the scene of a small village for her novel *Deep Secret* (another example of a crossover novel) about the flooding of a valley in Derbyshire in the last century and the making of a new reservoir. Robert Westall's *The Machine Gunners*, and *A Time of Fire*, both refer back to the Second World War as their pivotal experience.

In the first scene of *A Time of Fire*, the main character lives in a house near a street bombed during an air raid. His mother has just asked him to go to the corner shop for some matches; when he makes an excuse she goes herself. A few minutes later the shop is hit; his mother is killed. This event drives the remaining narrative. In the story that follows, the author's own experience of the war – he was ten in 1939 – is expanded by his adult knowledge and research to create scenes that almost never veer out of range of bombs, existing as consequences of that sudden, unexpected encounter with the enemy. The novel ends before the war is over; the characters undergo prolonged periods of anxiety and change as the conflict bites deep into their lives. People talk about 'losing every battle except the last'; they speak in idioms now out of use, such as 'what a swizz' and 'good riddance', while cities are overwhelmed by blitz. From a child's perspective, there might not be much hope. At the time of the retreat from Dunkirk ('The name to Sonny sounded like somewhere in Scotland'), no one has any high expectations:

> It paralysed him, standing there staring down at the newly buried potatoes. Mr Chamberlain, the Prime Minister, had been sacked, because he was a flop. Suppose things didn't get better? Suppose Mr Churchill was a flop as well? Suppose all the British were flops? Like the Poles, the Dutch, the Belgians...
>
> (Westall, 2002: 56)

Sonny's story – made real through the vividness of its picturing – may not match the bleakness and terror (written with attention to simple facts) that made Ian Serrallier's *The Silver Sword* our classic war text for children. Here is how Edek tells the story of his escape from Germany back into Poland – by hanging face down under the wagon of a train:

> 'Lying on my stomach, I found the view rather monotonous. It made me dizzy too. I had to shut my eyes. And the bumping! ... Then the train ran through a puddle. More than a puddle – it must have been a flood, for I was splashed and soaked right through. But that water saved me. After that I couldn't let go, even if I'd wanted to.'
>
> 'Why not?' said Jan, impressed.
>
> 'The water froze on me. It made an icicle of me. When at last the train drew into a station, I was encased in ice from head to foot. I could hear Polish voices on the platform. I knew we must have crossed the frontier. My voice was the only part of me that wasn't frozen, so I shouted. The station-master came and chopped me down with an axe. He wrapped me in blankets and carried me to a boiler-house to thaw out. Took me hours to thaw out.'
>
> (Serrallier, 1956: 84–5)

As well as the retelling of stories based on events familiar to audiences, writers for children have revisited scenes from myth and romance, as in the Arthurian stories retold by T. H. White, Marion Bradley, and others, or stories from the Greek myths in Charles Kingsley's *The Heroes.* Our knowledge of history always leaves new corners to explore. Rosemary Sutcliffe's novels about the Romans do just this, from the point of view of a youthful protagonist able to show us the unique conditions of place and period, while Philip Pullman's novel *The Tiger In The Well* recreates Victorian London's docklands and the slave labour forced upon immigrants in the city. We imagine, of course, that such evils only belong in the past, but the quality of realisation in this story makes it ever-present. As elsewhere in Pullman's fiction, adult characters can and do assume the face of an evil that acts in hiding, operates deliberately by concealment.

Research Ideas

To discover a story that takes you back into times made real and palpable through words is one of the most powerful experiences of reading available to children. They are not just learning about the past, but doing it in a way that quickens their sympathies and the imagination. But before you can write a story with this purpose you must yourself have responded to things, people, events in the past with an equal degree of excitement. Research will never supply the excitement in itself. Fortunately, for those moved to it, there is no shortage of stimuli. Living memory, when revived in conversation or interview, will always provide the sense of a voice speaking about the past, whether or not what's actually said is accurate and objective. Perhaps we should never expect it to be. Sometimes that voice itself can trigger the urge to write. But living memory usually travels only two or three generations back. Your grandmother may be able to remember the sayings and stories of her grandmother, who could remember hers, but only in a world where such things were passed on and that kind of memory for voices and family history was valued and cultivated. If you belong to a family of that sort then you're in luck, and not just as a writer.

The more usual route into the past requires some searching and persistence. Near where I work in York is the Yorkshire Film Archive, and many such archives exist in other regions. Watching scenes preserved in these archived films, some footage going back a hundred years, can help us develop a sense of the actual moment, what it contained as it moves forward inching ever closer to our present, a moment that's inhabited, like ours. This was real, we think: these faces, those hands, those horses piling snow, these soldiers on leave in the Great War, those clearing snow from railways stretching high over the moors as if they were excavating a quarry. The use of archive film for writing has yet to come into its own, and much of it figures children. Local and national newspapers hold stories going back for over a century. Local history societies may hold similar archive material. The emphasis on the local – always one of the source streams for fiction – means that you have a starting point. The setting you choose – a town, city, area of countryside – will be where you need to look. But your search can also be supplemented by internet sites – a writer friend of mine recently spent several hours looking up information on Humber Pilots, exploring the link between ships and shipping communities. In any museum we can now find re-creations of domestic living space, especially kitchens: a complete setting lacking only voices. The minor events and small forgotten corners of history are waiting to be recovered; it's these that carry the sense of the real.

Questions and Summary

Do I need to know something about the world children live in? Yes, and one way into this is to listen carefully to their voices – how they speak, what they say, how they communicate with each other and adults. You can find out what appeals to them in the stories they read, hear and tell. You also need to think about their perspective, their excitements, their concerns, their qualities of humour and energy, and to produce a sense of these in the atmosphere of your writing. Also think about your own children, your own childhood and that of your parents and grandparents – the generations before – and how their experience compares with your own.

Do books for children have to appeal to adults? If a story is one that is read aloud to a child, it must appeal to the person reading it, too. Crossover fiction attracts both child and adult readers, and usually involves older children or young adult characters. It can often (though not always) highlight problems in the relationship between adults and children, with the faults being mainly on the side of the adults. Adults also take an interest in this problem. They also like spectacular effects – the impact of vast spaces, primeval landscapes, fights between armies with outlandish weapons, armoured bears, huge forests; the good, the bad, the ugly and the stupid.

Do children prefer nice sentimental stories to harsh, realistic ones? Definitely not. The opposite is true. If you tend to think of the world of childhood as cosy and safe, you will have to change this view if you want to write successfully for children. You may feel sentimental about your own childhood but this view will not appeal to your readers. It's better to exaggerate the harshness rather than try to avoid it.

Is it easier to write for children than adults? Children's writing requires the same attention to detail as writing for adults. The difference is that child readers need clear narrative markers or counters: objects, events, people and places that signify immediately and are memorable. Fairy-tales always include strong counters such as a magic porridge pot, a glass slipper, a cottage made of sweets and chocolates, feathers dropped on the path through the woods to find your way home, a fairy godmother, a clock at midnight, a frog that speaks. Developing good narrative counters and embedding them in realistic narrative is a considerable skill. (See the comment by another writer on Jacqueline Wilson, p. 166, above.)

Is it important to have a child narrator? Most stories for children have child narrators, though this does not guarantee a successful story. Your narrator needs to be a good storyteller, with a feel for the story as a whole. Paddy Clarke in Doyle's novel tells wonderful anecdotes but can't see the overall shape of what is happening. Sometimes the shape is difficult to see, but readers need to be steered away from feeling too much confusion. Melvyn Burgess's novel *Junk*, for example, uses several narrators, speaking in the first person, one after the other. None of them can see where the story is heading, but the reader will have a pretty good idea. Third-person narration is usually focalised through a character's point of view, and often these characters are children. Overall, it's important to have a character whose response to his or her surroundings and to other characters is imaginative and definite, and who speaks in a way that child readers appreciate. To write for children you need to know what your main character is thinking, how he or she is reacting. You need to make the main character's attitude strong and clear. In fiction for children it is *the characters, especially the main character*, who must decide which events, places, actions, are the significant counters for him or her.

In children's fiction, how important is the relationship with adults? It is always a significant element in stories for children, though perspectives have changed. Stories show children taking on adult roles, and the adventure motif – going off on your own, doing your own thing, then returning to the comfort of home and family – no longer fits normal reality. Instead, home itself can be chaotic, and parents may be unable to offer enough stability. This situation is in constant flux, and new ways of describing the adult-child relationship will appear in stories for children. Crossover fiction ('crossover' also means changing from child to adult), shows children's highly critical view of the world they are about to enter.

Do you have to know a lot about specialised subjects such as magic, religion, myth and history? If you want to write about these subjects, then you have to feel their importance for yourself, imaginatively, and this should be the impulse that leads to research. Magic in children's fiction, obviously popular, has several manifestations, yet a constant feature is the difference between the magical and the real. Attention is often paid to ordinary reality (or to some symbol of the ordinary – the 'Shires' in *Lord Of The Rings*, for example) from which the narrative then takes flight and to which it returns. Magic changes power relationships, setting child characters free from their forced dependency on adults as well as liberating other energies.

Suggestions for Writing

1 Imagine a child character as your narrator. He or she knows (or has been told) about the physical limits of his or her world. Don't ever go beyond that point. Stay near. This or that area is forbidden. Children have more limits imposed on them than other people. Think about a child hero aged ten starting to test these limits – going there! Write as if inside his or her thoughts, as one or more of these limits is breached. Be aware that many parents don't feel comfortable with children straying too far away (or reading about children who are too adventurous). How will you deal with this issue? Try to make your story dramatic. There must be consequences – some frightening, others rewarding.

2 Explore the degree of fear and dread you can activate in writing a story for children, working on the principle that the more fear you engage, the better the story – assuming, too, that all the fear in the end will have been safely dispersed. Aim to get your readers *really afraid* before you end on a note of reassurance.

3 Try an experiment in reading where you ask children to read two pieces of fiction – *Paddy Clarke* and *The Bed and Breakfast Star* might form one double – and aim to get your child readers to tell you about their experience of reading these two fictions. Prepare your questions carefully beforehand. In the light of their answers, write the beginning of a story for children with a narrator of their age.

4 Invent a story for children with one or more of the following as a counter: a shed at the bottom of the garden; the head of a rhinoceros; a van arriving to take your home away; a place where you used to play and have fun in; a child's strong impression of a mother's or father's place of work; a building in the town where you lived when you were young; an interesting object owned by somebody else.

5 Shoes that won't move, or run away, a clock that goes backwards. Writing about magic often concentrates on objects or an object someone needs or finds useful. Write the start of a short story for children in which an object misbehaves, does the opposite of what it's supposed to, can't be controlled in the usual way. What happens? See how Alan Garner makes use of this device in *Elidor*, Chapter 10.

6 Suddenly the world has changed and the teachers in your school start to behave as if they were all your age. They look grown-up, the same as before, but something is very wrong. They argue, run about, fight, and throw things, won't walk sensibly in a queue, and will *not* be told. Observe how children your age think and act, then transfer this behaviour to your teachers. Find out how to get these impressions into writing, then into a story.

7 Retell the story of Little Red Riding-hood from the point of view of the wolf. Think of the age of your readers. If they are aged ten or older, introduce wit and humour into the story – the sort with the right appeal for this readership. Experiment with different angles and try some alternative voices for your character. What tone does he use? Savage, ironic, desperate, deceitful, or timidly wild? Remember that if you make the character of the wolf too nice, the story could lose its drama and urgency: it will appear as if there are no consequences.

8 Write a story in which three children run away from home and live in a barn up on a moor. The supermarkets all over the region have run out of food; there is no electricity or water. Civilisation has collapsed. In the barn they find an old mad woman and make friends with her. What happens?

9 Imagine some children living in your town or village two hundred years ago. Find out what the place was like at that time, in as much detail as possible, and what the way of life was like. Use this location as the setting of a story that happened in their time. You may uncover a real story or invent one.

10 Write a story in which one of the children – a boy – meets a girl from the future – in our world. They talk and each tells a story. They quarrel.

Revision and Editing

Look back over the first two pages of your writing. Identify the narrative markers or counters. If they are not obvious, will it help to make them so, or will your readers enjoy the story anyway? Try to make a frank and honest assessment.

Think about the voices in your story, especially that of your narrator. Is he/she speaking in a way that will be attractive to your readers, on their level, showing response and attitude, perhaps humour? Is your narrator a good storyteller?

If you aren't comfortable with what you've written, try writing in a speaking voice that comes naturally to you – *and* tells a story.

If you are writing a story with an outlandish setting and magical events, how do these compare with real-world circumstances and characters? Are there characters in your story who can make such a comparison?

Look closely at your writing style. Are the ideas accessible to your readers, the vocabulary appropriate? Do you refer to other stories, other characters, images, real-world events familiar to their particular culture group?

CHAPTER 6

DRAMA

Drama and Consequence

While writers of prose fiction have been free to explore the secret 'inner rooms' of their characters, to focus on their conscious and unconscious rhythms, the subject of writing in the drama arts (theatre, screenplay and radio) has shown how people express themselves together and to each other. Radio may be the exception; in this medium we can still represent inner voices occupying the mind and move from scene to scene with the speed of thought. In theatre and screenplay, however, no character can exist for long shielded behind his or her own isolated consciousness; he or she must come forward, confront, be confronted, and what he or she says or writes will be heard and read. Such a directive operates in fiction as well, but not to the same practical extent. Drama shows us both expression *and* reception. It must occur in spaces that are shared, and this aspect confirms its cultural history, one that reveals deep connections with music, mime, procession, ceremony and dance. Drama, as we shall see, derives its resonance from a sense of ritual and occasion. Writers whose original medium is not drama often observe its shift from inward to outward action. The poet Carol Rumens explains how when writing plays she has to adjust to this difference:

> I think part of my mind is constantly on drama alert. What makes a drama – it's first of all the day the play begins, that day which is unlike any other. I must have a sense of that moment – the inciting incident, the extraordinary day – and of course at least one character! I also need a story that contains outward as well as inward actions. Now there are lots of stories around but I want a story that I can write in quite a deep interior way. I want to be able to write with the poet part of myself involved.

> And that's difficult. At heart I am more interested in inward action. So I have to discipline myself to some degree and keep saying to myself, OK, now what will this character do? – how will I show, in action as well as images, what is felt?
>
> (Rumens, 2003: 19)

Whether or not the writer is an experienced dramatist, the right questions are just those that Carol Rumens asks: what will this character *do*? How will I *show?* Other questions might be, for example, what is there – for audiences, for writers – to be found in the present-day making and reception of drama? What is it people expect? What surprises them? What generates meaning for them and why? To answer these questions we can begin with a bold statement: drama hooks audiences through suspense. We are all acquainted with this effect. But we also suspect there is more to drama than making audiences hide behind the furniture. If we want to talk about suspense in connection with other kinds of response – shock, surprise, laughter, sense of meaning, of being moved – we might need to think more broadly and deeply about the impact of drama, and particularly how it depends on the moment. It is that *moment* of surprise, wonder and shock that seems to construct our experience as audiences. We are aware of a raised level of attention, not just our own but that of the characters involved, on screen, on stage, in the sound-space of radio, and we know that something has been said, or has just happened, that has raised the level of *consequence.* When the bride and bridegroom say 'I will... I do...' in the wedding ceremony, we presume they are saying something that has consequences. A state of consequence hangs over the couple, the assembled audience, and a similar sense attends the moment, when, say, Nora Helmer returns her wedding ring to her astonished husband in Act 3 of Ibsen's *A Doll's House*:

> NORA: Listen, Torvald. I have heard that when a wife deserts her husband's house, as I am doing now, he is legally freed from all obligations towards her. In any case I set you free from all your obligations. You are not to feel yourself bound in the slightest way, any more than I shall. There must be perfect freedom on both sides. See, here is your ring back. Give me mine.
>
> HELMER: That too?
>
> NORA: That too.
>
> HELMER: Here it is.

> NORA: That's right. Now it's all over. I have put the keys here. The maids know all about everything in the house – better than I do.
>
> (Ibsen, 1992: 71)

It seems at first that the term 'consequences' might be dispersed among a whole range of reactions to what happens in a play or a film. One question stage drama sometimes asks concerns the state of the future, of civilisation, the world, but the same rule still applies: without high levels of consequence achieved at regular moments within a text, drama would cease to be dramatic.

Here is a very different example from the one above, but no less pertinent, from the screenplay of Quentin Tarrantino's *Reservoir Dogs*. The character Freddy is a police undercover agent, about to join up with an armed gang planning a diamond heist in central Los Angeles. In the following memorable speech he has to convince the members of this gang without the least hint of doubt that he's on the wrong side of the law. His story must come over to them, and Holdaway is his trainer, a kind of director, helping him to act his part convincingly. If he fails, the consequences will be instant and fatal, and the whole police operation will fail. Freddy has got to get his part learned right. He and Holdaway meet on the roof of the L.A. State police building, out of sight of the streets:

> HOLDAWAY: An undercover cop has got to be Marlon Brando. To do this job you got to be a great actor. You got to be naturalistic. You got to be naturalistic as hell. If you ain't a great actor you're a bad actor, and a bad actor is bullshit in this job.
>
> FREDDY: (referring to the papers) But what is this?
>
> HOLDAWAY: It's an amusing anecdote about a drug deal.
>
> FREDDY: What?
>
> HOLDAWAY: Some funny shit that happened while you were doing a job.
>
> FREDDY: I gotta memorise all this? There's over four fucking pages of shit here.
>
> HOLDAWAY: It's like a fucking joke, man. You remember what's important and the rest you make your own. You can tell a joke, can't ya?

> FREDDY: I can tell a joke.
>
> HOLDAWAY: Well just think about it like that. Now the things you hafta remember are the details. It's the details that sell your story. Now your story takes place in the men's room. So you gotta know the details about that men's room. You gotta know if they got paper towels or a blower to dry your hands. You gotta know if the stall got doors or not. You gotta know if they got liquid soap or that pink granulated powder shit. If they got hot water or not. If it stinks. If some nasty motherfucker sprayed diarrhea all over one of the bowls. You gotta know every damn thing there is to know about that commode. And the people in your story, you gotta know the details about them, too. Anybody can tell who did what to whom. But in real life, when people tell a story, they try to recreate the event in the other person's mind. Now what you gotta do is take all them details and make 'em your own. This story's gotta be about you, and how you perceived the events that took place. And the way you make it your own is you just gotta keep on sayin' it and sayin' it and sayin' it and sayin' it and sayin' it.
>
> (Tarrantino, 1994:71–2)

Although this long speech could be used to illustrate many points on the subject of telling a story, its main function in *Reservoir Dogs* is that the audience will recognise it as carrying obvious and very dangerous consequences. Freddy's performance, when it happens, will convince the gang of experienced thieves planning the break-in, but we still share the anxiety of those moments: first, in the men's room where his story is located, second, when he tells it to the others, and third when Freddy the cop, now known as Mr Orange to the group, has been shot in the stomach during the break-in and could be dying from his wounds. At any moment before and during the robbery sequence, and during its aftermath, his role as undercover cop might be exposed. The speech above, therefore, has enormous consequences. Being an agent working for the police, everything he says and does has consequences. Everything said and done to him enhances the drama to an acute level, furthers the story, and indeed *is* the story.

We can contrast this speech with the series of exchanges between the men in black suits sitting around a table in a breakfast café at the start of the drama. There, very little that's said appears to have anything consequential about it. The conversation concerns a Madonna song 'Like a Virgin', and whether waitresses should be tipped. Consequence doesn't have to be present from the word go right through to the end. If it were, the audience would be exhausted, and left almost certainly *unconvinced.* If Mr Orange told his story about the men's room on a note of continuous high drama, suspicions would clearly have been aroused. The skill of convincingness – allowing people to recreate the event in their own minds – means you have to work up the scale of consequences gradually. You can't rush it; equally you can't leave it until too late. But one of the creative rewards of writing drama is that of discovering how to control consequence, how to deliver that sense of it to an audience, which means you are also discovering the precise moment when it should be done: delivery o*n time.*

The consequence of a speech or an action – or, indeed, a silence or lack of action – must be felt primarily by an audience thinking on behalf *of the characters*: what is happening, going to happen *to them. We want to know!* But there is another way of talking about consequence. What is happening, going to happen *to us. We want to know that too*! Some plays and films offer images of the human future. In the age of Ibsen many of them were ominous and negative, issued as warnings, as fears. All drama performs a collective function. Because of its relation to live performance, to an immediate and shared reception, it reminds us how we connect or fail to connect with each other as individuals, also as groups, as a culture.

A certain kind of British comedy (Morecambe and Wise, *Birds of A Feather, Only Fools and Horses),* thrives only when shared understandings exist in relation to accents, regions, minority groups, gender roles, status and power relations. All other forms of drama are similarly and perhaps irretrievably linked to an active background of voices, images, fears, rituals: all the public manifestations of everyday social life. It would be surprising, therefore, not to hear some pronouncements about the direction and future of that life, in other words, of consequences more or less generally feared and shared.

Drama as Ritual

One way to answer the question 'What is drama?' will be to do so using the idea of consequence, of the consequential in its pace, delivery and impact, and to point out suspense as a feature of what most audiences enjoy. Another, perhaps a little surprisingly, is to see drama as expressive ritual associated with public events such as weddings, funerals, acts of worship and ceremony, and taking place – as in law-courts, churches, government buildings – where the event is conducted in prescribed form. Suspense makes the audience wait for something, an event that will surprise and horrify them. They are excited because they think they know what might be about to happen, but will still be amazed by how it does.

But often these two forms of drama overlap. Just as Ibsen did with the scene of the rings in *A Doll's House*, many significant plays, not to mention TV soap episodes, concentrate their main action on events that bring together the public and private dimensions of life. We stay in for episodes on TV when Tracy Barlow names Steve as her baby's father, just as he's about to marry Karen, or when, at the funeral of Billy Grimshaw, his father Todd – estranged from his girlfriend's family – crouches at the edge of the grave and speaks to his baby son who was born dead. Both these scenes from Coronation Street make clear how story designers and writers of soaps know that a kind of mutual attraction exists between drama and public ritual, and that these together make a very volatile combination. How many scenes of catastrophe occur during TV weddings, christenings and funerals? Formal occasions attract disaster; everybody knows this. Every soap, too, has its legal battle: its courtroom debacle where things go terribly wrong and the innocent are convicted.

But let us be clear about what we might mean by ritual in this wider context of drama. Most of us wouldn't describe our friend's wedding as 'good drama' unless we were being ironic, or because something unpleasantly odd happened during the ceremony. We might be more inclined to say that the whole experience was moving, or special, by which we mean it sealed something, marked a division between past and future, or, using a term familiar to readers of this book, it 'shaped time'. Ritual can be drama, without the antics of Tracy at Steve's wedding, but only where 'drama' signifies an enhanced moment in which past and future divide, a new union or initiation gains public acknowledgement, a life at its end receives respect and dignity, a final farewell is said. All drama needs the sense of a moment heightened, lifted into significance in the long-term memory of the tribe. Public ritual can be a way of harnessing this appetite, hence its interest for scriptwriters, playwrights, writers of screenplays, who know how these time-shaping situations maximise the impact of a story.

This alliance of drama and ritual questions the barriers between so-called popular and high art. We can see a link between Billy Grimshaw's funeral in Coronation Street, May 2004, and the Sophocles play *Antigone*, written in Athens in the fourth century BC and existing in a version translated by Seamus Heaney, also appearing in May 2004. Both these dramas demonstrate the emotional power that attends burial of the beloved dead, and what happens when their closest relative is excluded from the ceremony or when the burial is prevented. *Antigone*, however, has already survived centuries and will continue to be translated in new versions, while the other, having lost its only currency as 'the latest Corrie story', will have faded to almost nothing by the time this book is published, so that those of us who saw the scene will have only the faintest recollection of the incident, if anything.

In Heaney's version, *The Burial At Thebes*, it is Antigone's dead brother Polyneices whom we hear described by Creon and denied any burial rites:

> He is forbidden
> Any ceremonial whatsoever.
> No keening, no interment, no observance
> Of any of the rites. Hereby, he is adjudged
> A carcass for the dogs and birds to feed on.
> And nobody, let it be understood,
> Nobody is to treat him otherwise
> Than the obscenity he was and is.
>
> (Heaney, 2004: 11)

His sister, Antigone, is outlawed because she threw dust on her brother's corpse. The father, outlawed by his own too-late confessed homosexuality, is refused attendance at his new-born son Billy's funeral. Both are forbidden by prohibitions, yet driven by love – the strong force, and by duty combined with love – probably the strongest force in all of our known cultural traditions. But somehow we see one as a major event in the history of our Western dramatic tradition, the other as mere ephemeral episode. Why is this? Could it be that the writers of *Coronation Street* were thinking only of suspense – habitually thinking only of that, (how to make 'drama ... the dramatic' means just that), or were they thinking of something else – how to move the audience, to make meaning? Whatever the aim, the episode itself contained other storylines; it did not concentrate the audience's mind quite so exclusively as a piece of Greek theatre. Its *theatrical context* (and therefore its force as ritual) couldn't have been more different, even though its content held unnoticed similarities.

Both episodes, however, draw strength from the same root: drama where the dysfunction of ritual enhances both suspense *and* meaning. The root also has high comic potential, whenever ritual formality shows cracks. For instance, the '*Jane Eyre*' moment – a marriage ceremony interrupted by that terrible voice at the back of the church answering the question: 'If any of you know cause or just impediment...' – was repeated, not only in *Four Weddings and a Funeral* but in another script by Richard Curtis, *The Vicar of Dibley,* starring Dawn French, where two parishioners of doubtful compatibility are confronted at their wedding by a voice from the back, a voice that adds, after a horrible silence, 'Sorry, wrong church'. This motif, popular in soaps and comedy programmes, could be described as one of festivity *disrupted. Secrets and Lies*, Mike Leigh's screenplay about a reunion between a mother and her mixed-race daughter, ends with a family birthday barbecue, and a revelation. Family gatherings (such as weddings and barbecues) are sacrosanct, even though we live in a secularised world, and are therefore susceptible to high levels of consequence.

The importance of ritual can't be approached without some acknowledgement of the power of myth in our cultural traditions. In the recent past the word 'myth' itself has aroused anxiety, particularly among writers. Poets, whom we might assume stand closest to myth, are the most vociferous in its favour, and also, it must be admitted, in its disfavour. Philip Larkin to my knowledge never wrote plays, but did express some thoughts often quoted on this issue. How far into the past should writers look for their subjects? Is there a tradition uniting ritual with myth, and myth with the public and popular rituals of our time? Do we attend a christening because we believe in sacred time, in holy places, in the sanctification of water? Because we believe the touch of the priest's hand on the forehead of the child signifies its deliverance from death? Or because we still harbour some residue of these beliefs? Do we read novels or go to films because we need to escape from real time into adventure time? Larkin's own take on the matter sounds quite forcefully unequivocal: 'As a guiding principle I believe that every poem must be its own sole freshly-created universe, and therefore have no belief in 'tradition' or a common myth-kitty...' Unequivocal, that is, unless we remind ourselves (or are reminded by writers on myth such as Mircea Elaide) that the idea of a 'sole freshly-created universe' – a new-born, integral new world – is itself a powerful mythic image. Larkin's famous comment itself, therefore, contains its own contradiction.

Action Motifs

At this point, before we go on to explore specific media, beginning with screenplay, it will be useful to highlight certain *action motifs* found in all drama writing. I have chosen six, though more could be included, and am aware that new ideas are likely to be regenerations of the ancient attributes of drama. The following motifs point back to what we know, as well as forward to new inventions:

Challenge

A protagonist challenges the rule of authority (Antigone herself is an example), possibly becomes leader of a group challenging law and order. He or she stands for the powerless against the powerful, and therefore exhibits *heroic* qualities. Challenge, of course, can lead directly to Fight, where one or the other must be defeated.

Threat

The established orders can see challengers as a threat, a serious one, and so take steps to prevent them. Threats also come from outside in the form of natural disasters, mechanical breakdowns or human error. Preventive measures may not work, or might work but only temporarily.

Fight

Challenge and Threat can easily lead to Fight. If this happens, we may see actual physical combat with serious, even fatal, consequences. Fight can be formal, ritualised – even in war, or haphazard and random – as often in a domestic setting where tempers suddenly flare on impulse. In both circumstances, Fight can create disorder; accidents are likely; chance can intervene; death is random. Scenes from the end of Shakespeare's *Hamlet* contain all these elements.

Gift

Gift demands nothing in return, unlike Offer and Reward. There are also forms of Gift that imply exchange and negotiation, a trade-off. Sometimes a Gift can be an Offer in disguise – the new earrings or roses or trip to the Bahamas may mean 'Forgive me' – the ring says 'Be my wife or husband'. The giver can make the promise of a gift that leads him or her to a series of problems. A Gift could be seen – and meant – as a Threat or a Challenge. Gifts, Offers and Rewards can be either accepted or rejected, with major consequences.

Wish

Wish almost always implies a desire for some kind of improvement or empowerment, a profound aspiration, or just for something nice to happen. Characters' wishes might cause others to oppose them, try to get them to change their wishes, or prevent them from attaining them. Wish always comes along with an obstacle, a chance of success, a possible disappointment. As a motif, it has huge dynamic, sometimes involving characters in a search or a quest. Wish can be for something very tangible and specific, or for something abstract – less control, more freedom.

Discovery

Discovery can be a shock: pleasant, unpleasant, or a combination of both. It can come at the start of a story, a trigger event, or near the end, leading the action towards crisis. The thing discovered can be a lost object, a new idea of oneself, a new impression of somebody else, a way to save the world from death rays. It can be known to the audience, to certain characters but not others – thus producing a sense of dramatic irony. It must play a part in the shaping of time, separating past from present.

FILM

Popular Film Narrative

Action motifs are the standard fare of popular film narrative. Challenge and Threat generate Wish, followed by Discovery, leading to Fight, followed by Offer and Reward. Whatever way the action motifs are arranged, there's little excuse for a writer to get bored with a story, or be unable to find some way forward. Action motifs also require that other elements in the drama – voice-over, dialogue, silent footage, flashback – have a point, make some contribution to the story. Idling and meandering – where dialogues jog along contentedly nowhere – can quickly be identified and avoided, for now we are telling a story and making all action, image, sound and event relevant and necessary to an outcome. Everything – from the pot of orchids in the murder room to the stuffed Edwardian chair on the terrace – must be a contribution to a story.

Writing a successful film screenplay comes to seem like the blue-print of a screenplay story itself, one of feature-film proportions, in which the central character – you, the writer – has a goal, meets with obstacles, overcomes them and succeeds. This effectively is the feature-film blueprint. To use another metaphor, the basic structure resembles preparing, cooking and serving a meal, the aim being your own pleasure and that of your guests. In the first part of the story (Act 1) you assemble the ingredients: characters, the context of their actions, define the central character (X) and his or her main drive or Wish. You then put X under serious pressure, (Act 2 – Threat, Challenge, Fight, Discovery), or 'cook the ingredients'. What is then served up – a resolution (Act 3) –

reveals how X, having overcome these obstacles, succeeds in fulfilling his or her stated need. This is the basic screenplay structure, and can be written in scenes arranged in linear sequences following the development of the action. You will need to test out this structure in movies you have seen, as well as looking for new structures.

It will be important to challenge this basic Act 1, 2 and 3 structure. Do feature films always show this pattern of character need, obstacle, action and resolution? For instance, a variation on this structure shows X discovering *other needs* than the one he/she sets out with, and ending by fulfilling those instead. This variation makes for a much richer story. In the film of *The Talented Mr Ripley*, for example, Tom is sent to Italy by the Greenleaf family, first to find Dickie Greenleaf, and second to persuade him to return to the USA. Tom has acquired this need as an obligation. He then develops another – to spend as much time with Dickie as possible and separate him from his fiancée. Finally, other wishes germinate: having murdered Dickie to disguise himself as his victim, remain in receipt of his fortune, and see the world. He does succeed in fulfilling these wishes, but is left in a state of complex ambivalence emotionally – a mixture of triumph and remorse.

In The Francis Ford Coppola film *Born on the fourth of July* (1996), the main character, a young American (played by Tom Cruise), joins the Marines to fight in Vietman. The year is 1968. His wish is to defend freedom, and free market capitalism, the values of his country and his family. He returns a veteran in the same year, paralysed from the chest down, unable to face his disillusionment, and with the war's abiding horrors deeply lodged in his memory, unable to convince himself that the cause has been, and still is, just and honourable. From defending the war and its aims, his wishes shift painfully but irrevocably towards protest. Rather than showing how obstacles in the path of need are overcome by X, screenplay structures can change the direction of need, and this variation deepens our understanding of character, deepens character itself, and offers a much richer psychological feast for its audience.

Short Fiction Films

Most audiences are so fully adjusted to the experience of watching a feature film of two to three hours' duration that the idea of a film lasting only ten to fifteen minutes, or sometimes only five or six minutes, is hardly likely to impress. Although the short fiction film has achieved international recognition as an art form since the late 1950s, and continues to generate opportunities for emerging new talent in screenplay writing and production, its power and impact are still not widely appreciated. Richard Raskin, in his valuable book *The Art Of The Short Fiction Film*, begins his celebration of the form by emphasising the qualities of *story* in short fiction films.

> When short fiction films are at their best, they tell their stories with such remarkable economy that they take our breath away. We find ourselves drawn into their world, caught up in the lives of their characters, moved or amused by the events that unfold, then once again finally eased out of the fiction, feeling profoundly enriched by the experience – all in a matter of five or ten or fifteen minutes.
>
> (Raskin, 2002: 1)

As he also explains, for film-school students, 'the experimental short is a way of making their mark and establishing their credentials as creative film-makers'. But for all students keen to develop their film-literacy and explore the possibilities of film through writing, the short fiction film offers insight into the process of how films tell a story, and also the manageable possibility of ideas being carried through to production.

Before discovering Raskin's book and its shot by shot analysis of nine short film screenplays, I had already been lucky enough to see some examples of this fascinating medium and to realise its potential. Here are some examples, in précis form, of recent short fiction films broadcast by Channel 4:

About A Girl, *by Brian Percival (Cinema 16: 2003)*

The sound-track of *About A Girl* unusually consists of a single monologue. It is spoken by the thirteen-year-old main character as she walks along a canal bank carrying a white plastic bag. What is in the bag – a few belongings? Is she leaving home? Where is 'home'? She speaks to herself about herself, her parents who now live apart, her friends who practise Michael Jackson-type dance routines up on the moors, who sing in the bus, and who dream of stardom and escape. It's all very predictable, but what brings the monologue to life is the character's speech, much of which consists of imitating other people's voices, especially her mother and father and her friends. The footage includes flashbacks illustrating these scenes and characters, so we feel that, through her, we meet others. We meet them as she sees them, as she hears them. The film has a basic short story structure – one main character surrounded by several minor characters, yet essentially alone. Her life holds several wishes at once – to be treated like an adult, to become famous, to get more attention from her parents, and to keep her secret.

Home, *by Morag McInnon (Cinema 16: 2003)*

In the first of this group of short films entitled *Home*, Bobby Wilson, a council worker, aged about 30, knocks on the door of a flat. The door opens. We see through his Point Of View (POV) a darkened hallway with a picture of Jesus in a frame on the wall. We enter a darkened room. 'Mr Young?' asks the kind Scots voice of Mr Wilson, but it's not a social call. A voice answers him and we get the sense of a big figure somewhere in the flat. Although it's daytime the curtains are drawn, and Bobby asks to have more light. No answer, so he opens the curtains himself. Another figure, similar to the first, has been standing in the room all the time, two of them, identical twin brothers, both wearing dark lounge suits. "We've got a room each now. ... We're very happy,' they tell Bobby Wilson. 'We're very happy here!' We see their two faces. The brothers are blind. In a short piece of dialogue with Bobby Wilson, it turns out they do ballroom dancing together; they partner each other; they win prizes. A trophy stands on a shelf near Bobby's head. He examines it. One of the brothers is making a pot of tea for their visitor; he brings it into the room with some teacups, trips over the carpet and falls. 'It doesn't matter.' One of them signs the form to say that now their mother has died they are the new joint tenants, with tenants' rights. Their fear was that they would have been evicted after her death. A sense of relief fills the half-lit rooms. Their overwhelming need is to go on living in this flat together, and this makes any approach from council officials a threat. Even so, it's not in their natures to react aggressively to threats. We feel, helplessly, they would accept what happens.

Bobby Wilson then pays a visit to another tenant on his list. He knocks, the door opens. There have been complaints about a smell, he tells the owner: 'Mind if I look around?' The tenant, a fierce, wizened hard-man Scot in his fifties, in a tee-shirt, aims a shower of filthy abuse at him as they edge around the flat. 'Just regulations,' Bobby explains... 'Everythin's fuckin' regulations!' shouts the tenant. 'Regulations my erse!' Nothing is found. On his way out Bobby notices another room, door shut. 'What's in there?' he asks again. He's insistent. The tenant opens the door. Inside, stretched out on a low-lying bed, is a donkey. 'Is it alive?' It gets up on its feet and stands there in the tiny room, its huge head bowed. The tenant attacks Bobby with a penknife, but is easily overpowered. The violence quickly subsides. He explains that the donkey lives here. This is its home. It used to give rides on the beach, but now it's old. The camera watches as Bobby Wilson leads the donkey out of the flat. 'Ye cannae take him away, he's all I've got. ... Ye'll find him a hame. Promise me!' This story shows initial aggression subsiding into acceptance and submission, as there is no way this character's wish (to keep the donkey with him) can be granted.

Skin Deep, *by Yusaf Ali Khan (National Film Archive)*

This writer explains that when growing up in Salford in the 1970s and 1980s it was safer to hide your ethnic identity. The film uses a mixed-race half-Asian actor, Darren Sheppard, to illustrate the point. The most powerful sequences in the film make it clear how the main character operates. In one identity he is at home with his Asian sister, parents and grandparents, while in another he risks his darkish skin-colour and joins a group of racist thugs who beat up Asian kids in the streets. Before going out the boy teaches himself to how shout racist abuse at children his own age (and ethnic background), whose skin colour just happens to be more physically obvious than his own. He practises this abuse by shouting in front of the bathroom mirror. We see his face in close-up as this happens, as he goes out, returns to the mirror, to his family, then back to the streets. Although challenged by the gang of thugs about his darkish skin-colour, he avoids their brutality by allowing himself to become assimilated. He takes on their identity, their violence against his own people. In a final scene with the mirror, his face in close-up surrounded by faces of white racist antagonists – a surreal fantasy – he shaves his skull, cutting the skin and causing blood to flow. It is a profound image of self-mutilation, a perverse *wish* to be racially invisible.

There are stories here but we encounter them through the briefest glimpse. What we see is a short sequence of moments in whole lives. A glimpse is all we have. Several of the films illustrate the importance of focalisation, so that we know whose view of the story we are sharing, whose eyes we are invited to look through, who its main characters are.

In *Come*, by Marianne Olsen Ulrichsen, (Ibid, 2002: 96–107) we first see the face of an old woman, then that of the young man she is remembering. We see her look down as her hand moves to touch a pocket-watch, then the face of a girl also looking down – it is her face when she was young. We now follow the young woman as she meets the man. People are dancing round a campfire by the sea. The man and woman go off together; she gives him a pocket watch; she says 'Come' to him; and they go to a cabin and make love. The old woman has the same watch in her hand, she places it in the pocket of someone near her, a man whose face we now see, who smiles.

Screenplay layouts for short fiction films can be written shot by shot, as in the following sequence from *Come*:

> Shot 15 (3 sec) Her POV: three young men sharing a bottle of brandy.
>
> Shot 16 (3 sec) She holds a pocket watch, rubbing its face with her fingers.
>
> Shot 17–23 (9 sec) We see his face then hers as they make eye contact.
>
> Shot 24 (1 sec) She smiles, holding the pocket watch by its chain.
>
> Shot 25 (1 sec) He looks down at it.
>
> Shot 26 (1 sec) His friend smiles at him.
>
> Shot 27 (1 sec) His watch pocket is empty.
>
> Shot 28 (2 sec) He looks up at her accusingly.
>
> Shot 29 (7 sec) She smiles knowingly then turns and walks away.
>
> Shot 30 (2 sec) The three men together.
>
> Shot 31 (8 sec) He has followed her, leaving his friends behind
>
> (Ibid:101–2)

This method does help to clarify how much action can be covered in very short periods. It also trains the eye and mind to the purpose of telling a story through images. Other methods can include treatments where the writer writes a description of the film's images, characters and events in about 1,000 words, thus providing a sense of the whole sequence, with minimum reference to individual shots. The precise angle and frame content of shots can be indicated quite simply, but without too much technical detail. The aim is to give a strong impression of action and point of view.

In Polanski's short film *Two Men And A Wardrobe*, two men come out of the sea carrying an old wardrobe towards the shore. In the course of the film they continue to carry it – through streets where they are taunted by a gang of youths, where people look at them with shock or ignore them. They use the wardrobe as a table, catch a fish out of the air and place it on the wardrobe mirror before eating it, endure various other encounters before carrying it back to the beach that is now completely covered in sandcastles. They lift their burden over these very carefully so as not to crush them. Reality effects themselves create opportunities for the surreal.

Both *Come* and *Two Men and A Wardrobe* repeat their opening images at the end. Both emphasise moments when characters act deliberately: the wardrobe men with the sandcastles, the girl with the pocket-watch. Both also empower objects with meaning, and illustrate close links between events. The wardrobe sequence becomes a tiny saga of pointless struggle that nevertheless brings people together. In the other short films, the pot of tea, the dancing trophy, are symbols of the brothers' connections with other people's customary worlds, yet these objects still seem imprinted with strangeness, de-familiarised by the narrative of dark rooms.

One development of the short film has been through its subject-matter. A tradition of the form has been to depict the life of the streets; poverty, sex, drug-culture, delivered with unsparing images and strong vernacular speech. This element of film culture is now finding its way into full-length features. In terms of their content, their bleakness, any of the scenes in Ken Loach's *Sweet Sixteen*, written by Paul Laverty, could have been developed from short film sequences. *City of God* and Alejandro Gonzales Innarita's *Ammores Perros* seem designed to foul the nest kept clean by decades of romantic heroism where goal-motivated characters reach their target. Another form of story appears, based on the casual not the causal, on randomness and contingency, on lives glimpsed and abandoned rather than whole and redeemable. Narrative structure is far from being a culturally neutral zone, and film narratives with their extremes of optimism and brutality, of wholeness and randomness, reflect cultural change by showing what audiences are increasingly prepared to witness. But not all short films belong to a mean-streets tradition. *Two Men and a Wardrobe*, and *Come*, for example, celebrate reunion and survival. The second of these reminds us once again that moments become dramatic not through conflict but through consequence.

RADIO

Radio drama, like the short fiction film, offers the chance to make use of a fascinating media. Sometimes described as the 'theatre of the mind', radio drama stands close to prose fiction, allowing a glimpse into the personal interior of thought. It can show us what has been left unsaid, can explore the hidden world of the individual mind as well as provide drama in its other uses: as spectacle, as festival and as ritual. Because it can paint scenes through words and generate atmosphere through voices, radio becomes a visual medium, too, creating a rich sense of place and occasion. Like poetry it can choose its subjects from anywhere in time, moving freely through a range of locations. All that matters is that the audience can follow, can make immediate sense of when and where, and, of course, of who is speaking to whom.

For a beginner there are obvious dangers. The writer cannot simply 'translate' scenes from theatre or prose fiction into radio, as if all actions and spaces have acoustic equivalents: 'Sound of someone sitting on a garden wall. A car approaches. Sound of a car window being wound down', etc. Or, forgetting we are wholly in a sound medium, 'She looks at him with playful contempt'. This is a feeling that could be conveyed through the tones of a voice. In fact, any emotional response can be suggested only in one of two ways – either through words and tones, or through silence.

Radio scripts need to be divided into sequences, or scenes, some lasting for several pages, others for no more than a few seconds. The BBC Internet guidelines to writing for radio encourages a variety of acoustic effects, especially when the impact is one of contrasts:

> A variety of sound is essential for holding the listener's attention and engaging their imagination. This variety can be achieved by altering the lengths of sequences, number of people speaking, space of dialogue, volume of sound, background acoustics and location of action. On radio, one room sounds very much like another if they're about the same size, but the difference between an interior and exterior acoustic is quite considerable. The contrast between a noisy sequence with a number of voices and effects and a quiet passage of interior monologue, is dramatic and effective.
>
> The best way to become familiar with the possibilities of the medium is to listen to radio plays as often as possible, and decide what works and what doesn't.

This makes good sense, but it's also worth remembering that however powerful and memorable a piece of radio drama, it is only so on the basis of four sound elements: voices, music, noise and silence. The aim of radio drama writing is to arrange these elements into a narrative.

To get some practice it's a good idea to start with a given story – one already in written form, with dialogues, silences, images and settings – and to produce the opening sequences for radio in five minutes of finished, detailed script. Raymond Carver's story (see pp. 132–5) would be an interesting and useful example. Given two voices – a man's and a woman's – short periods of silence, one or two longer silences, a telephone, you might then add various background noises. If the script were to continue, it might include other voices – that of his ex-wife, her parents, a doctor, voices at work, breakfast cooking, an alarm clock, traffic noise from a street outside their apartment, noises and voices indicating past and present as their imagination moves between different worlds. But always dominant would be their conversation – its tones, hesitancies and deliberations – then a phone unplugged and finally silence.

Imagine Jackie Kay's story didn't end with Melissa rejecting her father's suggestion about meeting up. He writes more letters, sends them, she reads them, he calls her on the phone. She resists. Eventually they meet. What happens? How would you use radio drama to explore these two characters: their pasts, their thoughts and actions? How would you convey Melissa's memories of her mother; his of his daughter and ex-wife; his thoughts about Trinidad and London; her thoughts about her mixed-race identity; about her lost child? Remember she's a character who wants to *suppress* consequences.

Another starting point would be to choose a feature film and investigate its opening sequences by re-writing it as a radio drama. If, for example, you chose the Michael Douglas film *Falling Down* about the character D-FENS (from the number-plate on his car) undergoing a mental breakdown during one day in the heat of the city, you would begin where the film begins: in D-FENS's car in an early morning traffic jam by a fly-over bridge. The radio is on, a fly buzzes in his window, the sounds of honking horns, shouts, revving engines, punctuate his thoughts – and what are his thoughts? A detailed sound and voice construction of the first five minutes of *Falling Down* would enable you to find out a lot about writing radio drama. Choose a film that interests you, creates impact in its first few minutes, and includes challenging sequences in terms of voices and sounds.

The next step would be to construct a story of your own invention, using some of the above radio techniques, and others. Such other effects might include:

- The actual words of letters and emails spoken by one or more voices in a drama;

- Voice-over (VO), where a character is narrating either alone or over background sounds, music or other dialogues;

- Interior voices (IV), where a character imagines the voice of another character. For example, in a crowded bar, a young boy hears (that is, imagines) his mother's voice telling him not to drink and drive, while the voices of friends offer him more vodkas. Another example might be a harassed school-teacher hearing (imagining) his head-teacher's voice asking for this week's register;

- Tone variation, where characters speak aloud to each other, or quietly – to themselves or another character – or speak using a mechanised device (indicated by D in a script) such as a telephone or mobile.

Fade, Stop, or Music indicates the end of one sound sequence and the beginning of another. A sequence can just stop and another begins after a short pause, or there can be a FADE OUT/FADE IN.

Another point to remember is that your listeners can switch off at any moment. You must try to prevent them from doing so. Also remember that you have a continuous track of sounds and silences to manage. You job is to interweave them so that you achieve a sustained level of audience interest and character consequence. The weave of sound has to be varied and well-organised enough to hold our attention, but not so varied and elaborate that it creates confusion.

- *Character and Voice.* Always make sure your audience knows who is speaking (unless, of course, you are writing a general crowd sequence). Characters need to be recognised by name, and to be distinguished from each other by voice.

- *Story and Time.* Start your script well into the story – near the end, if you can. Don't get involved in a preamble. Make sure you are moving your script forward through a time-period that is comprehensible to your listeners. Shifts from minutes to years to days to months then back to minutes again will cause listeners to switch-off. Try to confine your story to a definite short period of time – a few hours, part of one day, two or three days, no longer.

- *Place and World.* You can take us deep into the recesses of the mind of a character, and you can also cross continents; a character may suddenly remember a scene in the Philippines or

Trinidad – you can use your soundtrack to establish that world quickly.

- *Images*. Radio is a powerfully descriptive medium. With a few suggestions of where something is happening, your listeners' imagination will visualise whole landscapes, cityscapes, interior and exterior spaces. Think what lasting images you want to deliver. These may be narrative images of certain places or atmospheres. A radio drama version of Conrad's novel *Heart of Darkness* begins with the Roman militia invading Britain, ships moving through the wilderness of the Thames river-mouth. Then the sequence ends and Marlow begins his story, looking out over the same estuary. Narrative images of life in Europe, then in the Congo, are clearly significant to this story. Among Andrew Rissick's narratives of the Ancient Greeks is *King Priam and his Sons*, which begins with a series of mysterious images suggesting how the Gods appear to men: 'I am Hermes. I come out of the air like fire or thought, bring to the afflicted voices and visions. ... He is gone into the air with a man that came like a shadow.'

Do you want to convey a feeling for the state of life that exists at the time your story is set? How might you achieve this using only sound?

Plan each sequence carefully, so that you know how you are going to tell your story.

Remember that you are experimenting with a form that is probably new to you. If you succeed you will have learned some truth about the medium, and about the characters and the story. Learn to judge your script with the ear of a listener. It's with this quality in mind that radio has attracted writers of poetic drama.

THEATRE

With poetry and fiction, readers can have complete, privileged access to a character's secret, interior reflections without any other characters present. But in the theatre, every speech is an action involving someone else, instantly. Often, too, body movements and silences communicate in place of spoken words; a silence can be an action. In the theatre, an action is something done to a person or an object. Words are actions. A word can be an embrace, a touch, a shrug, a fist in the air. A silence, too, can be any of these. Action of some kind is inescapable. As I explained at the start of this chapter, one of the skills of writing for the theatre is to control the level of consequences involved in the action. One of theatre's essential insights is that your characters will also be trying to control the consequences. They will be aiming to maximise or minimise them, to make out that nothing very much matters when it does, or try to influence, pressurise, intimidate each other so that the consequences they wish for will result.

Experience of Theatre

First-hand experience of acting and production is not essential for writing, but it undoubtedly helps, and any book on writing plays should not omit this advice. Just as reading stories and poems stimulates the development of writing, so the experience of making theatre, as well as watching plays regularly, adds to your store of practical knowledge.

I want to begin by talking about the experience of directing a play with a group of English and drama undergraduate students. Pinter's short play *Family Voices*, originally written for radio, opens up the private worlds of its characters. Even though its use of language and treatment of its subject is unusual, its centre is the space where routines of living are experienced, where characters struggle for personal expression and define themselves by what they call 'home'. As a radio play it contains no instructions about pauses, silences, or a set, and even though it was staged in London as well as produced on radio, none of us had seen the stage production. With this play, the lack of stage instructions offered a challenge, and we had to work out how to control its impact on a live audience.

Pinter's text was written for three voices. Voice One, a young man aged about twenty, has left home. He sits in his lodgings writing a letter to his mother. His mother, Voice Two, is present on stage in the place he has abandoned. His father, Voice Three, is dead. When he speaks, therefore, it is from the ultimate point of distance and separation. The other two are closer to each other, but still miles apart (she sits and waits for a letter; it never arrives), so should the stage be divided: mother in sitting-room/son in lodging house? She sits at home perched on a large settee thinking mournfully of her son, he at a desk in his rented room in a large city. But almost as soon as the son begins to speak the audience knows he is writing a letter; they know to whom, and they also know this isn't the kind of letter he could send. All this distance might be fine for radio, but how could it work on stage?

In rehearsals we began to examine the space. The mother remains fixed; the son moves about. With the mother locked in her sitting-still position, the son moves out of his space and into hers, and even sits down next to her on her sofa as if in her lonely living room. While he describes the strange routine of life in his present, she describes what life was like in their past – her son at home, her husband and son going for walks together. He strides, gesticulates, and recreates in full view of the audience the strange inhabitants of the house where he now lives and acts out his encounters.

He suddenly crosses the stage and sits beside her. Even though they are living in different worlds – emotionally and in terms of place – do they look at each other? Does he make physical contact, touch her hand? He looks at her, but she only gazes away. If he touched her that would be an act requiring a response. But he doesn't need her response. He has escaped. By his behaviour the audience can see this. To sit by her side when she doesn't know where he is, is cruel, yet his speaking tone sounds anything but cruel. He has shed all the restrictions of her parental, protective gaze, and yet his tone sounds friendly and innocent of the break, even while he describes things surely calculated to arouse outrage. The audience can see he is teasing her, depositing her in the margins of his life. The routines that occupied that sitting room have been broken. Instead he describes other routines, other rooms, other people – a gay ex-policeman called Riley; a Mrs Withers; a schoolgirl called Jane 'who does her homework'; an old man, Mr Withers; a woman 'who wears red dresses'.

> VOICE TWO: Have you made friends with anyone? A nice boy? Or a nice girl? There are so many nice boys and nice girls about. But please don't get mixed up with the other sort. They can land you in such terrible trouble. And you'd hate it so. You're so scrupulous, so particular. ...
>
> Darling, I miss you. I gave birth to you. Where are you?
>
> (Pinter, 1983: 70)

Such desperation might seem poignant, but it is also a barely concealed attempt at re-possession. The audience can sense a rise in the level of consequences – for the mother, as she starts to ask questions she knows will not be answered or even received. In saying 'scrupulous ... particular', and saying that last line, she looks at him: it is just what she wants him to be, just what she wants him to hear. But nothing will come of what she wants. Her maximum expressions move him not at all.

In the last few minutes of the play, the father (Voice Three) arrives. He died, we are told, not knowing where his son was. Now he comes back. We decided he should reach the stage by walking towards it along the dividing aisle of the studio audience. His presence gains full control of all the available space; in other words he steals it back from the son. But will this invasion hold any consequences? The son has been winning the audience over and entertaining them by acting out the alarming, amusing, bewildering encounters with Jane, Riley, and the landlady Mrs Withers:

> She was in the Women's Air Force in the Second World War. Don't drop a bollock, Charlie, she's fond of saying. Call him Flight sergeant and he'll be happy as a pig in shit.
>
> You'd really like her, mother.
>
> (Ibid: 69)

and old Mr Withers:

> VOICE ONE: Mother, mother, I've had the most unpleasant, the most mystifying encounter, with the man who calls himself Mr Withers. Will you give me your advice?
>
> Come in here, son, he called. Don't mess about. I haven't got all night. I went in. A jug. A basin. A bicycle.
>
> You know where you are? he said. You're in my room. It's not Euston Station. Get me? It's a true oasis. …
>
> My name's Withers. I'm here or thereabouts. Follow? Embargo on all duff terminology. With me? … You're in a disease-ridden land, boxer. Keep your weight on all the left feet you can lay your hands on. Keep dancing. The old foxtrot is the classical response. … Up the slaves. Get me? This is a place of creatures, up and down stairs. Creatures of the rhythmic splits, the rhythmic sideswipes, the rums and roulettes, the macaroni tatters, the dumplings in jam mayonnaise, a catapulting ordure of gross and ramshackle shenanagins, open-ended paraphernalia. … Mind how you go. Look sharp. Get my drift? Don't let it get too mouldy. Watch the mould. Get the feel of it, sonny. Get the density. Look at me.
>
> And I did
>
> VOICE TWO: I am ill.
>
> VOICE ONE: It was like looking into a pit of molten lava, mother. One look was enough for me.
>
> (Ibid: 77–8)

Any audience must surely think this bizarre. 'Open-ended paraphernalia', for sure. But is it open-ended? It is, but also anything but. The jumbled rubbish of old Mr Withers's speech can be heard, and seen, as the old male chauvinist advice mechanism, springing into action with any passing youth who gets in its way. The emblem of it is: 'Look at me, *and respect me*', the act of a substitute parent – a command the son can't take at all seriously. To him, Mr Withers is just another old josser doing his stuff. The son's response in telling this story is a shrug.

But male advice revives again with the father. He appears, the judge, admonitory. He sits down between mother and son on the family settee. He speaks to each of them with avenging playfulness, but his threat is serious; it has to be felt as such by them *and* by the audience. Will the son's response be another shrug?

> VOICE THREE: I know your mother has written to you to tell you that I am dead. I am not dead. I am very far from being dead, although lots of people have wished me dead, from time immemorial, you especially. It is you who have prayed for my death, from time immemorial. I have heard your prayers. They ring in my ears. Prayers yearning for my death. But I am not dead.
>
> Well, that's not entirely true, not entirely the case. I'm lying. I'm leading you up the garden path. I'm playing about. I'm having my bit of fun, that's what. Because I am dead. As dead as a doornail. I'm writing to you from my grave. A quick word for old time's sake. Just to keep in touch. An old hullo out of the dark. A last kiss from Dad.
>
> I'll probably call it a day after this canter. Not much more to say. All a bit of a sweat. Why am I taking the trouble? Because of you, I suppose, because you were such a loving son. I'm smiling as I lie in this glassy grave.
>
> Do you know why I use the word glassy? Because I can see out of it.
>
> (Ibid: 80–1)

How does the son react? Respectfully this time? How does the mother? Turning directly to her, her dead husband articulates the words: 'Not much more to say. All a bit of a sweat.' It hurts her, is intended to. Facing her, he stares into her eyes.

We wanted the audience to feel his gesture as making a repulsive comment on his marriage. She submits, looks down. But with the father, the son is not submissive. His tactic is to ignore him and talk about his new family in place of the old one: a shrug *in supremis* and unanswerable:

> VOICE ONE: They have decided on a name for me. They call me Bobo. The only person who does not call me Bobo is the old man. He calls me nothing. I call him nothing. I don't see him. He keeps to his room. I don't go near it. He is old and will die soon.
>
> (Ibid: 81)

During this speech the son stares at the father, lowering his voice not his eyes. They are standing up and facing each other across the space of the stage. The comic attitude of the son's speech gives way to another tone – one of contempt. The audience must be able to sense that change, and to make a connection between old Mr Withers and the father.

Arranging this play for the stage tested our inventiveness. We had to make our own decisions about movements, gestures, actions, tones of voice and use of the stage space. We had learned and developed a kind of code, which we and the audience somehow understood. But it wasn't until later that I found myself reading a book that explained this code to me.

Status Interaction

Two years after directing this play, an American friend lent me a copy of *Impro* by Keith Johnstone. Johnstone had developed his ideas while working with actors and writers at the Royal Court in the early 1960s, and afterwards at theatre schools in Britain and North America. A point he makes is that once they have learned the rules of status transaction, actors can improvise without the inhibiting pressure to be original. His next point is that status transactions happen all the time in life. We recognise low and high status behaviour instinctively, but we can also train ourselves to observe it:

Low status (submissive)
Breaking eye contact then glancing back
Turning the body – hands, feet – inward
Sitting or shrinking while others stand
Keeping in one place while others move about
Moving the head and shoulders while speaking
Touching the face or mouth while speaking
Speaking quickly and in broken sentences
Introducing 'er' in mid-sentence (self-interruption)

High status (dominant)
Holding eye contact, breaking it, not glancing back
Stretching the body to fill space
Standing while others sit or shrink
Moving into unoccupied space
Detecting the centre of the space and occupying it
Keeping the head and shoulders still while speaking
Occupying space with hand gestures
Speaking slowly in coherent sentences
Introducing 'er' at the beginning of sentences (interrupting others)

When practicing improvisation, the effort to manage gesture, eye contact and positioning, can feel crude and unwieldy at first, but these effects will quickly free the actors by giving them certain sure and reliable rules. If the gardener plays high status towards the duchess, the effect will be a dramatic reversal with convention overturned, and audiences enjoy it when status positions change or become uncertain. The tutor-student relationship obviously implies a fixed status position, but one that may also be flexible. Students like it if I ask them to try and change this status relationship in a formal setting such as a lecture-room. They move about, throw things, try to leave; the lecturer, like the mother in *Family Voices,* is deposited on the margins and ignored. If I try to join in their conversations, my status becomes uncertain; that makes them uneasy.

In *Family Voices,* status transactions happen between characters within a closely related group. In one sense we see mother/father/son as one culture group. The mother thinks this culture group still operates. To the son, however, it is defunct and has already been replaced by another. But on the practical level, that is, on stage, *Family Voices* became a play about occupying the space, making eye contact, breaking it, lowering the voice and using a voice-tone inappropriate to the words being said. A conciliatory tone, a loving gesture, clashes with meanings and words that are effectively mocking, unfriendly, cruel. Through this *inappropriateness*, father and son challenge each other's status, and the son teases his mother's sincere utterances by imitating them. While the mother can only speak with an appropriate tone, father and son have become what Johnstone calls 'status experts', able to play high or low in a game of pretence and imitative mockery. The play ends with the father's cryptic statement:

> VOICE THREE: I have so much to say to you, but I am quite dead. What I have to say to you will never be said.
>
> (Ibid:83)

Is his tone here one of defeated withdrawal (low status)? Or the verbal equivalent of breaking eye contact – indeed all contact – deliberate (high status)? The text will not say, and its impact may depend entirely on how the actors are feeling at that precise moment, on how their status behaviour has influenced them up to the last moment of the performance.

Johnstone's comments on status made frequent reference, as we might expect, to Shakespeare's *King Lear*. Some years after my experience with *Family Voices*, The West Yorkshire Playhouse asked me to write a short play for younger audiences based on *King Lear*, using four actors from the cast of Jude Kelly's production. The text was to be in verse (though this requirement was flexible) yet written using the common expressions and rhythms of ordinary speech: for this audience nothing high-flown or Shakespearean. Of course, it's quite possible to write in speech-like language – the language of the speaking voice – and to generate effects, images, metaphors, especially those relevant to the condition of King Lear, for the king in the course of Shakespeare's play loses status so rapidly we might even say it haemorrhages from him. In my version of the play, entitled *NEVER*, Lear, a billionaire tycoon in the hydro-engineering industry, retires, gives away his money and power to his daughter Regan and her boy-friend (known in the play as a 'Soldier'), in exchange for board and lodging with them. The problem is that Lear is by now suffering a deep decline into senile dementia. His other daughter, Cordelia, disguises herself as Regan's maid in order to look after him. Lear, though, is too demented to recognise the daughter he truly loves and who loves him. Thus we have the basic Lear situation, and four characters.

The following short scene illustrates how Lear continues to believe he can use his status, even though he has none. Regan and the Soldier have taken over completely. Driven almost mad themselves by his deepening senility, the two decide not to kill him but dump him out in the countryside, actually the wilderness, near to a huge waterfall. They make him think, though, that he's actually in a residential care home. Here, they arrive at the spot with Lear in a wheelbarrow:

REGAN

We'll drop him off here then.
This is the place where he failed
to complete his masterpiece.
He gave it up.

North of here the Arctic ice
pours into miles of rivers.
A terrible waste of power:

two million volts, five hundred cities,
lights visible from space. The plan.
The big vision. The dam's half-built.
Before the fans turned water into heat
his powers of mind went ... phht, like that.
Wouldn't forward the finance.

Leave him here. He'll crawl his way to the edge,
or die of cold in the drizzle from the mountain.
He's come without his clothes. Still in his pyjamas.

They sit him down

SOLDIER

We didn't bring his rug.

Pause. Concerned

He needs his rug

REGAN

He's going to die.
All he needs is his skin.

LEAR

I'm cold.

Quietly

Uranus locked his children away in the earth.
They castrated him.

Shouting

From his lascivious blood the Furies spring.

Half singing

They put his trunk on the wrong train.
His balls they went to Gloucester.
I belong to Glasgow
And Glasgow belongs to me.
I left my heart in San Francisco.

Quoting forgetfully

His pancreas went to St Pancras,
His liver's in Liverpool Street.
I wouldn't be in his feet.
It comes right in the end.
The rhythm's awful.

Confused

Where's my wallet?
A ten-pound note's in it. Where is it?

REGAN

You won't need any money.
It's all on the house here.

LEAR

Just a tip to give the chef.

SOLDIER

Take this. Pocket money.

LEAR

This is the bill.
I've nothing to pay it with.
Where's my wallet … my pocket?

REGAN

Your pocket's here.
There's a ten-pound note inside.

LEAR

I've ordered. Why are they taking so long?

SOLDIER

We ate before we came.

REGAN

Try to remember.
You can't remember Maid's nice omelette
with lovely bread and butter, and a soft biscuit?

LEAR

Takes out the note.

Here's my pocket. It's empty.
Where's my pocket money?

SOLDIER

Give me an axe. I'll break his skull.

LEAR

I'm thirsty.

REGAN

We're going now, father.
You've got everything you need.
Next time we'll bring Cordelia.
Won't that be a nice treat?

Just call if you want anything.
You're safe and warm, and these
big stones will look after you.
I think we're lucky to have found
such a lovely place, don't you?
This pretty room?

Shall I put out the light?
Bye bye ... night night.

Regan and the Soldier exit. Lights fade

(Unpublished)

Would we describe this scene as realism? Hardly. But it does speak to the audience about the real – almost too appallingly real – position of a human being in a state of abjection associated with extreme old age. Though this time the consequences look like being fatal, (in the final scene Lear crawls over the huge falls and disappears in the sound of raging waters), the tone of his 'carers', his offspring, seems to be a knowingly light cruelty, as in *Family Voices*. Writing for the theatre confers a wide choice of language modes (the 'song' above, the references to Greek myths) and of ways of presenting characters; those above are unpleasant to the point of comedy ('All he needs is his skin'). Demented Lear thinks he's in a restaurant, thinks high status. ('I've ordered. Why are they taking so long?') The scene shifts through four verbal sequences: they arrive, Lear's mad shouts and songs, the confusion with money, they leave him to die. It does help to be aware of these shifts of sequence, to know how many there are in each scene, how long each one lasts, how one moves into another.

This scene can be played on an empty stage. The consequences of being in these surroundings are very high, very serious. But the point is made by how the characters refer to these surroundings, not by elaborate stage sets.

Naturalistic Representation

Another term for this approach to theatre is *illusionism* – the attempt to create the illusion that the events and characters we witness are real. As well as objects in a setting, the most definitive element in naturalistic presentation will be speech and dialogue. The sounds of ordinary speaking voices, sentences unfinished, interrupting each other, of mumbling, humour, scattered formalities: all these will most likely be found in a naturalistic setting. Although I did attempt that type of dialogue in the scene from *Never*, I was equally concerned with metaphor – the forest, waterfall, wilderness, as reflections of a mind. It's hard to know what people would usually talk about while pushing their aged relative up a forest track in a wheel-barrow at night. It's not so difficult if you are writing a scene in a country pub in Ireland, the wind blowing outside, a warm fire burning, and a few locals gathered round. Somebody might say 'These big stones will look after you', but it's more likely they'll talk something like this from Conor McPherson's play *The Weir*. Here the characters talk about putting a bet on a horse:

> FINBAR: Ah the principle of the thing is to win a few quid and don't be giving out.
>
> JACK: Who's giving out? I'm not giving out. All I'm saying is that the way I go at it, the principle's not, the science. It's the luck, it's the something that's not the facts and the figures of it.
>
> FINBAR: Jaysus. And do you and Kenny get down on your knees and lash a few quick Hail Marys out before he stamps your docket or something?
>
> JACK: Ah it's not like that. I'm not talking about that. For fuck's sake.
>
> (McPherson, 1994: 16)

This is a wonderful definition of luck, which is, of course, *not* chance. But the language is no more special or striking than it would be on any other night in this place, between these characters or people very much like them. Naturalistic means simply that – language as it is spoken, received and understood, under usual circumstances, given certain regional variations. How, then, does McPherson develop the drama, increase consequence, make contact with things, experiences, people, not 'usual'? Given only a country pub with a group of ordinary characters, how does he break the pattern of routine, rob the scene of its predictability? These 'usual circumstances' continue in the play. The characters talk, drink, tease and amuse each other. Nothing excessive. Then, when one of them arrives with a new guest, Valerie, a stranger to the area, they start to exchange anecdotes about ghosts, about the supernatural. Around these parts there used to be something known as a 'fairy road'. It runs through the house where Valerie is staying. The point is to entertain Valerie with some items of native folklore, a vital element of their narrative culture. Some are old stories going back five generations, others recent. Naturalistic speech in *The Weir* arrives laden not just with frequent expletives and quirky idiom but with stories that blur the distinction between the living and the dead. Finally it is Valerie's story – about her daughter who was drowned – that moves the characters, and the audience, to operate at the highest level of attention.

Here is Valerie's story about what happened after her daughter's drowning accident in a local town baths. For some time she didn't really know how to cope:

VALERIE: ...Just months of this. Not really taking it in like.

Pause

But, and then one morning. I was in bed. Daniel had gone to work. I usually lay there for a few hours, trying to stay asleep, really. I suppose. And the phone rang. And I just left it. I wasn't going to get it. And it rang for a long time. Em, eventually it stopped, and I was dropping off again. But then it started ringing again, for a long time. So I thought it must have been Daniel trying to get me. Someone who knew I was there.

So I went down and answered it. And. The line was very faint. It was like a crossed line. There were voices, but I couldn't hear what they were saying. And then I heard Niamh. She said, 'Mammy?' And I... just said, you know, 'Yes'.

Short pause

And she said... She wanted me to come and collect her. I mean, I wasn't sure whether this was a dream or her leaving us had been a dream. I just said, 'Where are you?'

And she said she thought she was at Nana's. In the bedroom. But Nana wasn't there. And she was scared. There were children knocking in the walls and the man was standing across the road, and he was looking up and he was going to cross the road. And would I come and get her?

And I said I would, of course I would. And I dropped the phone and I ran out to the car in just a tee-shirt I slept in. And I drove to Daniel's mother's house. And I could hardly see, I was crying so much. I mean, I knew she wasn't going to be there. I knew she was gone. But to think wherever she was... that... And there was nothing I could do about it.

Daniel's mother got a doctor and I... slept for a day or two. But it was... Daniel felt that I... needed to face up to Niamh being gone. But I just thought that he should face up to what happened to me. He was insisting I get some treatment, and then... everything would be okay. But you know, what can help that, if she's out there? She still... still needs me.

Pause

JACK: You don't think it could have been a dream you were having, no?

Short pause

VALERIE: I heard her.

Short pause

FINBAR: Sure, you were after getting a terrible shock, Valerie. These things can happen. Your... brain is trying to deal with it, you know? (*Pause*) Is your husband going to... come down?

VALERIE: I don't think so.

FINBAR: Ah, it'd be a terrible shame if you don't... if you didn't see... him because of something as, you know... that you don't even know what it was.

Short pause

BRENDAN: She said she knew what it was.

FINBAR: But sure you can't just accept that, that you, you know... I mean... surely you, you have to look at the broader thing of it here.

JIM: It might have been a wrong number.

BRENDAN: What?

JIM: It could have been a wrong number or something wrong with the phone, you know? And you'd think you heard it. Something on the line.

BRENDAN: But you wouldn't hear somebody's voice on the

fucking thing, Jim.

JIM: Just it might have been something else.

JACK: Here, go easy, Brendan, Jim's only trying to talk about the fucking thing.

FINBAR: Ah lads.

JACK: Just take it easy.

VALERIE: Stop. I don't want... It's something that happened. And it's nice just to be here and... hear what you were saying. I know I'm not crazy.

Short pause

(Ibid 39–40)

Notice how Valerie tells her story, and how her speech is arranged on the page, and punctuated, helping the actor to change her pace as she speaks. During this speech the actor will be aware of the theatre audience; she will hold their attention. But she will also be aware, as Valerie, of the way the men are listening. She needs to relive the experience, moment by moment, for them to follow it. And clearly they do follow it; they are moved; but this leaves them unable to know how they should communicate this response. The speech is about a story with huge consequences, including those which immediately followed. Is Valerie ill? (The doctor is called.) Should she just rest? Did she split from her husband because of it? But also her telling of it has consequences. The men must react. How? What do they think she is saying to them? That she heard the voice of her dead daughter? That she imagined it? Is she asking for confirmation? Is it a folk-tale, a banshee story? The banshee appears, traditionally, to a member of a family at the moment of the death of a close relative, but this 'ghost' appeared months later. This is not a story that follows the folk-tale pattern of experience, which is one reason why the men don't know what to say in reply. It also questions their Catholic religion – where *is* Niamh? (the mother's question, too).

Notice the different reactions of the men. What should we make of Jim's comment: 'It could have been a wrong number'? How will this be received: by the others, by Valerie, by the audience? Having broken with conversational habit, with the familiar, it's as if the characters don't know how to get it back.

Issues Theatre: Non-illusionism

The subject of a play can be the treatment of an issue: war, injustice, the state of the nation; treated partly through documentary, through the presentation of facts, and partly though role-play, the use of character and scene, as in the more traditional type of play. Sometimes we get a mixed form of theatre, containing private individualised characters, as in illusionist theatre, and others who represent a single viewpoint or value. Arthur Miller's *The Crucible* presents both the individualised character, John Proctor, victim of the Salem witch-hunts in seventeenth-century Massachusetts, and the more stereotyped character, Reverend Hale, the church's regional expert on devil-worship. Later we meet the even more stereotyped character, Judge Danforth, who assumes all accused are guilty until proved innocent, but we still haven't strayed from the idea of illusionism. To do so requires a basic change in the type of representation.

At this point, characters might wear masks, carry placards or even become placard-like in their speech. Status transactions occur between rival groups. Instead of a familiar domestic enclosure, the stage becomes a platform, a public space. Mime replaces private spontaneous action. Songs and chants disturb the surface of naturalistic speech. Performance is choreographed, gesture and timing become predicable. Image rather than plot stands in the foreground. In Peter Brook's corporate production of the Vietnam War protest play *US* (the title signifies 'us' the audience as well as 'United States', and both are under attack), the effect of napalm bombing is symbolised by the play's last sequence. One actor removes a butterfly from a matchbox, holds it between his fingers, strikes a match and sets fire to its wings. (A paper butterfly was used, but the point was that it could have been a real living creature tortured pointlessly.) The cast then refuses to leave the stage. The audience must make its own walk-out, an action which cannot help but seem like calculated indifference.

Caryl Churchill's play *Top Girls* constructs a forum for debating feminist issues and yet moves between modes of representation: illusionist and non-illusionist elements function independently in this play. It begins with an imaginary dinner party attended by significant women from past literature and history. Together they provide a telling illustration of the way narrative culture is gendered. In a final scene the issues are revived but in the domestic setting of a small back kitchen of a council house in East Anglia. Historical figures are public property; they come to us with large simplified 'issues' already attached, but can still be viewed in terms of a private perspective: What were they really like? Plays such as Brecht's *Galileo* and Alan Bennett's *The Madness of George III* re-examine the characters which history has stereotyped. Churchill's play suggests the more intimate perspective in the opening scene by making these stereotyped figures speak about major subjects that traverse history, while their *manner* of speaking resembles that of normal people at dinner parties, interrupting each other, trying hard to hold on to one topic, two or three speaking at once.

In later scenes in *Top Girls,* the private perspective widens; public debates are engaged in a private setting. However successful in business Marlene is, her relationship with her sister in that small kitchen will never form part of her public image. The private self is complex, baffling. When exposed, an apparently shadowless character has shadows; there are issues she cannot confront, losses untraced in her self-image of power. What character is and who or what constructs it becomes an issue itself.

Developments in Non-illusionism

I began this book assuming that all plays, poems and stories I quoted from or referred to would share at least one quality: that the writer is able to build up a world and encourage us to inhabit it imaginatively. In David Hare's play for radio and stage, *The Permanent Way*, developed by the writer in conjunction with the Out Of Joint Theatre Company, and first produced at York Theatre Royal in 2003, the actors speak directly to the audience from the stage, and out of a world we already share with them. The need to be in their own authentic world still exists, but it is one we know to be our own, verified by what we read, helplessly, in newspapers, hear on television news and special reports, exchange opinions about, throw up our hands in despair at. Hare and his company have sifted through spoken and written evidence connected with the Hatfield train disaster, and the privatisation of British Rail, two events tragically linked in the history of the British transport system. The distinction illusion/non-illusion has fallen away. We know we are hearing the real words of people actually involved, but spoken to us by actors in a non-illusionist style of representation. Here they discuss the trial that followed the crash:

> British Transport Policeman: We started with two weeks of technical discussion. At the end the judge says, 'No, there's no such charge in English law, because there's no controlling mind. To prove manslaughter you have to have a controlling mind.' And on the railways, everyone knows: there's no controlling mind. And that was it. The case fell at the first hurdle. The driver,

> he had his charge what they call 'set aside'. Because everyone knew. No justice in that. The driver to be prosecuted and no one else.
>
> Bereaved Mother: I'm not a rebel. I'm an M&S Supervisor, you believe in people, you believe in authority.
>
> British Transport Policeman: I did feel angry that Great Western Trains and Railtrack were not made to seem as guilty as they should have been seen to be.
>
> Bereaved Mother: Everyone around the table was dumbstruck. We didn't want anyone crucified. We didn't want blood and guts. All we wanted was someone to stand in the dock. That's all we expected. And we were told the law is not right for this.
>
> British Transport Policeman: Eventually Great Western were fined 3.5 million after pleading guilty to breaches of the Health and Safety at Work Act, 1974. Everyone said it was a lot but it didn't seem a lot to me...
>
> (Hare, 2003: 31–4)

Because the world of the play is so much our own, it follows that the consequences of what happens in it will be, too – are already – and so must be faced. This is the whole case made by *The Permanent Way*. If drama releases consequences – for the characters, for the audience – it also creates a tension; some will try to face those consequences, others to avoid them:

> John Prescott: ATP will be in the next Queen's Speech.
>
> Bereaved Mother: Prescott looked at me.
>
> John Prescott: You're a dangerous woman.
>
> Bereaved Mother: I said 'I know'.
>
> John Prescott: 'And do you know why? Do you know why you're dangerous?'
>
> Bereaved Mother: 'I know why. Because I'm not paid. And I won't go away.'
>
> (Ibid: 52)

Story Theatre

In the Young Vic Theatre in London, a group of young actors begin telling a story. It's as if an Ancient Greek Chorus from a play by Euripides had migrated to the north east of England (that's where the accents come from) and decided to *start* the action instead of just commenting on it. The play is *Skellig*, directed by Trevor Nunn, and scripted by the author of the original story, David Almond. The 'chorus' is actually the football team, who hardly appear in the story, but here functioning as storytellers they make a vigorous opening impression. Whenever the story moves too quickly for extended illusionist treatment, Almond brings on his storytellers and their rapid-fire language and gestures, their physical engagement with stage-space. Nunn explains his vision of the play – and of this type of play-making – as follows:

> Shakespeare begins his most exciting history play, *Henry V*, by bringing on a solitary storyteller, who he calls the Chorus – just like the Ancient Greeks. The storyteller is there, he says, to apologise that the actors have only a bare wooden stage and a few swords to tell the tale of the legendary warrior king, including all his amazing exploits fighting great battles. And then he says one of the most important sentences in the history of drama; he says the thing that in one way or another is what those up on stage have always said and will always say to the audience: 'Let us/on your imaginary forces work.'
>
> Very expensive big budget theatre can try to get an audience to believe that they are watching the 'real thing', just as film is invariably able to persuade them they are. But when the theatre has only bare boards – 'two planks and a passion' they used to call it – then only collusion with the *imagination* of the audience will bring about the necessary magic. 'Poor' theatre relies on imagination and so the form of theatre we call story theatre grew out of the poor theatre tradition.
>
> I have done many works of story theatre, including what seemed to many people like a mad, misplaced endeavor, to present a whole Dickens novel on stage. I chose *Nicholas Nickleby* and the intention was to find a way of staging the whole book, leaving out no strings of the story and including every incident, however impossible it might seem at first blush to stage such things.
>
> So my colleagues and I found the way of showing journeys by stage coach and cart and omnibus, we whirled from aristocratic haunts to poverty stricken tenements, we were undaunted by the need to have a rearing horse or people rolling ecstatically down a hill. We portrayed the elderly, the adult, youngsters and children. We moved from the crowded metropolis to the bleak north to the south coast and from

farce to comedy to tragedy – on, and with lots of songs.

It was I suppose a 'total' theatre experience, but none of it would have worked without the audience collectively contributing their imagination, to turn a few commonplace items at the disposal of the storytellers into the myriad different things we said they had become.

As Shakespeare knew four hundred years ago, when the audience contribute their imagination, they become part of the show, and when it works, the experience can be exhilarating and the memory of it indelible.

Here at the Young Vic, with its extraordinary history of being a poor theatre company for whom no endeavour is beyond their means, I am once again adapting a novel teeming with characters and once again with incidents that would seem impossible to stage. Words. Poetic words, heightened words, rhythmic words, descriptive words, everyday words and the words of magic and miracle

(Trevor Nunn, Programme Notes to *Skellig*, Young Vic Theatre, 2003)

Trevor Nunn's comments seem to me true to the life of theatre: its inventiveness, its commitment to creative language as its best resource, and to the collaborative process of making. Every piece of drama cannot help but show communication to be happening in two ways – first, between the individual actors on stage, and second, between the whole performance – its images, vitality and pace – and the audience. Theatre speaks within the space, and beyond it – to outside.

Although *Skellig* was originally written as a piece of children's fiction, Nunn clearly recognised its potential as theatre. The shape-shifting of forms of creative expression shows how work in progress sometimes moves between genres in the course of its development. While this book's approach to writing sees it mainly in terms of specific genres, the final point must be that genres are fluid, that the evolution of one idea can be achieved through a range of different forms. It's always worth looking again at a poem or personal narrative to find new ways of developing its imaginative strengths, and deciding to try an idea in a different genre can help this process along. Within a short story you finished writing some time ago or just recently, a scene might suddenly become recognisable as having the potential for drama. The workbook notes you wrote early on in the development of your writing might, on re-reading, take you by surprise: here is the material you've been looking for, the voices and scenes you need to start writing your first play.

Discussion and Workshop

Feature films are often divided into major sub-genres: Crime / Disaster / Sci-Fi, Horror / Sex, Jealousy and Romance / War / Biography / Fantasy / Entertainer (*Little Voice, The Full Monty, Billy Elliot*) / Adaptations. Do these distinctions imply different story structures or do they all more or less conform to the same blue-print? What differences of story-structure can we identify between these groups of film? Do they make use of action motifs? Look at a film adaptation of a novel. Does this film conform to a blue-print you recognise in other films that are not adaptations? Does it make use of action motifs? How does the structure of the film compare with that of the novel? Does the film include narrative image and narrative progression in its delivery?

In Act One of David Mamet's play *Oleanna,* a college tutor is playing high status with one of his female students. Read through the whole play and work out how each actor expresses his/her status position, how those positions change. Investigate these issues by acting out scenes from the play.

Investigate and explore (through workshops and/or discussion groups) some of the ways the following might influence new developments in the theatre and/or radio drama: reality TV shows; contemporary political conflicts; classical history and myth; Eastern religion and philosophy.

Divide into groups each containing two actors, one director. Each group works on and presents the following short scene from Caryl Churchill's play *Light Shining in Buckinghamshire.* Aim to emphasise the changes in status – between the two women, between them and the Great House.

TWO WOMEN LOOK IN A MIRROR

1st Woman comes in with a broken mirror. 2nd Woman is mending

1st Woman: Look, look, you must come quick.

2nd Woman: What you got there?

1st Woman: Look. Who's that? That's you. That's you and me.

2nd Woman: Is that me? Where you get it?

1st Woman: Up the house.

2nd Woman: What? With him away? It's all locked up.

1st Woman: I went in the front door.

2nd Woman: The front door?

1st Woman: Nothing happened to me. You can take things –

2nd Woman: That's his things. That's stealing. You'll be killed for that.

1st Woman: No, not any more, it's all ours now, so we won't burn the corn because that's our corn now and we're not going to let the cattle out because they're ours too.

2nd Woman: You been in his rooms?

1st Woman: I been upstairs. In the bedrooms.

2nd Woman: I been in the kitchen.

1st Woman: I lay on the bed. White linen sheets. Three wool blankets.

2nd Woman: Did you take one?

1st Woman: I didn't know what to take. There's so much.

2nd Woman: Oh if everyone's taking something I want a blanket. But what when he comes back?

1st Woman: He'll never come back. We're burning his papers, that's the Norman papers that give him his lands. That's like him burnt. There's no one over us. There's pictures of him and his grandfather and his great great – a long row of pictures and we pulled them down.

2nd Woman: But he won't miss a blanket.

1st Woman: There's an even bigger mirror that we didn't break. I'll show you where. You see your whole body at once. You see yourself standing in that room. They must know what they look like all the time. And now we do.

(Churchill, 1985: 207)

Explore how gender influences status. Re-write the above scene using two male characters. As above, one reports while the other reacts. What details would you have to change? Would the dialogue between the two have been different in any way?

Role play. Two people take part, but only one of them knows the story. This could be a meeting between a parent and head-teacher, a novelist and her agent, two friends who have lost touch with each other, a bride and groom. Something has happened which unsettles the relationship. Act out the meeting. If only one actor knows what has happened, the meeting will be played out with a greater sense of urgency and tension. The dialogue can then be developed into a script.

Suggestions for Writing

1 Develop a dialogue around two characters using action motif. For example, one of them is smoking in a non-smoking area. The other, an official, tells him/her to stop – a Challenge motif, possibly leading to Offer or Fight. A third character might become involved. What happens? Write a two-character dramatic sequence that explores one of the other action motifs. Develop your script with attention to one of the three specific media: stage, screenplay, radio.

2 Write a short dialogue for radio or the stage in which one character persuades another that he or she can now change their status from low to high. Something has happened – as in the sequence by Caryl Churchill above.

3 In writing for the natural speaking voice, it's often the case that as you get to know your characters, you begin to hear how they would speak – as a rhythm in your head, then their exact words. To develop this skill, begin with a single character. Write a monologue in his or her natural voice. At some point other characters might be involved, or this monologue could become the climax of a longer play.

4 Write a short fiction screenplay or radio play in which a carpet fitter arrives at an old woman's house. She lets him in and he fits the carpet while she talks. He is a deaf mute. Using memory sequences, see if you can find out how the story progresses or what significance this man has in the mind of the old woman. How do you convey the presence of a mute character on radio? (As an example, see Pinter's *A Slight Ache*.)

5 Write a short fiction screenplay in which a friendship undergoes an irrevocable change as a result of a decision or action by one of the characters.

6 Write a screenplay using one of the following as its title: The Spine, Grass, Blinded, Gently, Too Much Space, Role, The Sands.

7 Write the first ten minutes of a feature film screenplay that includes the set-up where a main character and wish are established for the audience. Choose the setting carefully – for suspense and consequence. The following comment by Syd Field from his book *Screenplay* will be a useful way to assess your progress: 'The first ten pages: Does it work? Does it set your story in motion? Does it establish your main character? Does it state the dramatic premise – i.e. what is the story about? Does it set up the situation? Does it set up a problem that your character must confront and overcome? Does it state your character's need?'

8 Issue play. As a group (actors/director/researchers) create a file on your computer containing images, evidence, data, interviews, comment and opinion all related to an issue (local, national or international), which you are aiming to represent dramatically. Your aim is to make the audience think, rather than to make up their minds for them. You might construct it out of the question: *What if…?* Develop a short play – forty-five minutes.

9 Re-writing. Re-tell a story using four actors, six separate prop objects, and limited sound effects – in forty-five minutes. Make plans, invent your own strategies, write the script as you rehearse and improvise. The story could be a folktale or fairytale that you want to make relevant to your present day adult audience, a story from classical or other ancient mythology, a story from Dickens (a good example would be *Great Expectations*), or from the work of a contemporary novelist.

10 Re-tell a real-life story connected to a place you know in the present or the past, or to people living as a group in the present or the past. Invent your own theatre strategies to get the story across to an audience in the space of forty-five minutes, with a minimum of resources ('Poor Theatre'), and a maximum of imagination.

Revision and Editing

Your characters must have aim and direction. Emotionally, are they travelling, or are they stuck? What is the soundtrack of thoughts at the back of their minds? Is it audible, inaudible, secret, revealed? Be sure that dialogues don't just wander pleasantly along. Make them go somewhere.

Are you aware of the level of consequence? Your characters might want to take control themselves. Let them do so, but allow yourself to have the ultimate say over what happens in your finished script.

Check whether your writing tells a story and tells it in a way that will excite, surprise, but not confuse the audience. If story is *not* your overall purpose, what is it? How clear are you about what it is you aim to achieve?

Think about the drama you are writing as a two-way form of communication. First, what are the characters saying to each other – are they giving and receiving significant messages – ones that have consequence and impact? Second, what does the scene itself give the audience in terms of its overall image and meaning? Think about these two flows of information and assess whether they *both* generate impact.

If your play is going to be read by a theatre director or radio producer, it needs to be presented on the page with an appropriate format. You will need to research details of presentation, through websites, through current published advice in your media. The BBC published advice on layout will help you revise and edit your script ready for submission and performance.

Before you submit your script to an assessor, which you will have to do if you want to make any practical gain from your writing, you will need to correct all minor errors – punctuation, spelling, sentence structure – just as you would if you submitted an article to a magazine, journal or a newspaper. Aim to submit an accurate script.

GLOSSARY

I have excluded literary terms, the definitions of which are easy to find elsewhere, also those that are given exact definition in the text, except where these articulate key ideas.

Action motif A story device with potential for conflict. Examples: Challenge, Threat, Offer, Gift, Fight, Discovery. One can lead to another as action develops.

Character rhythm Our access as readers to any created fictional character is through written words. As writers, we can give those words a pace and rhythm that corresponds with the character's own behaviour and attitude. Character rhythm easily develops into monologue, dialogue and free indirect speech (q.v.).

Cliché Tired or dead expression can be justified only when placed in the mouth of a *character*. In Alan Bennett's *Talking Heads*, for example, the term 'Soldiering On' (title of one of the monologues) is a cliché used by Muriel, the main character.

Closure Closure implies that the writer's own judgement – about what has happened, about the overall meaning of a piece – can be passed on authoritatively to readers. Most writers sensibly avoid this kind of finality. At the same time, the ending of a story, novel or play can be the most interesting part to write – and the most difficult – because you are in effect fine-tuning the reader's ultimate impressions. The aim is to enable readers to *participate* in the making of meaning.

Convergence An effect of writing in which readers and audiences seem to reach a moment of insight simultaneously with the writer, as if they are present when the right words are found and discoveries are made. The creative process therefore appears relatively transparent, less obscure. The equivalent of convergence is often described by actors as being 'in the moment' – you seem to exist wholly as the character; the lines the character speaks become your own.

Counters The narrative markers – an object, character, event, memory – recognised by readers as having recurrent high significance, especially in fiction for children. In Philip Pullman's trilogy, for example, high significance is attached to special objects: the alethiometer, the knife, the spyglass. This device is long associated with children's stories. Fairy tales and folktales also generate meaning through objects as counters.

Crossover fiction A term of recent invention, it applies to certain children's books which appeal to all-age readers. One reason for this appeal might be the way characters are situated – aware of the adult world they are about to enter, at a threshold, crossing over, learning what happens there.

De-familiarisation A term introduced by Viktor Schlovsky of the Russian School of Formalist Criticism in the early 1920s, it refers to an effect of writing that disrupts our normal habits of perceiving the real world, often by prolonging our attention to it, making it strange. Such an effect can be achieved by foregrounding the act of attention itself, as in William Carlos Williams's poem on p.74.

Enactment An effect of writing that, as we read, raises our level of attention. A performed poem can hold an audience by its use of timing and surprise, even suspense, just as well as a speech in a stage play, a dramatic scene in memoir or prose fiction, or in a piece of storytelling. Enactment includes speech qualities (q.v.) as well as focus and vividness.

Epistolary style In fiction, the use of a letter-writing style to indicate confidentiality, authenticity. Actual letters in stories can create turning points (q.v.), as in *The Curious Incident* where discovered letters reveal a deception, or in *Family Voices*, where unsent letters convey emotional distance.

Flashback A scene inserted to illustrate past events relevant to the story, flashback is a filmic device also used frequently in modern fiction. Readers and audiences need to retain a sense of the story's forward movement, however, so departures into flashback should be brief, significant, and return us to the present of the action.

Flash fiction A short prose fiction narrative usually less than 1,000 words in length. The piece should be complete, with a beginning, middle and end. It should demonstrate lack of superfluous action, economy of detail.

Focaliser The dominant point of view in a piece of narrative, usually presented using free indirect style or first-person narration. The focaliser is always one of the characters. First- and third-person narration can make use of different focalisers in turn as a story develops.

Free indirect style An effect of third-person narration (q.v.) in which the narrating voice echoes the thoughts, feelings, sense impressions of one of the characters. It allows access to hidden levels of thought and feeling, which the character may be suppressing or may not be able or willing to articulate (see Jackie Kay, *Trout Friday*).

Free verse Although it has no regular number of stresses or syllables per line (metrical regularity), and no obvious rhyme scheme, free verse can still retain vestiges of these more formal characteristics. Its lines of uneven length, for example, can still end with words of grammatical significance (see Elizabeth Bishop, p. 91). (There are exceptions to this tendency, see Sharon Olds, p. 81.) Free verse can make use of other verbal patterns – strong rhythms, internal rhymes, half-rhymes, as well as regular or irregular stanza forms.

Genre fiction A class of fiction – some might include in this fiction for children – aiming to meet its readers' expectations, so that situation, character, structure and style are governed by certain storytelling conventions. Genre fiction might include horror, thriller, fantasy, romantic fiction and science fiction, although the individual novel in any of these categories might go beyond the limits they impose.

Imagination The faculty of selecting (usually from memory) certain places, scenes, people and events as subjects for art. It feels as if such selecting is *involuntary*. Imagination can be triggered by sensations and can be developed and enhanced through artistic practice. Its further attributes include *shaping – a sense of artistic structure* – and the sense of entering the consciousness of someone, or some thing, an empathy with others. 'Imagination' can also carry a specific qualifying attribute, as in the 'vernacular imagination'.

Inciting incidents Also termed 'trigger events', these are incidents that release sequences of action or changes of mood, usually close to the start of a story. Short stories make use of inciting incidents as a regular starting point for action or change; in novels the incident may be a later development in the story.

Magic Writers wishing to include the magical in a story will benefit from thinking about the social history of magic, its connection with late medieval alchemy, also with primitive culture and folklore. Magic offers its recipients a form of power, evil in evil hands, never wholly explicable or reliable.

Modern fiction In one view, modern fiction mostly occupies the same world as that found in books on social and cultural history, from the eighteenth century to the present. But it can go well beyond the present, inventing new worlds, through fantasy, science fiction, and by depicting the impossible. As well as a concern with public themes and social behaviour, its attributes include the moment by moment telling of experience, a fascination with conscience and consciousness, the 'inner room' of the self, the telling, responding to, and overhearing of narratives, the reliability – or otherwise – of narrative.

Narration First-person narration ('I') requires strong attitude in the character of the speaker, yet sometimes can imply unreliability. Perhaps because of this uncertainty, this type of narration has been increasingly popular with contemporary fiction writers. Third-person narration can position itself at a distance from the story characters, or (as in free indirect style, q.v.), right inside their heads, or even inside their unconscious drives. First-person narration can sometimes develop access to the hidden lives of characters in the story. John Steinbeck's novel *East of Eden* (1952) is an interesting example of this.

Narrative culture The notion of an inherent background of stories, characters and significant events present in every cultural community, both regional and national. One element of narrative culture is the *history* – as known, as told and written – of a person or group, but narrative culture also includes divine, mythic, legendary and fictional narratives. Changes in narrative culture are of interest to writers. A major shift occurred with the rise of the novel. A culture's myths and social rituals (q.v.) with their emphasis on festival recur throughout its dramatic and fictional narratives, while film narratives influence the treatment of scenes in modern fiction. Narrative culture accounts for the current resonance (q.v.) of certain images. Scenes of street fighting and terrorism, for example, emerge in Elizabeth Cook's fictional treatment of the sack of Troy by the Greeks, see p. 111. Other developments in poetry and drama show a renewal of interest in classical themes, for example, the epic scale found in Ted Hughes's version of Ovid's *Metamorphoses.* Western religious traditions may depend exclusively on narrative, while others do so rather less. It's important, therefore (and not just for writers), to appreciate differences between cultures in their approach to narrative.

Narrative image An image (in a story, poem, film, play) of the background circumstances, the physical and cultural world, out of which events unfold into narrative progression.

Other A character exerting a major influence over a central character. The Other might be a spouse, sibling, relative or close friend, or an antagonist, an invader whose presence is disruptive. The Other becomes the reason why certain things happen, certain attitudes form. In works of contemporary fiction, the protagonist's relationship to the Other comes to replace that with external authority – a public world or encoded moral system.

Persona A first-person speaker who is not the author but is used by him or her to present a story, to deliver an opinion or insight. A persona can be a valuable device in all the creative genres, and is especially interesting to poets. For some reason we expect poets to speak directly in their own voice, which for many would be a restriction of poetry's breadth and inventiveness.

Point of view Sometimes referred to simply as POV, as in screenplay layouts. Point of view highlights the importance of personal response, the individual consciousness, including thoughts, feelings and sensations, as a character moves through the changing scenes and settings of a story.

Polyphony A term developed by Mikhail Mikhailovich Bakhtin to convey the many-voiced element that delivers modern fiction from single monologic discourse. A classic example is Magwitch's report of his trial in *Great Expectations* where he imitates the voices of his counsel and co-defendant whilst retaining his own London vernacular. The chapter 'Dialogue in the Modern Novel' in David Lodge's *After Bakhtin,* (1990) examines some recent examples of polyphony.

Realism In this book I develop two branches of the term: *topic realism* and *realist technique*. The first refers to a preference for real-world subject matter in the choice of scenes, attitudes and experiences, while the second is about 'making things real' through close-up focus and detailed depiction. *Magic realism* ignores the restrictions of topic subject matter and in its place chooses fantasy, fairy-tale, folklore or mythical characters and settings. Realist approaches still dominate modern fiction and also influence other genres.

Reality effects 'An old Chinese takeaway leaked orange liquid all over her suede shoes.', (Wilson, p. 162) is a good example of a reality effect, making one detail illustrate the general state of things you want to convey, strongly implying a sense of 'having been there'.

Resonance An image, word, reference or event has resonance if it tunes in to something in our cultural life, our understanding of our past, our hopes or fears for the future. Words can have resonance and gradually lose it – the word 'sin' for example. Resonance is therefore a measure of cultural change. In terms of music, a vibrating string has no resonance without the hollow body or box of the instrument. An image has resonance if it grips hold of our shared preoccupations. An example is the image of empty streets, London under attack in H. G. Wells's War of the Worlds.

Ritual A type of action (usually in public) in which each event is predictable. Ritual always follows prescribed rules. Even slight disruptions can therefore carry high levels of dramatic consequence.

Sequences Writing for the stage can benefit from a clear sense of sections in a scene, of sequences of exchange within a dialogue, as one topic shifts into another. Radio scripts rely heavily on very clear sequences of exchange, ending with a stop or fade out.

Status transactions In drama, characters can gain or lose status, generating high levels of consequence and therefore interest for audiences. Actors can train themselves through improvisation to exhibit high or low status traits, and to move between status levels.

Story world A state of things in which time is shaped by unusual events, changes, moments of consequence, challenge and crisis, where characters become more than usually aware of the moving edge of time.

Surrealism The idea of distortion has always appealed to writers and artists. It poses a link between the creative and mental disturbance. Both can be an attack on assimilation – on the sameness and dull familiarity of the so-called real world. In practice, even the appetite for shock comes from an understanding of how we receive messages, make links, act and think logically about ourselves. Realism and Surrealism continue along the same parallel as Reality and Magic in fiction for children, as if the surreal were the adult equivalent of the magical, a way of breaking free, going beyond, disregarding the need for convincingness. Voice One in Pinter's *Family Voices* (see pp. 206–8), when describing his new home in the city, often appears to have something surreal in mind.

Textual intervention The exploration of existing creative texts through innovative retellings.

Transmitter An object of focus, present for the whole poem, the whole act of attention, becomes a transmitter of meaning, shaping the poem's world. Ted Hughes, in *Poetry in the Making*, cites D. H. Lawrence's poem 'Almond Trees' in connection with this effect.

Turning point Where a main character crosses into a new emotional space, a turning point occurs. This can result from events, a change of mind, a reaction to something said or overheard.

Voice qualities Voice qualities such as tone, register, dialect and natural speech rhythms, imply energy and attitude, and frequently compel readers' attention, enriching a story with point of view, character interest and contrast. They also allow a place for contemporary speech, for regional and ethnic variations. Voice qualities, inherent in the creative genres, remind us of an oral tradition that long pre-dates the invention of writing.

BIBLIOGRAPHY

Titles referred to in the text

Almond, D. (1998), *Skellig*, London, Hodder

Armitage, S. (2005), 'The North', in *The Poetry Business*, Vol 36, Huddersfield, Faber

Armitage, S. (2003), *The Indispensible Home Doctor*, London, Faber and Faber

Atwood, M. (1983), *Bodily Harm*, London, Virago

Atwood, M. (1992), *Wilderness Tips*, London, Virago

Atwood, M. (1994), *Murder in the Dark*, London, Virago

Auden, W. H. (1994), 'Twelve Songs', in Richard Curtis, *Four Weddings and a Funeral*, London, Corgi

Ayckbourn, A. (2002), *The Crafty Art Of Playmaking*, London, Faber and Faber

Bakhtin, M. (1984), *Problems of Dostoevsky's Poetics*, ed. Caryl Emerson, Manchester, Manchester University Press

Banks, I. (1990), *The Wasp Factory*, London, Abacus

Bell, A. (1999), 'The Discourse Reader', in A. Jaworski and C. Coupland eds, *The Discourse Reader*, London, Routledge

Bell, R. (1994), *Scanning the Forth Road Bridge*, Cornwall, Peterloo

Berger, J. (1992), *Keeping a Rendezvous*, London, Granta

Bhatt, S. (1987), *The Reaper*, No 16, Santa Cruz, University of California Press

Bierce, A. (1991), 'Incident at Owl Creek Bridge', *Norton Anthology of American Literature*, 5th edition, New Jersey, Prentice Hall

Burningham, J. (2000) *Come Away From the Water, Shirley*, London, Red Fox

Bishop, E. (1991), *Complete Poems*, London, Chatto and Windus

Bohner, C. ed. (2002), *Short Fiction, Classic and Contemporary*, London, Prentice Hall

Bradbury, M. ed. (1990), *The Novel Today*, London, Fontana

Breeze, 'Binta' J. (1992), 'Testament' poem, in Afro-Caribbean reader, London, Norton

Bretton Women's Book Fund, (1983), 'You Can't Kill The Spirit, Yorkshire Women Go To Greenham', *People's History Of Yorkshire – Four*, Bretton Women's Book Fund: Leeds.

Browne, A. (1994) *Bear Hunt*, London, Puffin

Bryson, B. (1995), *Notes from a Small Island*, New York, Doubleday

Bryson, B. (1997), *A Walk in the Woods*, New York, Doubleday

Byatt, A. S. (2004), Introduction, in *The Annotated Brothers Grimm*, London, Norton

Carter, A. (1995), *The Bloody Chamber*, London, Penguin

Carver, R. (1997), *Collected Poems*, New York, Vintage Books

Carver, R. (1988), *Elephant*, London, Harvill

Causley, C. (1975), 'The Death of a Poet', from *Collected Poems 1951–75*, London, Macmillan

Chopin, K. (1894), 'The Story of an Hour'. First published in *Vogue*

Churchill, C. (1985), 'Light Shining in Buckinghamshire', *Plays One*, London, Methuen

Cinema 16 (2003) British Short Films

Cook, E. (2001), *Achilles*, London, Methuen

Copus, J. (2003), 'The Art of Illumination', National Poetry Competition winner, 2003, published in *IOS*

Crawford, R. and Imlah, M. eds (2000), *The New Penguin Book of Scottish Verse*, Penguin, London

D'Aguiar, F. (1993), *British Subjects*, Newcastle, Bloodaxe

Doherty, B. (2003) *Deep Secret*, London, Puffin

Doyle, R. (1995), *Paddy Clark, Ha Ha Ha*, London, Penguin

Duncan, I. (1968), *My Life*, London, Sphere Books

Eco, U. (1993), 'The City of Robots', in T. Docherty, ed., *Postmodernism: A Reader*, London, Harvester Wheatsheaf

Faithfull, M. (1994), *Faithfull*, London, Michael Joseph

Field, S. (2000) *Screenplay: The Foundations of Screenwriting*, New York, Dell

Fine, A. (1989) *Madame Doubtfire*, London, Puffin

Franzen, J. (2002), *The Corrections*, London, Perennial

Geddes, G. (1996), *Active Trading*, Cornwall, Peterloo

Gilman, C. P. (1981), *The Yellow Wallpaper*, London, Virago

Graham, W. S. (1977), *Collected Poems 1942–77*, London, Faber and Faber

Gunn, T. (1993), *Collected Poems*, London, Faber and Faber

Haddon, M. *Observer*, 11 April 2004

Hardy, T. (1930), *Collected Poems*, London, Macmillan

Hare, D. (2003), *The Permanent Way*, London, Faber and Faber

Heaney, S. (2004), *The Burial at Thebes*, London, Faber and Faber

Hegland, J. (1998), *Into The Forest*, London, Arrow Books

Herbert, J. (1979), *Lair*, London, Dent

Herr, M. (1990), in Don McCullin, *Autobiography*, London, Cape

Highsmith, P. (1990), *Plotting and Writing Suspense Fiction*, London, St Martins Press

Holub, M. (1990), *Poems Before and After*, Newcastle, Bloodaxe

Hoy, L. (1988) *Kiss File JC 110*, London, Walker Books

Hughes, T. (1986), *Poetry in the Making*, London, Faber and Faber

Hughes, T. (2004), *Collected Poems*, London, Faber and Faber

Ibsen, H. (1992), *A Doll's House*, New York, Dover Publications

Jaworski, A. and Coupland, C. eds (1999), *The Discourse Reader*, London, Routledge

Jeffreys, L. and Sansom, P. eds (2000), 'The Jewel You Lost. *Birthday Letters*, Ted Hughes', *Contemporary Poems, Some Critical Approaches*, Huddersfield, Smith Doorstop

Johnson, L. K. (1991), *Tings An Times, Selected Poems*, Newcastle, Bloodaxe

Kay, J. (2002), 'Trout Friday', from *Why Don't You Stop Talking?*, London, Picador

Keating, P. J. (1991), *The Haunted Study*, London, Grange Books

Keats (1996) 'Ode On A Grecian Urn', in Ferguson, Salter and Stalworth (eds) *The Norton Anthology of Poetry* (4th Edition)

Kerouac, J. (1991), *On the Road*, London, Penguin. (First published 1957)

King, S. (2001), *On Writing: A Memoir of the Craft*, London, Hodder, New English Library

Kureishi, H. (1990), *The Buddha of Suburbia*, London, Faber and Faber

Larkin, P. (2003) *Collected Poems*, London, Faber

Lawrence, D. H. (1995), *Sons and Lovers*, London, Penguin. (First published, 1913)

Lee, H. ed. (1985), '*Happy Endings*' by Margaret Atwood, *The Secret Self, Short Stories by Women*, London, Dent

Lessing, D. (1995), *Under My Skin*, London, HarperCollins.

Lessing, D. (2003), 'The Old Chief Mslangha', in D. Lessing, *This was the Old Chief's Country*, London, Norton

Lochhead, L. (2000), in R. Crawford and M. Imlah eds, *The New Penguin Book of Scottish Verse*, London, Penguin

Lodge, D. (1988), *Nice Work*, London, Penguin

Lodge, D. (1990) *After Bakhtin*, London, Routledge

Lodge, D. (1992), *The Art of Fiction*, London, Penguin

Lopez, B. (1987), *Arctic Dreams*, Toronto, Bantam Books

MacCaig, N. (1988), *Voice Over*, London, Chatto & Windus

Mamet, D. (1984), *Glengarry Glen Ross*, London, Methuen

McCullers, C. (1999), *The Ballad of the Sad Café*, London, Penguin. (First published in Britain, 1953)

McPherson, C. (1994), *The Weir*, London, Nick Hern Books

Mills, P. (1993), *Half Moon Bay*, Manchester, Carcanet Press

Mills, P. (2000), *Dinosaur Point*, Huddersfield, Smith Doorstop

Mills, P. (2002), 'The Jewel You Lost: *Birthday Letters, Ted Hughes*', in L. Jeffreys and P. Samson, eds, *Contemporary Poems, Some Critical Approaches*, Huddersfield, Smith Doorstop

Morgan, E. (2000), *New Selected Poems*, Manchester, Carcanet

Morpurgo, M. (2002), *The Sleeping Sword*, London, Egmont

Morrison, T. (1994), *The Bluest Eye*, London, Penguin. (First published, 1970)

Munden, P. and Wade, S. eds (1999), *Reading The Applause*, Huddersfield, Talking Shop

Murdoch, I. ([1970] 2001) *A Fairly Honourable Defeat*, London, Vintage

Murray, L. (2001), *Learning Human*, Manchester, Carcanet Press

National Film and TV Archive, The British Film Institute (www.bfi.org.uk/research viewingservice)

Nunn, T. (2003), Programme Notes to '*Skellig*', London, Young Vic Theatre

O'Brien, T. (1995), *In the Lake of the Woods,* London, Flamingo

Olds, S. (1996), *The Wellspring*, London, Cape

Ong, W. (1995), *Orality and Literacy*, London, Routledge

Paulin, T. (1996), *Writing to the Moment, Selected Essays*, London, Faber and Faber

Phillips, C. ed. (1997), *Extravagant Strangers, A Literature of Belonging*, London, Faber and Faber

Pierre, D. C. B. (2003), *Vernon God Little*, London, Faber and Faber

Pinter, H. (1976), 'Writing for the Theatre', in H. Pinter, ed, *Plays One*, London, Faber and Faber

Pinter, H (1983), *Family Voices*, London, Methuen

Pinter, H. (1963), *The Collection* and *The Lover*, London, Methuen

Plath, S. (1963) *Ariel*, London, Faber

Plath, S. (1977), *Johnny Panic and the Bible of Dreams*, London, Faber and Faber

Pope, R. (1995), *Textual Intervention, Critical and Creative Strategies for Literary Study*, London, Routledge

Pritchett, V. S. (1984), 'Introduction' to the *Oxford Book of Short Stories*, Oxford, Oxford University Press

Pritchett, V. S. (1993), 'You Make Your Own Life', in *The Complete Short Stories*, London, Hogarth Press

Pullman, P. (1991) *The Tiger in the Well*, London, Penguin

Raskin, R. (2002), *The Art of the Short Fiction Film*, North Carolina, McFarland

Redgrove, P. (1994), *My Father's Trapdoors*, London, Cape

Rich, R. (2004), *The School Among the Ruins*, Norton, London

Rowling, J. K. (1997), *Harry Potter and The Philosopher's Stone*, London, Bloomsbury

Rumens, C. (2003), *Writing in Education*, 28, National Association of Writers in Education

Sage, L. (1994), *Angela Carter, Writers and their Work*, London, Northcote House

Salinger, J. D. (1986), 'A Perfect day for Bananafish', in *For Esme With Love And Squalor and Other Stories*, London, Penguin

Salinger, J. D. (1995), *The Catcher in the Rye*, London, Penguin (first published 1951)

Sansom, P. (2000), 'Song', in *Point of Sale*, Manchester, Carcanet

Serraillier, I. (1956), *The Silver Sword*, London, Cape

Shields, C. (2002), *Unless*, London, HarperCollins

Shklovsky, V. (1917), 'Art as Technique' in J. Rivkin and M. Ryan, eds, *Literary Theory, An Anthology*, Oxford, Blackwell

Skilton, D. (1977), *Defoe to the Victorians: Two Centuries of the English Novel*, London, Penguin

Stand Magazine (1980), Vol. 3, Newcastle, Stand

Steinbeck, J. (1952) *East of Eden*, London, Heinemann

Stevenson, R. L. (1994), *Treasure Island*, London, Penguin. (First published 1883)

Sweeney, M. (2002), *Selected Poems,* London, Cape

Syal, M. (1997), *Anita and Me*, London, Flamingo

Tarrantino, Q. (1994), *Reservoir Dogs*, London, Faber and Faber

Tredre, R. (1995), *Observer*, 22 January

Vonnegut, K. (1969), *Slaughterhouse Five*, London, Penguin

Westall, R. (2002), *A Time of Fire*, London, Macmillan

Weissbort, D. (1986), *Leaseholder, New and Selected Poems*, Manchester, Carcanet

Welsh, I. (1996), *Marabou Stork Nightmares*, London, Vintage

Wilkins, A. (1982), *The Trees Along This Road*, Watsonville, CA., Blackwells Press

Williams, W. C. (1968a), *Selected Poems*, New Directions

Williams, W. C. (1968b), 'Proletarian Portrait', in *The Selected Poems of William Carlos Williams*, New York, New Directions

Wilson, J. (1995), *The Bed and Breakfast Star*, London, Corgi

Wilson, J. (1999), *How To Survive Summer Camp*, Oxford, Oxford University Press

Woolf, V. (1998) *To The Lighthouse*, Oxford, Oxford World's Classics

Further Reading

Atwood, M. (2002), *Negotiating with the Dead*, Cambridge, Cambridge University Press

Bell, J. and P. Magrs (2001), *The Creative Writing Coursebook*, London, Macmillan

Berry, C. (1993), *Voice and the Actor*, London, Virgin

Brande, D. (1983), *Becoming a Writer*, London, Papermac. First published 1934.
Brook, P. (1980), *The Empty Space*, London, Penguin
Brook, P. (1989), *The Shifting Point, Forty Years of Theatrical Exploration, 1946–1987*, London, Methuen
Calvino, I. (1982), *The Uses of Literature*, New York and London, Harcourt Brace
Crook, T. (1999), *Radio Drama, Theory and Practice*, London, Routledge
Doubtfire, D. (1996), *Creative Writing*, London, Hodder, Teach Yourself Books
Dundes, A. (1965), *The Study of Folklore*, New York, Prentice Hall
Eagleton T. (2000), *The Idea of Culture*, Oxford, Blackwell
Esslin, M. (1980), *The Theatre of the Absurd*, London, Penguin
Field, S. (2003), *The Definitive Guide to Screenwriting*, London, Ebury Press
Le Guin, U. (1998), *Steering the Craft, Exercises and discussions on Story Writing*, Portland, OR, The Eighth Mountain Press
Haffenden, J. (1985), *Novelists at Interview*, London, Methuen
Haffenden, J. (1981), *Viewpoint: Poets in Conversation*, London, Methuen
Hyland, P. (1997), *Getting Into Poetry*, Newcastle, Bloodaxe
Jaworski, A and Coupland, C. eds (1999), *The Discourse Reader*, London, Routledge
Jeffreys, L. and Sansom, P. eds (2000), *Contemporary Poems, Some Critical Approaches*, Huddersfield, Smith Doorstop
Jellico, A. (1987), *Community Plays*, London, Methuen
Johnstone, K. (1981), *Impro*, London, Methuen
Johnstone, K. (1999), *Impro for Storytellers*, London, Faber and Faber
Kitchen J. and M. Paumier Jones, eds (1996), *In Short, A Collection of Brief Creative Non-fiction*, London, Norton
Livingstone, D. (1993), *Poetry Handbook*, London, Macmillan
Lodge, D. (2002), *Consciousness and the Novel*, London, Secker and Warburg
McKee, R. (1999), *Story: Substance, Structure, Style, and the Principles of Screenwriting*, London, Methuen
Paulin, T. (1998), *Writing To The Moment, Selected Critical Essays 1980–1996*, London, Faber and Faber
Penn, W. S. ed. (1993), *The Telling of the World, Native American Stories and Art*, New York, Stewart, Tabori and Chang
Rich, A. (1993), *What Is Found There, Notebooks on Poetry and Politics*, London, Virago
Sansom, P. (1994), *Writing Poems*, Newcastle, Bloodaxe
Schmidt, M. (1999), *Lives of the Poets*, London, Phoenix
Sellers, S. ed. (1989), *Delighting the Heart, Notebook by Women Writers*, London, The Women's Press
Singleton, J. and M. Luckhurst, eds (2000), *The Creative Writing Handbook*, London, Macmillan
Singleton, J. (2001), *The Creative Writing Workbook*, London, Palgrave,
Sweeney, M. and J. Hartley-Williams (2003), *Writing Poetry*, London, Hodder, Teach Yourself
Vogler, C. (1999), *The Writer's Journey*, London, Pan
Wainwright, J. (2004), *Poetry: the Basics*, London, Routledge
Woolf, V. (1992), *A Room of One's Own*, London, Penguin

INDEX